SAINT LOUIS

—THE—

OF THE

WORLD.

THIRD EDITION.

MISSOURI DEMOCRAT PRI..., FOURTH AND PINE.

SAINT LOUIS:

THE

FUTURE

GREAT CITY OF THE WORLD.

BY L. U. REAVIS.

THIRD EDITION.

Henceforth St. Louis must be viewed in the light of her future—her mightiness in the empire of the world—her sway in the rule of states and nations.

ST. LOUIS:
PUBLISHED BY ORDER OF THE ST. LOUIS COUNTY COURT.
MISSOURI DEMOCRAT PRINT
1871.

Dedication.

TO JAMES B. EADS,

THE MAN OF REAL GENIUS AND MARKED FIDELITY TO HIS FRIENDS,

THE CITIZEN OF GENUINE PATRIOTISM AND RARE PUBLIC

SPIRIT, THE MAN WORTHY OF HONOR

BECAUSE SELF-MADE,

THIS WORK,

DEVOTED TO THE FUTURE OF A CITY WHOSE

BEST HOPE IS IN SUCH MEN, IS

DEDICATED BY

THE AUTHOR.

TABLE OF CONTENTS.

EXPLANATORY.

A Presentation of Causes in Nature and Civilization, which in their reciprocal action tend to fix the position of the FUTURE GREAT CITY OF THE WORLD in the Central Plain of North America, showing that the center of the World's Commerce and Civilization, will, in less than One Hundred Years, be organized and represented in the Mississippi Valley and by ST. LOUIS, occupying as she does the most favored position on the Continent and the Great River; also a complete representation of the Great Railway System of St. Louis, showing that in less than ten years she will be the greatest Railway Center in the World.

L. U. R.

PROPHETIC VOICES ABOUT ST. LOUIS.

St. Louis alone would be an all-sufficient theme; for who can doubt that this prosperous metropolis is destined to be one of the mighty centers of our mighty Republic?—CHARLES SUMNER.

Fair St. Louis, the future Capital of the United States, and of the civilization of the Western Continent.—JAMES PARTON.

NEW YORK TRIBUNE,
NEW YORK, *February* 4, 1870.

DEAR SIR: I have twice seen St. Louis in the middle of winter. Nature made her the focus of a vast region, embodying a vast area of the most fertile soil on the globe. Man will soon accomplish her destiny by rendering her the seat of an immense industry, the home of a far-reaching, ever-expanding commerce. Her gait is not so rapid as that of some of her Western sisters, but she advances steadily and surely to her predestined station of first inland city on the globe.

Yours, HORACE GREELEY.

L. U. REAVIS, ESQ., *Missouri*.

I also remember that I am in the city of St. Louis — destined, ere long, to be the greatest city on the continent (renewed cheers); the greatest central point between the East and the West, at once destined to be the entrepot and depot of all the internal commerce of the greatest and most prosperous country the world has ever seen; connected soon with India by the Pacific, and receiving the goods of China and Japan; draining, with its immense rivers centering here, the great Northwest, and opening into the Gulf through the great river of this nation, the Father of Waters — the Mississippi. Whenever — and that time is not far distant — the internal commerce shall exceed our foreign commerce, then shall St. Louis take the very first rank among the cities of the nation. And that time, my friends, is much sooner than any one of us at the present time actually realizes. Suppose that it had been told to you — any one of you here present, of middle age — within twenty years past, that within that time such a city should grow up here, with such a population as covers the teeming prairies of Illinois and Indiana, between this and the Ohio, who would have realized the prediction? And so the next quarter of a century shall see a larger population west of the Mississippi than the last quarter of a century saw east of the Mississippi; and the city of St. Louis, from its central location, and through the vigor, the energy, the industry, and the enterprise of its inhabitants, shall become the very first city of the United States of America, now and hereafter destined to be the great republican nation of the world.—[*Extract from a speech delivered in St. Louis, October* 13, 1866, *by* GEN. B. F. BUTLER.

Now, sir, when I see this country, when I see its vastness and its almost illimitable extent; when I see the keen eye of capital and business fastened with steady, interested gaze upon the trade of the West, and all our Eastern cities in hot rivalry are reaching out their iron arms to secure our trade; when I see the railroads that are centering here in St. Louis; when I see this city, with 60,000 miles of railroad communication and 100,000 miles of telegraphic communication; when I see that she stands at the head-waters of navigation, extending to the north 3,000 miles, and to the south 2,000 miles; and when I see that she stands in the center of the continent, as it were; when I see the population moving to the West in vast numbers; when I see emigration rolling toward the Pacific, and all through these temperate climes I hear the tramp of the iron horse, on his way to the Pacific Ocean; when I see towns and villages springing up in every direction; when I see States forming into existence until the city of St. Louis becomes the center, as it were, of a hundred States, the center of the population and the commerce of this country — when I see all this, sir, I feel convinced that the seat of empire is to come this side of the Alleghanies; and why may not St. Louis be the future Capital of the United States of America?—[*Extract from a speech of* SENATOR YATES.

If it were asked whose anticipations of what has been done to advance civilization, for the past fifty years, have come nearest the truth — those of the sanguine and hopeful, or those of the cautious and fearful — must it not be answered that none of the former class had been sanguine and hopeful enough to anticipate the full measure of human progress since the opening of the present century? May it not be the most sanguine and hopeful only, who, in anticipation, can attain a due estimation of the measure of future change and improvement in the grand march of society and civilization westward over the continent?

The general mind is faithless of what goes much beyond its own experience. It refuses to receive, or it receives with distrust, conclusions, however strongly sustained by facts and fair deductions, which go much beyond its ordinary range of thought. It is especially skeptical and intolerant toward the avowal of opinions, however well founded, which are sanguine of great future changes. It does not comprehend them, and therefore refuses to believe; but it sometimes goes further, and, without examination, scornfully rejects. To seek for the truth is the proper object of those who, from the past and present, undertake to say what will be the future, and, when the truth is found, to express it with as little reference to what will be thought of it as if putting forth the solution of a mathematical problem.—[J. W. SCOTT.

Office of The Tribune.

New York, Feb. 4 1870.

Dear Sir: I have twice seen St. Louis in the middle of winter. Nature made her the focus of a vast region embodying a vast area of the most fertile soil on the globe. Man will soon accomplish her destiny by rendering her the seat of an immense industry, the home of a far-reaching, ever-expanding commerce. Her growth is not so rapid as that of some of her Western sisters, but she advances steadily and surely to her predestined station of first inland city on the globe.

Yours,

Horace Greeley

L. U. Reavis, Esq.

ST. LOUIS,

THE

FUTURE GREAT CITY.

Great cities grow up in nations as the mature offspring of well-directed civil and commercial agencies, and in their natural development they become vital organs in the world's government and civilization, performing the highest functions of human life on the earth. They grow up where human faculties and natural advantages are most effective. They have a part in the grand march of the human race, peculiar to themselves, in marking the progress of mankind in arts, commerce, and civilization; and they embellish history with its richest pages of learning, and impress on the mind of the scholar and the student the profoundest lessons of the rise and fall of nations. They have formed in all ages the great centers of industrial and intellectual life, from which mighty outgrowths of civilization have expanded. In short, they are the mightiest works of man. And whether we view them wrapped in the flames of the conqueror, and surrounded with millions of earnest hearts, yielding in despair to the wreck of fortune and life at the fading away of expiring glory, or the sinking of a nation into oblivion; or whether we contemplate them in the full vigor of prosperity, with steeples piercing the very heavens, with royal palaces, gilded halls, and rich displays of wealth and learning, they are ever wonderful objects of man's creation, ever impressing with profoundest conviction lessons of human greatness and human glory. In their greatness they have been able to wrestle with all human time. We have only to go with Volney through the Ruins of Empire; to trace the climbing path of man, from his first appearance on the fields of history to the present day, by the evidences we find along his pathway in the ruins of the great cities, the creation of his own hands. The lessons of magnitude and durability which great cities teach may be more clearly realized in the following eloquent passage from a lecture of Louis Kossuth, delivered in New York City:

"How wonderful! What a present and what a future yet! Future? Then let me stop at this mysterious word, the veil of unrevealed eternity.

"The shadow of that dark word passed across my mind, and, amid the bustle of this gigantic bee-hive, there I stood with meditation alone.

"And the spirit of the immovable past rose before my eyes, unfolding the picture-rolls of vanished greatness, and of the fragility of human things.

"And among their dissolving views there I saw the scorched soil of Africa, and upon that soil, Thebes, with its hundred gates, more splendid than the most splendid of all the existing cities of the world—Thebes, the pride of old Egypt, the first metropolis of arts and sciences, and the mysterious cradle of so many doctrines, which still rule mankind in different shapes, though it has long forgotten their source.

"There I saw Syria, with its hundred cities; every city a nation, and every nation with an empire's might. Baalbec, with its gigantic temples, the very ruins of which baffle the imagination of man, as they stand like mountains of carved rocks in the desert, where, for hundreds of miles, not a stone is to be found, and no river flows, offering its tolerant back to carry a mountain's weight upon. And yet there they stood, those gigantic ruins; and as we glance at them with astonishment, though we have mastered the mysterious elements of nature, and know the combination of levers, and how to catch the lightning, and how to command the power of steam and compressed air, and how to write with the burning fluid out of which the thunderbolt is forged, and how to dive to the bottom of the ocean, and how to rise up to the sky, cities like New York dwindle to the modest proportion of a child's toy, so that we are tempted to take the nice little thing up on the nail of our thumb, as Micromegas did with the man of wax.

"Though we know all this, and many things else, still, looking at the times of Baalbec, we cannot forbear to ask what people of giants was that which could do what neither the puny efforts of our skill, nor the ravaging hand of unrelenting time, can undo through thousands of years.

"And then I saw the dissolving picture of Nineveh, with its ramparts now covered with mountains of sand, where Layard is digging up colossal winged bulls, large as a mountain, and yet carved with the nicety of a cameo; and then Babylon, with its beautiful walls; and Jerusalem, with its unequaled temples; Tyrus, with its countless fleets; Arad, with its wharves; and Sidon, with its labyrinth of work-shops and factories; and Ascalon, and Gaza, and Beyrout, and, further off, Persepolis, with its world of palaces."

The first great cities of the world were built by a race of men inferior to those which now form the dominant civilization of the earth, yet there are many ruins of a mold superior, both in greatness and mechanical skill, to those which belong to the cities of our own day, as found in the marble solitudes of Palmyra and the sand-buried cities of Egypt. It is true, however, that ancient grandeur grew out of a system of idolatry and serf-labor, controlled by a selfish despot or a blind priesthood, which compelled a useless display of greatness in most public improvements. In our age, labor is directed more by practical wisdom than of old, which creates the useful more than the ornamental; hence we have the Crystal Palace instead of the Pyramids.

But, leaving the ancient cities, we are led to inquire, "Where will grow up the future great city of the world?" At the very outset of this inquiry it is necessary to clearly comprehend a few underlying facts connected with the cities of the past and those now in existence, and note the influence of the more important arts and sciences that bear upon man's present intellectual and industrial interests, and, if possible, to determine the tendency of the world's civilization toward the unfolding future.

The first great fact we meet with is, that the inevitable tendency of man upon the earth has been to make the circuit of the globe by going westward, within an isothermal belt or zodiac of equal temperature, which encircles the earth in the north temperate zone. Within this belt has already been embraced more than three-fourths of the world's civilization, and now about 850,000,000 people. It is along this belt that the processions of nations, in time, have moved forward, with reason and order, "in a pre-determined, a solemn march, in which all have joined; ever moving and ever resistlessly advancing, encountering and enduring an inevitable succession of events."

"It is along this axis of the isothermal temperate zone of the northern hemisphere that revealed civilization makes the circuit of the globe. Here the continents expand, the oceans contract. This zone contains the zodiac of empires. Along its axis, at distances scarcely varying one hundred leagues, appear the great cities of the world, from Pekin in China to St. Louis in America.

"During antiquity this zodiac was narrow; it never expanded beyond the North African shore, nor beyond the Pontic sea, the Danube, and the Rhine. Along this narrow belt civilization planted its system, from oriental Asia to the western extremity of Europe, with more or less perfect development. Modern times have recently seen it widen to embrace the region of the Baltic sea. In America it starts with the broad front from Cuba to Hudson's Bay. As in all previous times, it advances along a line central to these extremes, in the densest form, and with the greatest celerity. Here are the chief cities of intelligence and power, the greatest intensity of energy and progress Science has recently very perfectly established, by observation, this axis of the isothermal temperate zone. It reveals to the world this shining fact, that along it civilization has traveled, as by an inevitable instinct of nature, since creation's dawn. From this line has radiated intelligence of mind to the North and to the South, and toward it all people have struggled to converge. Thus, in harmony with the supreme order of nature, is the mind of man instinctively adjusted to the revolutions of the sun, and tempered by its heat."

> "Through the ages one increasing purpose runs,
> And the thoughts of men are widened with the process of the sun."

It is a noteworthy observation of Dr. Draper, in his work on the Civil War in America, that within a zone a few degrees wide, having for its axis the January isothermal line of forty-one degrees, all great men in Europe and Asia have appeared. He might have added, with equal truth, that within the same zone have existed all those great cities which have exerted a powerful influence upon the world's history, as centers of civilization and intellectual progress. The same inexorable but subtle law of climate which makes greatness in the individual unattainable in a temperature hotter or colder than a certain golden mean, affects in like manner, with even more certainty, the development of those concentrations of the intellect of man which we find in great cities.

If the temperature is too cold, the sluggish torpor of the intellectual and physical nature precludes the highest development; if the temperature is too hot, the fiery fickleness of nature, which warm climates produce in the individual, is typical of the swift and tropical growth, and sudden and severe decay and decline, of cities exposed to the same all-powerful influence. Beyond that zone of moderate temperature, the human life resembles more closely that of the animal, as it is forced to combat with extremes of cold, or to submit to extremes of heat; but within that zone the highest intellectual activity and culture are displayed. Is it not, then, a fact of no little import that the very axis of this zone — the center of equilibrium between excess of heat and cold — the January isothermal line of forty-one degrees — passes nearer to the city of St. Louis than to any other considerable city on this continent? Close to that same isothermal line lie London, Paris, Rome, Constantinople, and Pekin; north of it lie New York, Philadelphia, and Chicago, and south of it lies San Francisco. Thus favored in climate, lying in the very center of that belt of intellectual activity beyond which neither great man nor great city has yet appeared, St. Louis may, with reason, be expected to attain the highest rank, if other conditions favor.

A second underlying fact that presents itself is that nearly all the great cities of the world have been built upon rivers, whether in the interior or near the ocean's edge: such as Babylon, on the Euphrates; Thebes, on the Nile; Nineveh, on the Tigris; Rome, on the Tiber; Paris, on the Seine; London, on the Thames; New York, on the Hudson; Cincinnati, on the Ohio; St. Louis, on the Mississippi; and Constantinople, on the Bosphorus; while Carthage, St. Petersburg, and Chicago belong to interior waters, and Palmyra and the City of Mexico to the interior country.

A third fundamental fact is, that the arts and sciences do more to develop interior cities, and multiply population upon the interior lands, than upon the seaboards or coast lands. Steam engines, labor-saving machines, books, the value and use of metals, government, the enforcement of laws, and other means of self-protection—all have tended more to make the people of the interior more numerous, powerful, and wealthy than those who dwell along the shores of the oceans.

A fourth fundamental fact is, that, to all modern civilization, domestic transportation by water and rail is more valuable to nations of large territorial extent than ocean navigation. This fact is founded not only upon the assumption that a nation's interests are of more importance to itself than to any other nation, and it hence necessarily does more business at home than abroad, but also upon the fact that the exchanges of domestic products within this country, it is estimated, already exceed in value six thousand millions yearly, while the whole value of all foreign exchanges is less than one thousand millions a year. With every year, as the country advances in population and industry, its domestic exchanges gain upon its foreign; and those cities, like New York, which much depend largely upon foreign trade, are overtaken in the race for commercial supremacy by inferior cities more favorably located for transacting the far greater business of domestic interchange.

A fifth fundamental condition upon which to base a high civilization, a prosperous, wealthy, and numerous people, who are destined to build great cities, is a country well adapted by nature with suitable climate and resources of soil, minerals, timbers, water-powers, and navigable advantages.

A sixth and final fundamental fact is, that the most favored and surely to be a prosperous, wealthy, and numerous people, are those who are favored in land and country so far as to be able to organize the producer and consumer, side by side, with full and equal advantages to work out the great problems of usefulness in life, and share the liberty, the happiness, and intelligence which the world affords.

The growth of a city is analogous to the growth of a man, and auxiliary to our six fundamental facts are the three following requisites to human life and individual prosperity:

I. The necessity for food.
II. The necessity for clothing.
III. The necessity for shelter.

There can be no civilized life without all of these requisites; and as they are the products of labor and skill, where they can be produced in the greatest abundance and used to the greatest advantage, and the most extensively, will almost certainly be the place where the great city will grow up—where our problem will be solved. Added to these should be ample facilities for the intercommunion of the people, one with another, and for the ready exchange of commodities forming foreign and domestic commerce. These may be enumerated as good roads, railways, and navigable channels, with attendant cheap freights.

Thus, with this statement of fundamental facts, we are enabled to proceed to a discussion of the causes in nature and civilization, which, in their reciprocal action, tend to fix the position of the future great city of the world.

We have seen that the human race, with all its freight of commerce, its barbarism and civilization, its arms and arts, through pestilence and prosperity, across seas and over continents, like one mighty caravan, has been moving forward since creation's dawn, from the East to the West, with the sword and cross, helmet and distaff, to the conquest of the world; and, like a mighty army, leaving weakness behind and organizing power in the advance. Hence, we can easily realize that the same inevitable cause that wrested human power from the cities of the ancients, and vested it for a time in the city of the Cæsars, and thence moved it to the city of London, will, in time, cross the Atlantic Ocean, and be organized and represented in the future great city of the world, which is destined to grow up on the American Continent; and that this power, wealth, and wisdom, that once ruled in Troy, Athens, Carthage, and Rome, and are now represented by the city of London—the precursor of the final great city—will, in less than one hundred years, find a resting place in North America, and culminate in the future great city which is destined to grow up in the central plain of the Continent, and upon the great Mississippi river, where the city of St. Louis now stands.

In this westward march of civilization, we know that the center of the world's commerce, which was once represented by the cities of the Mediterranean, has moved westward to the Atlantic Ocean, and is now represented by the city of London. The tendency is still westward, and that London cannot remain the center for any considerable length of time is universally evident. Human power is moving westward with an irresistible tendency, and is destined to be organized on the American Continent in its most absolute and gigantic form.

There may be those who will assume that New York is to be the successor of London, and even surpass in population and commercial supremacy that great city of the trans-Atlantic shore, before the position of the final great city is fixed. This is not possible. We have only to comprehend the new character of our national industry, and the diversity of interests which it and our rapidly increasing system of railways are establishing, to know that it is impossible. The city of New York will not, in the future, control the same proportionate share of foreign and domestic commerce of the country that she heretofore has. New Orleans and San Francisco will take some of the present valued trade, and, together with other points which will soon partake of the outpost commerce, the trade to and from our country will be so divided as to prevent New York from becoming the rival, much less the superior, of London, as Mr. Scott has so earnestly contended. Then, in the westward movement of human power and the center of the world's commerce, from the city of London to the New World, it is not possible for it to find a complete and final resting place in any city of the Atlantic seaboard, but it will be compelled to move forward, until, in its complete development, it will be organized and represented in the most favored city in the central plain of the Continent. Besides the diffusion of our external commerce through so many channels upon our seaboard, so as to prevent its concentration at any one of the seaboard cities, there are elements at work in the interior of the country which will more surely prevent the city that is to succeed London from growing up on the Atlantic shore of our Continent. Every tendency of our national progress is more and more to our continental development—a living at home, rather than going abroad to distant markets. There is an inherent principle lurking among all people of great continental nationality and resources, which impresses them stronger with home interests than with external and distant fields of action; and this principle is rapidly infusing itself among the people of these great valley States; therefore, it is needless to look into the future to see our great cities on either seaboard of our Continent, for they are not destined to be there. But most certainly will they grow up in the interior, upon the lakes, the rivers, and the Gulf; and among these cities of the interior we are to look for the future great city of the world—that which London now heralds, and which the westward tendency of the world's civilization will in, less than one hundred years, build up as the greatest industrial organism of the human race.

Leaving the Atlantic seaboard and coming west of the Appalachian mountains, we at once enter the domain of the Mississippi Valley, which comprises an area of 2,445,000 square miles, and extends through thirty degrees of longitude and twenty-three degrees of latitude. In this valley, which is still new in its early development, there are already many large and flourishing cities, each expecting, in the future, to be greater than others. First among these stand Chicago, Cincinnati, St. Louis, and New Orleans—four cities destined, at no distant day, to surpass, in wealth and population, the four cities of the Atlantic seaboard—Boston, New York, Philadelphia, and Baltimore. Assuming, then, that the future great city is to be in the Mississippi Valley, we are to ascertain which of the four cities it is to be, or whether some new and more prosperous rival will present itself for the great mission. As the great city is to be in the future, we must view it as the growth of the well-developed resources of our country; and, all things being considered, it is but just to say that, inasmuch as it will be an organism of human power, it will grow up in or near the center of the productive power of the Continent. That Chicago, Cincinnati, St. Louis, and New Orleans have each many natural advantages, there can be no question. There is, however, this difference: the area of surrounding habitable country, capable of ministering to the wants and supplying the trade of a city, is broken, in the case of New Orleans, by the Gulf and the lake, and by regions of swamp; in the case of Chicago, it is diminished one-third by the lake; while Cincinnati and St. Louis both have around them unbroken and uninterrupted areas, capable of sustaining a large population. But if we ask to which of these cities belong the greatest advantages, must we not answer, it is the one nearest the center of the productive power of the Continent? Most certainly, for there will grow up the human power. And is not this center St. Louis? We have only to appeal to facts to establish the superior natural advantages of St. Louis over any other city on the Continent.

But, before we enter upon a discussion of the productive powers of the Continent, let us look for one moment at the elements of human want upon which civilization is founded; and this brings us back to a consideration of our auxiliary and essential requisites to our six fundamental facts. Under all circumstances, and in every condition of life, in country or clime, the first and greatest necessity of man is food; and, with a civilization and an industry universally founded upon the principle of "for value received," it is incontrovertibly true that, in that part of the country where the most food can be produced and supplied at the cheapest rates to the consumers, there will be an essential requisite to encourage and sustain a dense population. Then, without entering into a detailed investigation of the advantages afforded to Chicago, Cincinnati, and New Orleans, for obtaining an all-sufficient supply of cheap food, we shall at once assume that St. Louis is central to a better and greater food-producing area or country than either one or the other three cities; and that no man can disprove the assumption, is most certainly true.

St. Louis is, substantially, the geographical center of this great valley, which, as we have already seen, contains an area of 2,445,000 square miles, and will, in the mature development of the capacity of its soil, wield, at least, the products of 1,000,000 square miles. That we may infer, approximately, the capacity of the more central portions of this valley for food producing purposes, we call to the calculation an estimate, made by the Agricultural Bureau, of the cereal products of the Northwest for the next four decades:

Year.	Bushels.
1870	762,200,000
1880	1,219,520,000
1890	1,951,232,000
1900	3,121,970,000

We consume in this country an average of about five bushels of wheat to the inhabitant, but, if necessary, can get along with something less, as we have many substitutes, such as corn, rye, and buckwheat. A low estimate will show that our population will be in:

Year.	Population.
1870	42,000,000
1880	56,000,000
1890	77,000,000
1900	100,000,000

Accordingly, we can use for home consumption alone of wheat in:

Year.	Bushels.
1870	210,000,000
1880	280,000,000
1890	385,000,000
1900	500,000,000

This calculation is made for Illinois, Missouri, Iowa, Wisconsin, and Minnesota; and by taking into the account Nebraska, Kansas, the Indian Territory, and Arkansas, four additional States which naturally belong to the account of this argument, we at once swell the amount of food for the next three decades to a sufficiency to supply hundreds of millions of human beings, at as cheap rates as good soil and human skill and labor can produce it.

Nor do these States comprise half of the food-producing area of the Valley of the Mississippi. Other large and fertile States, more eastern, and southern, and western — Indiana, Ohio, Kentucky, Tennessee, Alabama, Mississippi, Louisiana, Texas, Kansas, and Nebraska—do now, and will continue to, contribute largely to the sum total of the food produced in the Valley States. And when we consider that less than one-fifth of the entire products of the whole country in 1860 was exported to foreign countries, thus leaving four-fifths for exchange in domestic commerce between the States, and that such is the industrial and commercial tendency of our people to a constant proportional increase of our domestic over our foreign exchange, we see an inevitable tendency in our people to concentrate industrially and numerically in the interior of the Continent. And when we take into the account that not more than eighteen per cent. of the soil of the best States of this valley is under cultivation, we are still more amazed at the thought of what the future will produce, when the whole shall have been brought under a high state of improved culture. Then the food-producing capacity of this valley will be ample to supply more people than now occupy the entire globe, and with the superior advantages of domestic navigation that St. Louis has over any of the valley cities, and the still additional advantages which she will have in railway communications, and her proximity to rich soils, where can a people be supplied with more and cheaper food than here? Not only are the superior advantages afforded for the production of an abundance of cheap corn and wheat for food, but also for the growth of rye, oats, barley, sugar, and all kinds of vegetables and fruits essentially necessary for the wants of those who inhabit the land. In addition to the food taken direct from the soil, St. Louis is better situated than the other three cities for being amply supplied, at the lowest possible rates, with the best quality of animal food. Not only is there every advantage on all sides to be supplied with animal food from the constantly increasing products of agricultural districts adjacent to the city, but in twenty hours ride by railway we reach the great pastoral region of our country, where, in a few years, cattle and sheep will swarm over the wide prairies in infinite numbers, where they are kept in reserve to supply the markets of the constantly increasing people. Already the domestic animals — quadrupeds — are more numerous in civilized life than were the wild quadrupeds among the aboriginal savages of this country. In the year 1860, taken together, horses, asses and mules, oxen, sheep and swine amounted to more than one hundred millions, or more than three times the human population of the Union. Considering the great pastoral region of our country which will, before many years, be brought into use, the increase of quadrupeds will, no doubt, be greater than that of man; at least, for the next fifty years, the increase on the pastoral region will exercise a valuable influence in aiding to establish good and sufficient markets in the large cities of the Valley States, thus concentrating and strengthening the power of the interior people, who will find ample food at all times. And, in every view of the subject of food, there seems to be no question as to the advantage St. Louis will possess for an abundance and for cheapness over the other three cities, holding, as she does, the nearest relation to the producer, and with better facilities for obtaining it.

Next to food, as a prime necessity, is the want of clothing. The principal materials out of which to make clothing are wool, cotton, linen, and leather. Each of these can be produced cheapest and best in and adjacent to the food-producing regions, or, at any rate, the wool and the leather. In fact, in the final advancement and multiplication of the human species upon the planet, for the want of room cotton will have to be abandoned, and only those animals and vegetables cultivated that can serve the double purpose of supplying food and clothing, and material for the mechanic arts. This will compel cattle and sheep, and wheat and corn, to be the principal food. The flesh of the sheep and the cow will supply food, and the hides, leather and the wool, clothing. The grain of the corn and the wheat will also form food, while the stalk will enter into many uses in art. The hog will finally be compelled to give up the conflict of life; his mission will be fulfilled, and man will require a more refined food for his more refined organization. Fish will not be in the way of man in his higher and more multitudinous walk upon the earth, and, consequently, will continue to supply a valuable portion of his food. Cotton will, ere long, be driven to an extreme southern coast, and, finally, gain a strong foothold in Central America and other more extreme southern countries, and, at last, yield to superior demands. But, to return: St. Louis, on account of the large area of rich, and, in most part, cheap lands, surrounding her in every direction, has equal, if not better advantages, for being supplied with ample materials for cheap and good clothing than any other city on the Continent; and, with superior advantages, as we shall show after awhile, for the manufacture of the materials into clothing, she will stand first in facilities to supply food and clothing to her ever-increasing people.

Next to food and clothing comes the necessity for shelter, or houses, which are essential to a high civilization. The materials out of which houses are mostly made, in American cities, are stone and brick, while the farmer builds of stone and wood. Of these building materials an inexaustible supply is to be found in almost any direction we may go out, for three hundred miles, from St. Louis. It may be said that, inasmuch as Chicago has the advantages of cheaper lumber, she has the advantage over St. Louis in building material; but this does not follow. The new and best buildings of Chicago are made of stone and brick, brought from distant places; while St. Louis stands on an immense foundation of good limestone, from which thousands of perch are quarried annually, and worked into first-class buildings. Besides, within fifty and one hundred miles from the city, in the southeastern part of the State, are inexhaustible beds of choice qualities of as fine building stone as the Continent affords; also, extensive forests of the most valuable timbers, suited for the mechanic arts and for building material. Brick, of first-class quality, are made in various parts of the city, and supply the demand for building purposes. Nor can any of these supplies be exhausted for ages to come. Stone and wood are found in abundance in all parts of the Valley States, wherewith to supply the farmer with cheap building materials.

Thus, we have seen that the three essential requisites, food, clothing, and shelter, necessary to man's wants and the purposes of civilization, can be supplied in abundance and cheapness to St. Louis, with greater advantages than to any other city belonging to the Valley States; and these must render her the greatest market and the best depot for such materials that the Continent affords.

Passing, then, from these essential requisites, let us take up another line of discussion, that bears more directly upon the future development of American commerce and American civilization. I refer to the productive power of the Continent, which is the basis of our physical and material life. In what does the productive power of the Continent consist? The answer must be, that it consists in the soils suited to agricultural purposes, the coal-fields, the mineral deposits, the valuable forests, the water-powers, the domestic navigation, and all o'erspread with a temperate and healthful climate. Although the largest coal and iron deposits of the Continent are already known, the geology of the entire extent is so imperfectly known that there still remain undisturbed in many of the Territories, and even in some of the States, valuable deposits of these two substances, which, ere long, will be unearthed and made subservient to the wants of our people.

Beginning with the soils of the country, it is well understood, by those acquainted with its surface, that the largest and richest body of soil, best suited for corn, wheat, oats, rye, and hay-growing, is spread over the Valley States. In fact, no country in the world has so large an area of rich land as belongs to the States of the Mississippi Valley. In capacity for producing the various products in the department of agriculture, it has already been referred to in the discussion of the subject of food, and will require no further consideration.

Next to the corn-fields above come the coal-fields below, and the iron deposits. These are the material upon which modern and more advanced civilization is founded, more than upon any other substances which the arts have brought into use. Says Prof. Taylor:

"The two important mineral substances, coal and iron, have, when made available, afforded a permanent basis for commercial and manufacturing prosperity. Looking at the position of some of the geat depositories of coal and iron, one perceives that upon them the most flourishing population is concentrated—the most powerful and magnificent nations of the earth are established. If these two apparently coarse and unattractive substances have not directly caused that high eminence to which some of these countries have attained, they at least have had a large share in contributing to it."

M. Aug. Vischers also says, that "coal is now the indispensable aliment of industry; it is a primary material, engendering force, giving a power superior to that which natural agents, such as water, air, &c., procure. It is to industry what oxygen is to the lungs, water to the plants, nourishment to the animal. It is to coal we owe steam and gas."

Whoever will look into the development of commerce and civilization during the greater part of this century will find that coal and iron have given them their cast and development in Europe and America. Nor have either of these attained their highest use. On examination, we find that St. Louis is far better supplied than Chicago, Cincinnati, or New Orleans, with coal and iron; in fact, she stands in a central position to the greatest coal-fields known on the globe. Surrounded on the one side by the inexhaustible coal-beds of Illinois, and on the other by the larger ones of Missouri, Iowa, and Kansas, who can doubt her advantages in the use of the most important substance for the next two thousand years? On the one side we have Illinois, with her 30,000 square miles of coal, which is estimated by Prof. Rodgers to amount to 1,227,500,000,000 tons, which is much greater than the deposits in Pennsylvania—they amounting, according to the same authority, to 316,400,000,000 tons. On the other side we have Missouri, with more than 26,887 square miles, amounting to more than 130,000,000,000 tons. Iowa has her 24,000 square miles of coal; Kansas, 12,000 square miles; Arkansas, 12,000 square miles; and the Indian Territory, 10,000 square miles. Nearly all the other States are likewise bountifully supplied, but these figures are sufficient to show the position of St. Louis to the greatest coal deposits in the world. We can only approximate to the value of these resources by contrast. It is the available use of these two substances that has made England — a little island of the sea, not so great as the State of Iowa — the great heart of the world's civilization and commerce. She, with her 144,000,000,000 tons, or 12,000 square miles, of coal, with its greater development and use, reckons her wealth, in substantial value, at $100,000,000,000; while our nation, with our 3,740,000,000,000 tons, or 500,000 square miles, of less developed and not so well used coal, and more than twenty-five times as large, are only reckoned to be worth $23,400,000,000, with an annual increase of $921,700,000. It is true, our nation is only in its infancy, but these facts and the contrast teach us how mighty we can be, if we do but use these apparently coarse and unattractive substances, coal and iron, as the best wisdom and skill will enable. We possess thirty-four times the quantity of coal and iron possessed by England, and perhaps double as much as that possessed by all other portions of the earth. These resources are availably located; they are in proximity to the widest plains and richest soils known to man. They are developed by ocean-like lakes or magnificent rivers, and are, or will be, traversed by railroads from ocean to ocean. Their value is incalculable, their extent boundless, and their richness unequaled. They are mines of wealth, more valuable than gold, and sufficiently distributed over this great valley to supply well-regulated labor to 400,000,000 producers and consumers. Adjacent to our coal-fields are our mountains of iron of a superior quality, and of quantity inexhaustible. Thus is St. Louis favored with coal and iron in such endless supplies as to always render them as cheap as the American market can afford. The rich deposits of precious metals which belong to the great mountain system of our continent, being on the west side of the valley, have already, and will necessarily yet more, contribute to building up the interior of the country than either coast region; and though this interest never can be so valuable as that of coal and iron, it is of immense value and important in its bearing upon the subject under discussion. Already the account has been made large, as the following table shows, but not the half has been taken from those rich and extended mines:

Table showing the Growth of Coinage of the United States from 1793 to 1867.

YEARS.	GOLD.	SILVER.	COPPER.	TOTAL.
1793 to 1800, 8 years........	$1,014,290 00	$1,440,454 75	$79,390 82	$2,534,135 57
1801 to 1810, 10 "	3,250,742 50	3,569,165 25	151,246 39	6,971,154 14
1811 to 1820, 10 "	3,166,510 00	5,970,810 95	191,158 57	9,328,479 52
1821 to 1830, 10 "	1,903,092 50	16,781,046 95	151,412 20	18,835,551 65
1831 to 1840, 10 "	18,791,862 00	27,199,779 00	342,322 21	46,333,963 21
1841 to 1850, 10 "	89,443,328 00	22,226,755 00	380,670 83	112,050,753 83
1851 to 1860, 9½ "	470,838,180 98	48,087,763 13	1,249,612 53	520,175,556 64
1861 to 1867, 7 "	296,967,464 63	12,638,732 11	4,869,350 00	314,475,546 74
Total, 74 years.............	$885,375,470 61	$137,914,587 14	$7,415,163 55	$1,030,705,141 30

Valuable forests of the best timbers used in mechanical industry are to be found in the southeastern part of the State, and will, in due time, furnish material for agricultural implements, furniture, and the various uses to which timber is applied. Water powers, not surpassed in any part of New England, are to be found in many parts of the southern half of the State, and which, when properly improved, will contribute largely to the commercial interests of St. Louis.

There still remains to be considered the domestic navigation of the Mississippi Valley. This includes, in its broadest scope, the Gulf and the greater lakes, with the Mississippi river and her tributaries, which comprise the finest inland navigation on the globe. These rivers afford more than 20,000 miles of navigable water, which form transportation facilities for the commerce of the most productive portions of the great Valley States. The following remark of Col. Benton is very expressive of the magnitude and importance of the river system of this great valley:

"The river navigation of the Great West," said he, "is the most wonderful on the globe, and, since the application of steam power to the propulsion of vessels, possesses the essential qualities of open navigation. Speed, distance, cheapness, magnitude of cargoes, are all there, and without the perils of the sea from storms and enemies. The steamboat is the ship of the river, and finds in the Mississippi and its tributaries the amplest theater for the diffusion and the display of its power. Wonderful river! Connected with seas by the head and by the mouth, stretching its arms toward the Atlantic and the Pacific, lying in a valley which is a valley from the Gulf of Mexico to Hudson's Bay; drawing its first waters not from rugged mountains, but from the plateau of the lakes in the center of the Continent, and in communication with the sources of the St. Lawrence and the streams which take their course north to Hudson's Bay; draining the largest extent of richest land, collecting the products of every clime, even the frigid, to bear the whole to market in the sunny South, and there to meet the products of the entire world. Such is the Mississippi; and who can calculate the aggregate of its advantages and the magnitude of its future commercial results?"

St. Louis is centrally situated in this great system of domestic navigation, and cannot fail to be, in all the future, the most important city and depot identified with its interests. In the nature of river navigation, a smaller class of boats is required for the upper waters than those which can be most economically used in deeper streams, and hence arises a necessity for transfer, at some point, from up-river boats to those of greater tonnage; and at that point of transfer, business must arise sufficient of itself to sustain a considerable city. The fact that St. Louis is this natural point of transfer between the upper waters of the Mississippi, Missouri, and Illinois, and the great channel thence to the Gulf, is not to be overlooked in estimating its natural advantages. To the domestic navigation we add the railway system of the Valley States, which will, in a few years more, comprise more than 100,000 miles; and, by reference to the map illustrating this new inland agency for the easy exchange of products and people, we behold at a glance a most wonderful system traversing all parts of these States. In the rapid construction of these lines of communication, St. Louis is fast becoming the greatest railway center on the Continent, as well as in the world, and, with her advantages for domestic navigation, she is soon to be provided with the best commercial facilities of any city on the globe; and to her 20,000 miles of river navigation will be added, in less than fifteen years, a continental system of railway communication; and with all these constantly bearing an ever-increasing commerce to her markets, who cannot foresee her destiny among the cities of the world? These thousands of miles of railway can be built the cheapest of any extended system in the world, as they are unobstructed by mountain ranges; they will also be the straightest, shortest, and best routes from point to point, for the same reason. Granting that she will become the center of the greatest railway communication and of river navigation in the country, we must take into the account the question of freights, as an item of interest which will bear directly upon the subject of the growth of all American cities. Cheap freights will have a direct and important bearing upon the matter of distributing food and raiment to the people of the Valley States, and also of giving to their products the advantages of the best market. To settle this question in favor of St. Louis, involves but two points necessary to be considered: the first, the universal competition constantly existing between the various rival railroads of the Valley States, which will, of necessity, make the freights to St. Louis as cheap as to any other city; the second point is, that St. Louis stands in the midst of the greatest producing and consuming region of the country, and in this she cannot fail to have the advantage over any rival city that may aspire for empire in the republic or the world. Situated, then, as she is, in the very heart of the productive power of the country, and destined, at a very early date, to be connected by railway and by water, in the most advantageous way, with every city and harbor upon our seacoast, and with every inland city and productive region where industry and wealth can find opportunity, we are led to consider her future as a commercial and manufacturing city, and her advantages to become a distributing point for the future millions of industrious and intelligent of our race who are yet to inhabit this Continent, under one flag and one language.

Let us go a little deeper into the discussion. Having pointed out a condition of advantages which nature, by an inscrutable wisdom, has organized sufficiently strong to insure, under a well-directed civilization, the production on our Continent of the future great city of the world, it is a part of the argument to point out some of the essential incidental wants and conditions which must control the use of products in civilized life, in order to make them subserve the highest use in supplying the wants of man.

The first essential want of any productive people is markets, whereat to dispose of their surplus products, mechanical or agricultural, at profitable prices. Markets are a want of population in all lands. Mr. Seaman says, in the first series of his valuable work on the progress of nations, that "population alone adds value to lands and property of every kind, and is, therefore, one of the principal sources and causes of wealth." And why is it so? Simply because it creates a market by causing a demand for property and products; it enhances their price and exchangeable value, rewards the producer for his industry, and encourages and increases industry and production. Population thus creates markets, and markets operate to enhance prices and to increase wealth, industry, and production. Markets are, therefore, among the principal causes and sources of value and of wealth, and stimulants of industry. The farmer, mechanic, miner, and manufacturer are all beneficial to each other, for the reason that each wants the products of every other in exchange for his own, and thus each creates a market for the products of all the others, and thereby enhances prices and stimulates their industry. Hence the advantage to the farmer of increasing mechanical, manufacturing, and mining industry, as far as practicable, in his own country, in order to create a market for his products and to encourage domestic commerce.

Agricultural products alone cannot furnish the materials of an active commerce, and two nations almost exclusively agricultural have seldom much intercourse with each other. Tyre, Carthage, and Athens, in ancient, and Venice, Florence, Genoa, and the Netherlands, in more modern times, were the greatest of commercial nations at their respective eras, as Great Britain is now, because they were also in advance of all other nations in the mechanic arts and manufactures, and their commerce was based on their mechanism and manufacturing industry, which furnished the principal subject-matter and materials for making exchanges and carrying on commerce with foreign nations. Then it is that the people of this great valley must look to the proper and highest use of the resources and materials which nature has so bountifully bestowed. Capital and skill must be made to supply the ever-increasing demand of this growing people, and thus it will become the mightiest in art, the most bountiful in the field, and the richest in commerce, "and in peace more puissant than army or navy, for the conquest of the world;" and, stimulated to loftier endeavors, each citizen, yielding to irresistible attraction, will seek a new life in the great national family.

But it is argued by some that a city cannot be successful in the pursuit of both commercial and manufacturing interests. This cannot be maintained as a correct position. There never has been any war between commerce and the mechanic arts. There can be none. They are the twin offspring of industry and intelligence, and alike dependent on each other for prosperity. The false conception of the relations they hold to each other, and the condition of prosperity they impose upon a city, come from a failure to perceive the true interests. The principles of economy regulate them both, and it is rarely that a city situated, as they are, on a harbor, on the coast, or an available point on a river, where commerce can find its easiest exchange, is equally advantageously situated with reference to the raw material necessary to enter into the mechanic arts on such terms of competition as to enable the producer to compete with rival products in the market of the country. It is because cities are so situated that a strict adherence to the rules of economy cannot admit of the union of commerce and mechanic arts in the same city, that some suppose that a commercial city cannot be made a manufacturing city, and that a manufacturing city cannot be made a commercial city.

The following remarks, from a writer in the New York *Times*, is a valuable item in our argument: "No one who desires to understand the whole subject of his country's future should fail to seek the metropolitan center of that country. The question which puzzles the people, and even the newspapers, of late, is this, 'Where is Paris, the London, or the Jerusalem, of the nation?' I know New York has yet the clearest title to that claim, but of late St. Louis has spoken much and often in her own behalf—with what truthfulness, I propose to examine. Chicago has been heard, Cincinnati puts in her voice, Philadelphia prides herself upon her strength and beauty, Boston calls herself the hub, and others put in their claims. Now, next to New York, I am disposed to regard the claim of St. Louis. Before slavery died this claim was not worth much, but that dead weight is now removed. Standing here, then, in St. Louis, an Eastern man, I cannot resist the impression that I am in the future commercial, if not political, metropolis of the land. A thousand voices conspire to enforce this impression upon the not very prophetic mind. I would make no invidious flings at the check of Chicago, the conceit of Boston, the cool silence of a New Yorker, as he points to a forest of masts and a million of people, the nonchalant airs of the City of Brotherly Love, and the peculiar habits of Cincinnati. Chicago has the railroads, she says. Granted. A metropolis of railroads, without a river deep, pure, and broad enough to afford drink to her present population, suggests the idea that railroads cannot make a city. Fitchburg, in Massachusetts, has more railroads than any New England town. What does that bring her, save the name of being Fitchburg? Shipping alone, which you have in New York, cannot make a city. Philadelphia may keep on annexing every town in Pennsylvania, and Jersey, too, and that cannot make a metropolis. The pork trade flourishes in Cincinnati, but even so respectable a constituency as a gentlemanly porker, who loves luxury, lives on the fat of the land, and is otherwise excessively aristocratic, cannot make a metropolis. In fact, no great cosmopolitan center can be made out of one specialty. Manchester is greater than London in its specialty, but Manchester's specialty must always keep it constrained, and prevent its ever becoming a center. Cologne, with 'seventy-nine well-defined, distinct, and separate' perfumes, has made it the city of odors, but Cologne can never be a capital. Shoes make and kill Lynn at once. Lowell and Lawrence have reached their highest glory. Chicago is a depot for speculators in grain, and Cincinnati abounds in hogs, but this is the end of their glory. New York and St. Louis are alike in this: you will find every specialty in about equal proportion. St. Louis only needs one thing to make it to the West what New York is to the East—railroads. She is not even an inland city. Light-draught sailing vessels can sail from St. Louis to London. All that she further needs is age. Up to 1866, capital was slow to venture and settle down in this city. Save a few thrifty Germans, the population of St. Louis was southern. This was her condition up to this time, so that she is, practically, a city of only ten years' growth."

There is another principle that enters into the account, which may be termed the involuntary or fortuitous cause—a kind of happening so! It is the highest form of incidental action in commerce. Often commerce, as if by the control of an unknown law, will change from one city to another, and impoverish the one and give vitality and strength to the other. These changes, at first thought, seem to be as inexplicable as the eddy movements of the water in the stream.

They are changes that usually have their origin in the action of a single man in the timely use of money, sometimes by a distant cause, sometimes by legislation; but never does commerce forsake an available point for the development of mechanical industry. Looking at St. Louis, with her location for internal commerce and mechanical industry without a parallel on the earth, we can safely say that she is destined to unite in one great interest a system of commerce and manufacturing that will surpass in wealth and skill that of Old England. It is true, her iron furnaces and glass factories will be built some distance outside of her corporate limits, but the wealth and the labor will be hers, and beneath her sway will be united side by side, in the most profitable relations and on the largest scale, the producer and consumer; and they, actuated by a universal amity, will seek the most liberal compensation, attain the highest skill, aspire to a better manhood, and learn to do good. The manufacturing of wood into its various uses will also form a very important part of the industry of this city, as will also the manufacturing of fabrics of various kinds. Thus, with a great system of manufacturing industry, compelling the coal, the iron, the wood and the sand to serve the purposes and wants of the commercial interests, as well as to enter into all channels through which capital flows and which industry serves, both wealth and population will be developed and concentrated in the highest degree. The time fixed for the future great city of the world to grow up, as the most consummate fruit of man's civilization, is within one hundred years from our date.

Let us look still deeper into this matter, and consider the new agencies and influences that tend in modern times with such irresistible force to concentrate mankind in the great interior cities of the Continents. The greatest of these agencies compels a more rapid development of the internal commerce of modern nations than in past times, and the consequent organization and concentration of human power in the interior cities.

There is not a living man whose experience, if he knows the facts written in the records of his own land, does not teach him of the continental growth and the consequent interior development of the country, in support of the argument under consideration. So great are the facts, that the constant development oft he internal trade of our continent is rapidly reversing the proportion of our domestic to our foreign commerce, so as to soon show the latter to stand in comparative value to the former, as the cipher to the unit; and that the immense growth of our domestic and internal commerce will guide and control our industry, and establish and organize human power and civilization in our own land in conformity to the most economic principles of production, supply and demand, there is no manner of doubt. This done, our foreign commerce will only be ancillary to the enjoyments of our people, and contribute to the development of cosmopolitan ideas among the world's inhabitants, more than to the creation of wealth among the nations.

It may be asked, to what cause must this change in the relative value of foreign and domestic commerce, and the influence of each upon civilized man, be referred? The answer is, that steam is the cause. It is the most wonderful artificial agency to advance public and private wants that man has yet made subservient to his will. It almost serves his entire mechanical wants—

"It sows, it sculls, it propels, it screws;
It lifts, it lowers, it warps, it tows,
It drains, it plows, it reaps, it mows;
It pumps, it bores, it irrigates,
It dredges, it digs, it excavates;
It pulls, it pushes, it draws, it drives,
It splits, it planes, it saws, it rives;
It carries, scatters, collects, and brings,
It blows, it puffs, it halts, it springs;
It breaks, condenses, opens and shuts,
It picks, it drills, it hammers, it cuts;
It shovels, it washes, mixes, and grinds,
It crushes, it sifts, it bolts, it binds;
It thrashes, winnows, punches, and kneads,
It molds, it stamps, it presses, it feeds,
It rakes, it scrapes, it bores, it shaves,
It runs on land, it rides on waves;
It mortices, forges, rolls, and rasps,
It polishes, rivets, files, and clasps;
It brushes, scutches, cards, and spins,
It puts out fires, and papers pins;
It weaves, it winds, it twists, it throws,
It stands, it lies, it comes, it goes;
It slits, it turns, it shears, it hews,
It coins, it prints—aye, prints the news."

Thus we have a suggestive statement, in *measure*, of many of the varied uses of steam. Its value cannot be estimated, nor can the wonderful influence which its use, during the last half century, has exerted upon civilized man be measured.

We, then, again repeat that it is this agency that is rapidly transforming the ancient order of the world's industry and commerce to a new application and a new power; and will compel the cities of the interior, in the future, to outgrow in all time the coast cities. It is this agency, more than all other mechanical agencies, that has lifted mankind from the vassal empires of Cyrus, the Cæsars, and Charlemange, to the great empires of our own time. It is this agency that will forever develop domestic commerce to a vastly greater value than that of foreign commerce, and, consequently, is the most powerful agent to produce the great city of the future that the genius of man has made subservient to his wants.

But let us not be understood as desirous ot undervaluing foreign trade. We hope and believe that its greatest blessings and triumphs are yet to come. Many of the articles which it brings to us add much to our substantial comfort, such as woolen and cotton goods, sugar and molasses; and others, such as iron and steel, with most of their manufactures, give much aid to our advancing arts But if these articles were the products of domestic industry—if they were produced in the factories of Lowell and Dayton, on the plantations of Louisiana and in the furnaces, forges, and workshops of Pennsylvania and Missouri—

why would not the dealing in them have the same tendency to enrich as now that they are brought from distant countries?

A disposition to attribute the rapid increase of wealth in commercial nations mainly to foreign commerce, is not peculiar to our nation or our time; for we find it combated as a popular error by distinguished writers on political economy. Mr. Hume, in his essay on commerce, maintains that the only way in which foreign commerce tends to enrich a country is by its presenting tempting articles of luxury, and thereby stimulating the industry of those in whom a desire to purchase is thus excited—the augmented industry of the nation being the only gain.

Dr. Chalmers says: "Foreign trade is not the creator of any economic interest; it is but the officiating minister of our enjoyments. Should we consent to forego those enjoyments, then, at the bidding of our will, the whole strength at present embarked in the service of procuring them would be transferred to other services—to the extension of home trade; to the enlargement of our national establishments; to the service of defense, or conquest, or scientific research, or Christian philanthropy." Speaking of the foolish purpose in Bonaparte to cripple Britain by destroying her foreign trade, and its utter failure, he says: "The truth is, that the extinction of foreign trade in one quarter was almost immediately followed up either by the extension of it in another quarter, or by the extension of the home trade. Even had every outlet abroad been obstructed, then, instead of a transference from one foreign market to another, there would just be a universal reflux towards a home market that would be extended in precise proportion with every successive abridgment which took place in our external commerce." If these principles are true—and we believe they are in accordance with those of every eminent writer on political economy and if they are important in their application to the British isles—small in territory, with extensive districts of barren land, surrounded by navigable waters, rich in good harbors, and presenting numerous natural obstacles to constructions for the promotion of internal commerce; and, moreover, placed at the door of the richest nations of the world—with how much greater force do they apply to our country, having a territory twenty times as large, unrivaled natural means of inter-communication, with few obstacles to their indefinite multiplication by the hand of man; a fertility of soil not equaled by the whole world; growing within its boundaries nearly all the productions of all the climes of the earth, and situated 3,000 miles from her nearest commercial neighbor.

Will it be said that, admitting the chief agency in building up great cities to belong to internal industry and trade, it remains to be proved that New York and the other great Atlantic cities will feel less of the beneficial effects of this agency than St. Louis and her Western sisters? It does not appear to us difficult to sustain, by facts and reason, the superior claims in this respect of our Western towns. It should be borne in mind that the North American Valley embraces the climate, soils, and minerals usually found distributed among many nations. From the northern shores of the upper lakes, and the highest navigable points of the Mississippi and Missouri rivers, to the Gulf of Mexico, nearly all the agricultural articles which contribute to the enjoyment of civilized man are now, or may be, produced in profusion. The North will send to the South grain, flour, provisions, including the delicate fish of the lakes, and the fruits of a temperate climo, in exchange for the sugar, rice, cotton, tobacco, and the fruits of the warm South. These are but a few of the articles, the produce of the soil, which will be the subjects of commerce in this valley. Of mineral productions which, at no distant day, will tend to swell the tide of internal commerce, it will suffice to mention coal, iron, salt, lead, lime, and marble. Will Boston, or New York, or Baltimore, or New Orleans, be the point selected for the interchange of these products? Or shall we choose more convenient central points on rivers and lakes for the theaters of these exchanges?

It is imagined by some that the destiny of this valley has fixed it down to the almost exclusive pursuit of agriculture, ignorant that, as a general rule in all ages of the world, and in all countries, the mouths go to the food, and not the food to the mouths. Dr. Chalmers says: "The bulkiness of food forms one of those forces in the economic machine which tend to equalize the population of every land with the products of its own agriculture. It does not restrain disproportion and excess in all cases; but in every large State it will be found that wherever an excess obtains, it forms but a very small fraction of the whole population. Each trade must have an agricultural basis to rest upon; for in every process of industry, the first and greatest necessity is that the workmen shall be fed." Again: "Generally speaking, the *excrescent* (the population over and above that which the country can feed) bears a very minute proportion to the natural population of the country; and almost nowhere does the commerce of a nation overleap, but by a very little way, the basis of its own agriculture." The Atlantic States, and particularly those of New England, cannot claim that they are to become the seats of the manufactures with which the West is to be supplied; that mechanics, and artisans, and manufacturers are not to select for their place of business the region in which the means of living are most abundant and their manufactured articles in greatest demand, but the section which is most deficient in those means, and to which their food and fuel must, during their lives, be transported hundreds of miles, and the products of their labor be sent back the same long road for a market.

Such a claim is neither sanctioned by reason, authority, nor experience. The mere statement exhibits it as unreasonable. Dr. Chalmers maintains that the "excrescent" population could not, in Britain even, with a free trade in bread-stuffs, exceed one-tenth of all the inhabitants; and Britain, be it remembered, is nearer the granaries of the Baltic than is New England to the food-exporting portions of our valley, and she has also greatly the advantage in the diminished expenses of transportation. But the Eastern manufacturing States have already nearly, if not quite, attained to the maximum ratio of excrescent population, and cannot, therefore, greatly augment their manufactures without a correspondent increase in agricultural production.

Most countries, distinguished for manufactures, have laid the foundation in a highly improved agriculture. England, the north of France, and Belgium have a more productive husbandry than any other region of the same extent.

In these same countries are also to be found the most efficient and extensive manufacturing establishments of the whole world; and it is not to be doubted that abundance of food was one of the chief causes of setting them in motion. How is it that a like cause operating here will not produce a like effect? Have we not, in addition to our prolific agriculture, as many and as great natural aids for manufacturing as any other country? The water-power of Missouri alone is greater than that of New England; besides, there are immense facilities in the States of Kentucky, Minnesota, and Ohio, as well as valuable advantages possessed in all the Valley States. But to these water-powers can be added the immeasurable power of steam in developing manufacturing industry in our own as well as other States of this valley.

If our readers are satisfied that domestic or internal trade must have the chief agency in building up our great American cities, and that the internal trade of the great Western Valley will be mainly concentrated in the cities situated within its bosom, it becomes an interesting subject of inquiry how our leading interior city will, at some distant period — say one hundred years — become the great city of the world, and gather to itself the preponderance of the industry and trade of the continent.

But our interior cities will not depend for their development altogether on internal trade. They will partake, in some degree, with their Atlantic and Pacific sisters, of the foreign commerce also; and if, as some seem to suppose, the profits of commerce increase with the distance at which it is carried on, and the difficulties which nature has thrown in its way, the Western towns will have the same advantage over their Eastern rivals in foreign commerce, which some claim for the latter over the former in our domestic trade. St. Louis and her lake rivals may use the outports of New Orleans and New York, as Paris and Vienna use those of Havre and Trieste; and it will surely one day come to pass that steamers from Europe will enter our great lakes and be seen booming up the Mississippi.

To add strength and conclusiveness to the above facts and deductions, do our readers ask for examples? They are at hand. The first city of which we have any record is Nineveh, situated on the Tigris, not less than 700 miles from its mouth. Babylon, built not long after, was also situated far in the interior, on the river Euphrates. Most of the great cities of antiquity, some of which were of immense extent, were situated in the interior, and chiefly in the valleys of large rivers meandering through rich alluvial territories. Such were Thebes, Memphis, Ptolemais and Rome.

But when we consider that our position in vindication of the superior growth of interior cities over outports is sustained by the civilization of the ancient nations, as found in the examples of their great interior cities, and that, too, when water facilities ruled the commerce of the world, must not all opposing argument in favor of seaboard cities be of naught when we bring to the discussion the power and use of steam, the railway system, and the labor-saving and labor-increasing inventions which the arts afford? Comprehending this mighty reversal in the order and means of industrial civilization, must we not say, with Horace Greeley, that "salt water is about played out"?

Of cities now known as leading centers of commerce, a large majority have been built almost exclusively by domestic trade. What country has so many great cities as China — a country, until lately, nearly destitute of foreign commerce?

There are now in the world more than 300 cities containing a population of 50,000 and upwards; of these more than two-thirds are interior cities, containing a population vastly greater than belongs to the outport cities. It should, however, be kept in mind that many of the great seaports have been built, and are now sustained, mainly by the trade of the nations respectively in which they are situated. Even London, the greatest mart in the world, is believed to derive much the greater part of the support of its vast population from its trade with the United Kingdom. At the present time not one-fifteenth of the business of New York city is based upon foreign commerce, but is sustained by the trade growing out of our home industry.

Though the argument is not exhaustive, it is conclusive. It is founded in the all-directing under life-currents of human existence upon this planet, and from its principles there is neither variableness nor shadow of turning away. Man's home is upon the land; he builds his master-works upon its sure foundations. It is upon the land that he invents, contrives, plans, and achieves his mightiest deeds. He spreads his sails upon the seas and battles with the tempest and the storm; and amid the sublimities of the ocean he travels unknown paths in search of fame. The ephemeral waves obliterate the traces of his victories with the passing moments; upon the land, time alone can efface his works.

The organization of society as one whole is yet too imperfect to call for the use of one all-directing head and one central moving heart, and it will only be the ultimate, the final great city, that will fully unite in itself the functions analogous to those of the human head and heart, in relation to the whole family of man.

The center of this great commercial power will also carry with it the center of the moral and intellectual power. One hundred years, at our previous rate of increase, will give more than four duplications, and more than six hundred millions of people, to the present area of our country. But, allowing twenty-five years for a duplication, and four duplications, we would have six hundred millions at the close of one hundred years. Of these, not less than four hundred millions will inhabit the interior plain and the region west of it; and not over two hundred millions will inhabit the margin east of the Appalachian mountains. The productions of these four hundred millions, intended for exchange with each other, will meet at the most convenient point central to the place of the growth or manufacture of their products. Where, then, let us inquire again, is most likely to be the center of the most ample and best facilities for the exchange, in the future, of the commodities of that great people? Where will that point be? Which of the four cities we have under consideration is best suited for this great purpose? Must it not be St. Louis, commanding, as she will, the greatest railway and river communication? It cannot be a lake city, for neither of them can command, with so great advantage, the great surplus products of the country. It cannot be Cincinnati, for she is not so well situated in the center of the productive power of the continent. It cannot be New Orleans; higher freights upon the products of the country will be against her. It cannot be New York nor San Francisco, for all our six fundamental facts stand against them, and unerringly point to the central plain of the continent, where the four hundred millions of people will prefer to transact business.

Human power, as already stated, is moving westward from the old world, as well as from our own Atlantic seaboard. But a few facts are necessary to demonstrate the truth of this statement: First, in evidence that human power is moving westward from the old world, we have but to refer to the reports of the State Department at Washington upon our foreign commerce to learn that our imports are greater than our exports, and our internal commerce far greater than our foreign commerce; and by reference to the various reports on emigration, we learn that thousands are coming from Western Europe, yearly, to our shores, while but few of our own people are seeking homes on the other side of the Atlantic. Second, in evidence of the westward movement of human power from the Atlantic States, the following statistical facts are given; and although our tables show, in the most conclusive manner, that human power is moving westward, yet since they were made up, many thousands of new miles of railways have been added to the great system of the Mississippi Valley, and at least three-fifths of the number of miles of railways of the entire country are now in the Valley of the Mississippi.

Nor can these facts, in their magnitude and character, be considered of casual concern to the American citizen; for they are the most important in our national progress. They are the irrefutable evidences of the historic and sublime march of the American people in the course of the star of empire in its majestic career across the continent.

The following Table will show the number of miles of railroad in operation in the United States for each year since 1830, also the ratio of such mileage to the area and the population of the several States.

Year.	Miles in operation.	Annual increase of mileage.	Year.	Miles in operation.	Annual increase of mileage.	Year.	Miles in operation.	Annual increase of mileage.
1831........	23	......	1844......	4,377	192	1857......	24,408	2,491
1832........	95	72	1845......	4,633	256	1858......	26,968	2,460
1833........	229	134	1846......	4,930	297	1859......	28,789	1,821
1834........	380	151	1847......	5,599	669	1860......	30,635	1,846
1835........	633	253	1848......	5,996	397	1861......	31,256	621
1836........	1,098	265	1849......	7,365	1,369	1862......	32,120	864
1837........	1,273	175	1850......	9,021	1,656	1863......	33,170	1,050
1838........	1,497	224	1851......	10,982	1,961	1864......	33,908	738
1839........	1,913	416	1852......	12,908	1,926	1865......	35,085	1,177
1840........	2,302	389	1853......	15,360	2,462	1866......	36,827	1,742
1841........	2,818	516	1854......	16,720	1,360	1867......	39,276	2,449
1842........	3,535	717	1855......	18,374	1,654	1868......	42,255	2,979
1843........	4,026	491	1856......	22,017	3,643	1869......	47,254	4,999
1844........	4,185	159	....	....	......	....	....	....

STATEMENT

Showing the area, population, and railroad mileage in the several States, and their relation to each other, on or near January 1, 1870.

STATES, ETC.	Area in sq. miles.	POPULATION.		Miles of RR	Cost.	Cost per mile.	1 MILE OF R.R.	
		Total.	To sq. mile.				To sq. mile.	To inhabitants.
Maine	31,776	665,600	20.03	680	$ 24,694,200	36,315	46.71	977.9
New Hampshire	9,280	340,000	36.64	702	23,479,092	33,446	13.22	484.3
Vermont	10,212	320,000	31.33	621	25,043,408	41,864	16.42	514.4
Massachusetts	7,800	1,350,000	173.08	1,480	88,361,920	59,704	5.27	912.2
Rhode Island	1,306	200,000	153.14	125	5,092,125	40,737	10.45	1,600.0
Connecticut	4,674	525,000	112.32	692	26,453,700	38,225	6.75	758.6
New York	47,000	4,400,000	93.62	3,658	184,476,598	50,431	12.89	1,202.4
New Jersey	8,320	900,000	108.17	1,011	62,594,043	61,913	8.22	890.2
Pennsylvania	46,000	3,500,000	76.69	4,898	254,877,226	52,037	9.39	714.5
Delaware	2,120	125,000	58.96	210	7,828,590	37,279	10.10	595.5
Maryland and District of Columbia.	11,184	800,000	71.54	588	34,398,599	58,501	19.02	1,360.5
West Virginia	23,000	400,000	17.39	387	26,508,726	68,498	59.43	1,033.6
Ohio	39,964	2,650,000	66.31	3,448	137,020,072	39,739	11.59	768.5
Michigan	56,451	1,200,000	19.45	1,325	57,151,225	43,133	42.60	905.7
Indiana	33,809	1,750,000	51.77	2,853	102,143,106	35,802	11.85	613.8
Illinois	55,410	2,567,532	44.21	4,036	178,704,476	42,791	13.17	607.0
Wisconsin	53,924	1,300,000	25.09	1,512	57,974,616	38,343	35.66	925.8
Minnesota	83,531	600,000	7.19	795	25,249,200	31,760	105.09	754.7
Iowa	55,045	1,250,000	22.74	2,095	82,557,665	39,407	26.28	596.6
Missouri	65,350	1,600,000	24.50	1,800	98,991,000	54,995	38.17	934.6
Nebraska, Wyom'g, and Utah	300,000	250,000	.83	1,058	....	....	283.55	236.3
Kansas	81,318	600,000	7.38	1,150	46,621,000	40,540	87.34	644.4
Colorado	....	....	....	293	8,790,000	30,000	....	....
Virginia	40,904	1,300,000	31.78	1,483	52,312,825	35,275	27.59	876.6
North Carolina	50,704	1,050,000	20.78	1,130	23,148,050	20,485	44.87	829.2
South Carolina	29,385	700,000	23.82	1,101	5,123,691	25,491	26.71	636.3
Georgia	58,000	1,100,000	18.97	1,652	33,537,252	20,301	35.11	671.9
Florida	59,268	150,000	2.53	446	9,705,852	21,762	132.69	336.3
Alabama	50,722	980,000	19.32	1,081	27,191,474	25,154	46.92	906.6
Mississippi	47,156	800,000	16.96	990	29,021,850	29,315	47.66	808.1
Louisiana	41,346	730,000	17.69	375	15,116,375	40,577	110.26	1,946.6
Texas	237,504	750,000	3.16	583	21,013,652	36,044	407.39	1,286.4
Kentucky	37,600	1,250,000	33.24	852	....	35,776	44.01	1,467.1
Tennessee	45,600	1,050,000	23.03	1,451	....	25,987	31.42	723.6
Arkansas	52,191	500,000	9.58	128	....	43,562	407.74	3,906.2
California	188,981	600,000	3.17	702	52,840,944	75,272	269.20	854.7
Nevada	112,090	100,000	.89	60	....	....	1587.90	1,333.3
Oregon	95,274	80,000	.84	402	10,307,682	25,641	278.83	248.7
				47,853				

The above table, with some slight changes, is taken from Mr. Poor's *Railroad Manual* for 1870–71. In some particulars it is incorrect. It falls short in giving the present population of the country. Our present census will show us to have more than 42,000,000 inhabitants. It is estimated that our present railway system, as exhibited by the above table, cost $2,000,000,000, which is the annual value of the commerce of our Western rivers.

STATISTICAL TABLE,

Prepared from the United States Census Reports, showing the Controlling Power and Progress of the Mississippi Valley.

Description of Resources	Atlantic Slope.		Mississippi Valley.		Pacific Slope.	
	1850.	*1860.*	*1850.*	*1860.*	*1850.*	*1860.*
Population	13,255,254	15,903,802	9,813,117	14,993,427	107,271	491,153
Area, square miles	323,197	423,197	1,899,811	1,899,811	627,256	627,256
Land improved in farms, acres	63,965,491	73,882,853	48,885,479	87,034,199	181,644	3,537,668
Land unimproved in farms, acres	84,598,954	93,679,468	90,736,948	142,567,264	4,191,998	7,763,090
Cash value of farms	$1,991,599,378	$3,132,561,500	$1,232,941,038	$3.446,702,533	$6,033,010	$67,780,934
Value of farming implements and machinery	$78,826,805	$105,820,439	$72,389,639	$134,292,513	$371,194	$3,985,091
Live stock, horses	1,441,447	2,054,269	2,460,078	3,987,645	32,194	207,260
" asses and mules	760,785	270,187	396,128	641,056	2,411	5,805
" milch cows	3,435,181	3,194,557	2,931,345	4,450,022	18,568	281,151
" working oxen	816,236	755,084	866,348	1,393,995	18,160	45,832
" other cattle	4,619,672	4,545,368	5,372,321	9,099,605	280,276	1,075,314
" sheep	10,663,775	8,704,355	11,013,228	12,644,001	36,218	1,221,919
" swine	10,167,505	9,767,182	20,152,783	23,254,291	33,925	554,672
Value of live stock	$280,479,888	$502,975,639	$257,926,413	$617,616,940	$5,774,215	$44,325,528
Wheat, bushels	47,630,178	53,396,897	48,474,581	102,057,361	336,973	7,219,988
Rye, bushels	12,805,283	15,287,195	1,382,214	4,958,375	316	55,844
Indian corn, bushels	180,029,595	201,638,663	359,912,515	636,456,595	25,053	682,486
Oats, bushels	82,865,111	98,216,624	63,656,947	72,350,255	72,114	2,130,306
Rice, pounds	205,439,416	179,427,085	9,874,081	7,730,807	....	2,140
Tobacco, pounds	94,102,203	215,472,069	105,646,057	218,732,827	1,395	3,565
Ginned cotton, bales, 400 lbs. each	899,615	1,278,646	1,546,178	4,108,270	....	136
Wool, pounds	27,881,509	26,502,154	24,581,022	30,765,734	44,428	2,997,035
Peas and beans, bushels	5,696,433	8,585,405	3,514,321	6,263,209	9,147	213,381
Irish potatoes, bushels	46,906,072	69,996,473	19,016,138	39,749,331	144,586	2,403,063
Sweet potatoes, bushels	19,834,295	21,391,242	19,432,803	20,488,724	1,060	214,860
Barley, bushels	4,216,763	6,169,419	938,741	5,258,605	11,511	4,457,867
Buckwheat, bushels	7,111,179	13,012,306	1,639,101	4,180,596	332	80,411
Value of orchard products	$5,268,494	$10,657,206	$2,435,701	$8,072,064	$18,971	$1,262,615
Wine, gallons	73,861	356,645	89,333	1,081,187	58,055	249,360
Value of market garden produce	$3,805,066	$10,261,210	$1,285,580	$4,584,374	$189,384	$1,273,904
Butter, pounds	200,161,424	257,882,960	111,968,204	167,217,182	295,478	4,572,630
Cheese, pounds	80,042,817	73,239,325	25,124,948	28,920,068	68,128	4,524,545
Hay, tons	10,213,398	10,836,040	3,308,028	6,822,187	7,216	359,769

STATISTICAL TABLE—CONTINUED.

Prepared from the United States Census Reports, showing the Controlling Power and Progress of the Mississippi Valley.

DESCRIPTION OF RESOURCES.	ATLANTIC SLOPE.		MISSISSIPPI VALLEY.		PACIFIC SLOPE.	
	1850.	*1860.*	*1850.*	*1860.*	*1850.*	*1860.*
Clover-seed, bushels	316,945	555,224	152,027	180,531	6	1,533
Grass-seed, bushels	300,226	282,184	116,583	563,227	22	4,629
Hops, pounds	3,291,549	10,148,740	205,422	272,014	58	1,162
Hemp, dew-rotted, tons	232	301	32,961	52,979	....	1
Hemp, water-rotted, tons	57	76	1,621	3,788	....	114
Hemp, other prepared, tons	....	3,574	....	13,660	....	....
Flax, pounds	3,355,485	2,622,285	4,343,641	2,093,355	1,190	4,505
Flax-seed, bushels	513,140	142,130	349,067	424,668	5	69
Silk cocoons, pounds	4,855	1,172	6,088	10,772	....	....
Maple sugar, pounds	22,577,904	28,030,706	11,675,532	11,989,699	....	....
Cane sugar, hogsheads, 1,000 lbs each	3,673	3,072	233,141	227,910	....	....
Molasses, gallons, in 1850	760,030	....	11,940,879	....	82	....
Cane molasses, gallons, in 1860	....	1,005,600	....	13,968,396	....	....
Maple " " "	....	484,378	....	1,277,770	....	46
Sorghum " " "	....	575,372	....	6,056,909	....	26,342
Beeswax, pounds, 1860	....	539,633	....	721,827	....	1,327
Honey, pounds, 1860	....	10,359,970	....	12,541,339	....	18,353
Beeswax and honey, in 1850	5,944,794	....	8,908,986	....	10	....
Value of home-made manufactures	$18,160,123	$8,414,632	$16,525,229	$15,739,436	$8,392	$402,788
Value of animals slaughtered	$60,799,400	$92,478,822	$50,564,074	$115,818,366	....	$4,433,444
Value of agricultural implements produced	$4,639,844	$8,903,815	$2,202,767	$8,883,594	....	$15,205
Value of flour and meal produced	$88,151,908	$113,196,213	$45,857,566	$103,851,894	$1,888,332	$6,096,262
Value of lumber sawed and planed	$37,134,449	$46,752,976	$19,037,922	$42,987,879	$2,349,605	$6,171,431
Value of iron foundings	$15,340,012	$21,884,915	$4,771,505	$6,661,741	....	....
Railroads, miles of	6,948	15,345	1,641	15,174	....	74
Railroads, miles of, built in ten years	....	8,397	....	13,533	....	74

Such has been the rapid development of our stupendous system of railways, that more than three-fifths of the roads of the country belong to the States of the great Valley. Add to these the material wealth of the country, as returned by the census of the year 1860, and everywhere evidence is palpable to show that human power is moving westward. The foregoing table is a conclusive exhibit of the fact.

ordinary stage carries past the city about 1,500,000 gallons of water per second, or enough in six seconds to supply the present necessities of its inhabitants for a whole day. It is not only abundant, but is one of the most wholesome waters known. It is true that in time of high water it contains a large per centage of sedimentary matter, brought down by the swift current of the Missouri river, but of this it is easily freed by settling and filtering. And it is worthy of mention here that the old inhabitants of our city are so far from being averse to this admixture of sedimentary matter, that they almost regret that the new works now in course of construction will furnish them settled or clear water.

The first waterworks in St. Louis consisted of a reservoir on the Big Mound, supplied by a small engine from the Mississippi river. It was constructed in 1829–30, and designed to contain 300,000 gallons. The city of St. Louis then numbered 5,852 inhabitants. In 1850, the population being then 77,860, a larger reservoir was completed, holding about 8,000,000 gallons. This reservoir has also been out of use for many years. The reservoir by which the city is now supplied was finished in 1855, when the city contained 125,000 inhabitants. The water is pumped into it by three pumps located at the foot of Bates street, and having a total capacity of about 11,000,000 gallons per day. One of these pumps was procured by the present Board of Water Commissioners in 1868, the other two not having sufficient capacity to supply the city beyond a contingency. Previous to the year 1860 it had become apparent that the existing works would soon be insufficient to supply the city. In fact, the area of the city had been extended so much, and in the direction of grounds so much higher than the reservoir, that a large portion of the territory included within the new limits could not be supplied. The question of new and more extended works was agitated for several years, but without any result, until the Governor of the State, under a law passed in January, 1865, appointed a Board of Water Commissioners. These gentlemen appointed Mr. James P. Kirkwood, the acknowledged head of hydraulic engineers in the United States, since his completion of the Brooklyn waterworks, their Chief Engineer.

In October, 1865, Mr. Kirwood submitted several plans of works to the Commissioners. The one adopted by them was subsequently rejected by the Common Council, to whom, according to the then existing law, belonged the final decision of the matter. The members of the Board of Water Commissioners resigned, and a new Board appointed by the Governor, having retained Mr. Kirkwood's services, submitted new plans to the Common Council for approval, after Mr. Kirkwood had modified his former plans so as to bring them in accordance with the expressed opinion of the Council. There seeming to be but little hope that the conflicting opinions of the members of our City Council would ever admit of their approving any plan, a new law was passed by the Legislature which placed the whole matter in the hands of a commission of three members, and authorized them to apply the proceeds of three and a half millions of bonds, to be issued by the city, to the construction of the works. The new Board appointed as their Chief Engineer Mr. Thomas J. Whitman, an engineer of long experience in hydraulic works. Mr. Kirkwood had declined to accept the position again, but consented to act as consulting engineer.

The plan of their predecessors, with some slight alterations, was adopted by the new Board, and after acquiring the necessary land they proceeded at once with the construction of the works. These works, of which we will give a brief description, are now nearly finished, and will, within two months, furnish the city with an abundant supply of pure and wholesome water.

The water is taken from the Mississippi river, at what is called Bissell's Point, close to the northern boundary of the city. It first enters an iron tower, 80 feet high, sunk to the rock, and provided with gates at different heights, so that the water may be taken at any desired depth below the surface. In this tower are several strainers and screens to free the water from foreign matter before entering the pump-well. From this tower a pipe of 5½ feet interior diameter, and 300 feet in length, conducts the water to the pumping engines, that are to lift it into the settling reservoirs. These engines are two in number, and are duplicate engines of the Cornish-bull class—steam cylinder 64 inches diameter, 12 feet stroke, and plunger 54 inches in diameter and 12 feet stroke, each of a capacity to pump 17,000,000 gallons in twenty-four hours. The foundations for these engines are of the most substantial character, and to provide for the rapidly increasing demand, have been constructed large enough to hold three engines, although one engine, working half time, could supply the present average demand of the city. To free the water from the sedimentary matter, or to settle it, particularly at seasons of high water, four settling reservoirs, each 240 by 660 feet, and averaging in depth about 20 feet, have been constructed close to the river bank. The water pumped by the low-service engines is, by an appropriate set of gates, admitted at will into either of these four reservoirs; there it is left at perfect rest for twenty-four hours, during which time, according to experiments made on the subject, about nineteen-twentieths of the sedimentary matter falls to the bottom. During the next day the water is drawn off by a system of gates so arranged as not to stir up the sediment, and allow the water to discharge at all times near its surface; the last three or four feet of water is not drawn off, but on the fourth day is allowed to run out into the river through proper sluice-gates, taking with it most of the sediment, while the remainder is washed out with the aid of an engine, and the reservoir is then ready for a new supply. Thus, each of the four reservoirs passes through the cycle of operation during four days. The water, after leaving the settling reservoirs, runs by gravity through a covered conduit about one-half mile long, into a small reservoir near the high-service engines, called the clear-water well, and from it through a short conduit to the high-service engines. These are two in number, with steam cylinders of 85 inches diameter and 10 feet stroke, and pump cylinders 50 inches diameter and the same stroke. To give an idea of the size of these engines, we will state that the walking beam of each engine alone weighs 32 tons, and the fly-wheel 36 tons; in fact there are only one or two engines in existence that have a larger capacity than these, each of which must be able, according to contract, to raise sixteen and a half million gallons to a height of 270 feet within twenty-four hours. These engines were built by the Knap Fort Pitt Foundry Company, at Pittsburg, Penn. They pump through a force main five miles in length, and of 36 and 30 inches diameter, into the storage reservoir on Compton Hill. To relieve the engines and force main from any concussion, a stand pipe is now in process of construction which, when completed, will have a height of 242 feet above the ordinary high-water level of the river. It is about one-half mile from the high-service engines, and will, from its summit, present a view of the whole city, and of the river for many miles in its course. Before reaching the storage reservoir two pipes of 20-inch diameter branch off into the city and connect it with the present system of distribution, while a third feeder of the same size starts from the storage reservoir so as to secure continual motion, and thereby prevent the water from becoming foul.

The storage reservoir covers about seventeen acres of land, and is built near the city boundary, at the most elevated point within its limits. The elevation of its water surface will be twenty-six feet above the highest street grade, and will be ample to supply the upper story of every house in the city. We must not omit to mention in this connection that the greatest portion of the 8,000 tons of large pipe needed in the construction of these works has been cast in this city by the enterprising firm of Shickle, Harrison & Howard.

As before stated, the Commissioners expect to have the works ready to supply the city within a few months; and unless some delay impossible to anticipate occurs, St. Louis will soon be able to boast of having the most liberal supply of wholesome water of any city in this country. What beneficial influence the completion of these works will have on the comfort and health of its inhabitants, and on the prosperity of its manufacturing interests, may be easily imagined.

MISSOURI AND HER RESOURCES.

Missouri is the great central State of the World's Republic. Geographically considered, nearly equal portions of the American Union stretch out from her borders towards the North, South, East, and West. Its dormant and latent energies being once awakened and developed, Missouri must become the Empire State of the Center, as New York is of the East. Its climatic position is altogether propitious, the surface not being greatly elevated, and the State lying between the temperate parallels of 36° 30′ and 40° 30′ N. latitude, and between the meridians of 89° 2′ and 95° 52′ W. longitude.

The greatest length of the State, from East to West, is 320 miles, and its width, from North to South, 280. These dimensions embrace an area of 67,380 square miles, equal to 43,123,200 acres of land; being about one-third larger than England, and possessing twice the productive capacity of that wonderful country. Missouri is larger than any State east of the Mississippi, and possesses as much fruitful and arable soil as any of her sister States, whether East or West. Not less than 36,000,000 acres of land in Missouri are well adapted to furnish all the products of a temperate clime.

No State is better supplied with fountains and streams, as well as with great rivers. It is bounded and bisected by the Mississippi and Missouri, two of the largest and longest rivers in the world; rivers whose fountains are more than three thousand miles away, fed by the waters of the Itasca, or the eternal storms that breed and brood about the cliffs and canons of the Rocky Mountains, whose affluents water a score of States and Territories, and whose accumulated floods are poured into a torrid sea. One thousand miles of these great rivers lie within or upon the boundary of Missouri. The principal streams flowing into the Mississippi from this State are the Salt, Meramec, White, and St. Francois, the two latter being more properly rivers of Arkansas; and the main affluents of the Missouri are the Osage, Gasconade, LaMine, Chariton, Grand, Platte, and Nodaway.

Nature has given to Missouri vast resources in agricultural and mineral wealth, also abundant facilities for commanding and managing the internal commerce of the West. St. Louis, her commercial capital, is near the confluence of the two great rivers. There she stands, like the Apocalyptic angel, "with one foot on the land, and the other on the sea," beckoning to her the white-winged messengers of commerce from every ocean, and stretching out her iron fingers to grasp the internal trade of half a continent.

The geographical and mineralogical features of Missouri are not only peculiar, but such as add greatly to the value of its products. What is known as the "Ozark range"— not of mountains, but of hills — passes through the south half of the State from west to east; sometimes appearing merely in the shape of elevated table-lands, and then again broken into rough and rugged hills. Most of the latter, however, are rich in metals or minerals, such as iron, lead, zinc, copper, coal, etc. Much the larger portion of this hilly region, too, is susceptible of cultivation; and for raising sheep, or the culture of the cereals, fruits, and especially grapes, no better land can be found anywhere east of the Rocky Mountains. As the first settlers in Missouri generally sought the rich alluvial and prairie soils of the northwestern and central portions of the State, the vast and fruitful region lying in the southwest, south, and southeast was neglected, and deemed almost worthless. Large quantities of this land, so rich in minerals, and readily yielding fine crops of grain and fruit, have, within a few years, been sold for 12½ cents per acre. That time has passed, however, and thousands of enterprising immigrants, both farmers and miners, are making for themselves pleasant and profitable homes in the south half of Missouri.

The soil along the river bottoms of Missouri is rich as the famed valley of the Nile. Only a little less fruitful, and much more easily put into cultivation, are the millions of acres of rich prairie land in the northwest and central portions of the State. The capacity of this State for producing food for both men and animals is something enormous. Whenever there is a full development of the State's resources, Missouri will furnish happy homes for five millions of people; one-half making bread, not only for themselves, but to feed two or three millions of miners, mechanics, merchants, and professional men; and the whole State receiving every year many millions more for her exports than she pays for imports.

Looking at the two grand districts of Missouri a little more in detail, and beginning with the extreme southeast, we find an extensive bottom-land along the Mississippi, extending from Cape Girardeau south to the Arkansas river. It includes many swamps, which are rendered almost impenetrable by a dense growth of trees. The most extensive of these, called the Great Swamp, commences a few miles south of Cape Girardeau, and passes south to the mouth of the St. Francois, penetrating far into the State of Arkansas. This peculiar feature gave to Missouri its southeastern "pan-handle," or projection south of 36° 30′, the once charmed parallel between freedom and slavery. The early settlers in the region below Cape Girardeau, and south of the proper boundary of the State, could not reach any settlements in Arkansas, on account of the swamps, and prayed to be attached to Missouri, where they were in the habit of trading and getting their corn ground.

Turning northward from the swamp region, and following up the course of the Mississippi, we find a belt of high lands reaching all the way up to the mouth of the Missouri. The highest part of this range is between St. Genevieve and the mouth of the Meramec, where the ridge rises from three to four hundred feet above the waters of the Mississippi. This ridge of high lands is the Ozark range, before alluded to, cut asunder by the Father of Waters, extending westward through the State, not losing its rough and rugged character until it is lost in a ridge of high prairie.

In the country north of the Missouri, constituting about one-third of the State, the country is more level, but sufficiently undulating to secure good drainage; and the soil is generally excellent, a large portion of the country being a rich prairie, watered by numerous streams, each with its belt of timber. Altogether the richest soil and most productive portions of Missouri are to be found in the western and northwestern counties of the State. The Platte country, in the northwest, and Clay, Jackson, and Lafayette counties, in the west, have long been famed for their wonderful yield of hemp, grain, and stock.

THE CLIMATE

Of Missouri is peculiar. Being situated about half way between the great Southern Gulf and the semi-arctic regions of the North, with but slight barriers on either side, she is subject, like all Western States of the same latitude, to frequent changes of temperature. But notwithstanding the great and sudden transitions as indicated by the thermometer, Missouri may be considered a very healthy State. Pulmonary diseases very rarely originate here. In most parts of the State plowing and putting in crops commence in March, and the forests are in full foliage early in May; while in the extreme southern counties cotton is raised, and young stock manage to live through the winter with little or no care.

Taking the State with all its advantages — its fruitful soil and healthful climate, its vast wealth of metals and minerals, its facilities for transportation by rail or river, its present wealth and prospective greatness — and there is scarcely another State in the American Union that affords such attractions and inducements either to the capitalist or the emigrant.

HISTORY.

Although the life of Missouri, as a State, has only extended through half a century, yet it has been the busiest and most progressive half century in the annals of the world, and its characteristics have been stamped upon the history and fortunes of the State. Missouri had its origin amidst the first great political troubles and disputes of the American Republic. A compromise gave legal existence to the State, and this compromise was finally washed out in the blood of a civil war. The fraternal strife which for four years transformed the most beautiful country and the grandest political empire in the world into a great battle-field, gave a full share of its bloody fortunes to Missouri. Some of the fairest portions of the State were almost depopulated, and whole sections passed through the ordeal of blood and fire, and when the desolation had gone by, presented nothing but unpeopled and smoking ruins. But after the night came the day, and the horrid wounds inflicted by civil war began to be healed by the angel of peace. It was sharp and painful surgery that cut away the old excrescence, but it left the body politic healthier, and all the people happier and more prosperous than ever before.

Under the old regime, the States of Illinois and Indiana, although far behind us in natural resources, were outstripping Missouri in the march of empire. Although the great advantages of the State brought many immigrants in spite of the system then in vogue, yet our sister States across the Mississippi were, at the commencement of the war, far in advance of us as regarded population and material wealth. This state of things is being rapidly changed by the multitudes of immigrants from the Eastern and Middle States and the Old World, who are seeking homes on our rich prairies, in our fruitful valleys and extensive forests, or in our exhaustless mines of iron, lead, and zinc.

POPULATION.

The present population of Missouri may be safely put down at nearly, if not quite, 2,000,000. The first census of the State, when it was admitted into the Union in 1821, showed a population of 70,647. From that date the number of inhabitants very nearly doubled each decade up to 1860, when the population of Missouri, including white, free colored, and slaves, amounted to 1,172,797. The war drained the State, not only of material wealth, but of multitudes of people; but the return of peace, and the increased and ever-increasing tide of immigration, will bring the State up to three millions before the year 1880. Of the present inhabitants of Missouri about one hundred thousand, or one in fifteen, are colored. Considering the condition these people have been in for generations past, they have conducted themselves with great propriety since their formal emancipation in 1865. A large majority of them are not only making an honest support for themselves and families, but, by their industry and frugality, accumulating a decent competence. On the south side of the Missouri river especially, there is a large German element in the population. Wherever these people make homes in the country, and plant vineyards or cultivate small farms, you may look with confidence for present prosperity and future wealth. Every town or neighborhood in Missouri that has been planted by Germans is now actually wealthy, or has the elements of certain prosperity in the future.

EDUCATION.

But let us pass from these general views of a great State and its varied resources to some of the details which constitute the grand result. When we speak of the wealth of a State, we should not so much consider its rich mines, its fruitful soil, its genial climate, and its natural channels of commerce and communication, as its people. The people are all that give real wealth to any country. Without inhabitants, the fairest lands upon which the sun shines would be of no more value than a barren beach or a rocky cliff. But, then, the people must have intelligence in order to give value to the country they inhabit. Savages make a land poorer instead of richer by their presence. And just in proportion as a community rise in the scale of civilization, intelligence, refinement, and moral worth, their lands and houses go up in their money value.

In this matter Missouri made a grand investment at the very start, and her school fund has been so well husbanded and increased by legislation that she has now a system of public instruction that may challenge comparison with that of any State in the Union. It is not meant by this that the educational machinery of the State is everywhere in perfect working order, but that the foundations of the system are laid deep and secure; and if any child of Missouri grows up in absolute ignorance, it will be because it refused the light that is offered almost "without money and without price."

The following items will serve to indicate the present working of the common school system in Missouri: Number of children in State between five and twenty-one years, 584,026 for the year 1869; number of children in public schools, 249,729. It would be safe to estimate that 150,000 students were in the numerous colleges, seminaries, private and parochial schools, during the same year. Number of teachers in public schools, 7,145; number of public schools in the State, 5,307; number of public school-houses, 5,412; value of public school-houses, $3,087,062.

The richly-endowed Industrial College, incorporated with the State University, at Columbia, offers not only an academic but an agricultural education to all who desire to become scientific as well as practical farmers. Other incorporated and leading institutions of learning in Missouri are: North Missouri Normal School, at Kirksville; William Jewett College, at Liberty; Grand River College, at Edinburgh; Plattsburg College, at Plattsburg; McGee College, at College Mound; Christian University, at Canton; Washington University and St. Louis University, both at St. Louis; St. Paul's College, at Palmyra; and Bethel College, at Palmyra.

MANUFACTURES.

No great community, living in a fertile and productive country, can be long or largely prosperous unless it shows a certain amount of independence, or rather an ability and disposition to supply most of its ordinary wants. A simple monopoly is always an evil, tending to enrich a few and impoverish the multitude. Before the war, the Southern States made cotton and sugar, and looked to the North almost entirely for breadstuffs. Since the war they have learned to produce a large portion of their food supplies, and, as a result, will soon be more prosperous than ever before.

Missouri has a food-producing capacity sufficient to sustain thirty or forty millions of people. But it is by no means her policy to devote all her energies to raising corn, wheat, and pork, trusting entirely to other States and foreign countries for the ten thousand articles and implements demanded by the present civilization and the various industries connected with it.

Missouri has illimitable quantities of the raw material, and wonderful facilities for generating the necessary power to transform that raw material into the thousand forms suited to the wants of civilized men. Until lately we have done but little in the way of manufactures beyond making wheat into flour, corn into whisky, hemp into bagging and rope, tobacco into shapes to suit smokers and chewers, and iron into stoves and heavy castings. But a new era has dawned upon the State. We have discovered that we can make a thousand articles of primary and pressing need just as well as they can be made in New or Old England. In the single article of iron, the capital invested in its manufacture has quadrupled within the last four or five years. Capitalists from abroad, who have studied our resources and facilities for manufacturing iron, have become satisfied that Missouri must soon become one of the largest iron-producing States in the world; and they are adding millions to the working capital employed in this branch of industry.

The time is approaching when we shall not have to import our railroad iron from Europe, much of our pottery and queensware from other States, our glass and hardware from the good city of Pittsburg, and many of our woolen and cotton goods from New England. When that time comes, Missouri will have achieved her great destiny as the Empire State of the Mississippi Valley.

CREDIT OF MISSOURI.

A country possessing such vast stores of material wealth as Missouri, although much of it is still undeveloped, should have proper credit and consideration in all bureaus of finance throughout the world. A State that could be sold under the hammer to-day for more than a thousand millions of dollars should have her bonds as good as gold. They are nearly so, in spite of the heavy railroad debt incurred before the war. This debt is being rapidly canceled, and very soon Missouri 6's will stand at par or a premium. It may not be improper to add in this connection, that the assessed value of the taxable property in Missouri in 1868, with such addition as the assessors themselves allow to be correct in estimating the real cash value of property, amounted to $1,177,000,000, and this vast amount will be increased to at least $1,250,000,000 the present year.

STOCK-RAISING.

Perhaps there is no one of the great Western States of the American Union better adapted to stock-raising than Missouri. Abundant crops of grain and corn are almost as certain as the return of the seasons. The climate in most parts of the State is mild enough to preclude the necessity of much shelter or long feeding in winter. Small streams, with their meandering branches and bubbling fountains, lie like a net-work all over the State; and some of these streams are so impregnated with salt as to supply stock with all they need of this article.

The following exhibits the number and value of horses, mules, cattle, sheep, and hogs, in 1868:

		VALUE.
Horses	375,400	$19,203,427
Mules	86,299	4,822,988
Cattle	933,517	12,169,234
Sheep	1,385,805	1,951,078
Hogs	1,952,532	3,734,006
Total	4,733,453	$41,880,733

VALUE OF LAND IN MISSOURI.

It is doubtful whether any other State in the Mississippi Valley can furnish good land at so moderate a price as Missouri. On the south side of the Missouri river there are more than a million of acres (much of it good land) still to be given away as homesteads. In the same portion of the State there are millions of acres, mostly lying south of the Osage river, that can be bought for from fifty cents to five dollars an acre. Much of this land is equal to any in the whole country for vineyards, fruit, and sheep farms. In the extreme southeastern quarter of the State there is an immense body of the richest land in the world, which can be restored to use by drainage, and that, too, at a moderate cost, compared with the value of the land to be redeemed. Not only can a large portion of the land in the south half of Missouri be obtained very cheaply, but even the finely cultivated farms along the valley of the Missouri and all over the rich prairies of the western, central, and northern portions of the State, can be purchased lower than the same kind of land and improvements in Illinois. No country in the wide West offers stronger inducements to the enterprising and industrious immigrant than Missouri. If he is a farmer, our fruitful soil awaits the hand of the cultivator, to whom it will return "thirty, fifty, or an hundred fold." If he is a miner or mechanic, his hands shall find plenty of work, with liberal pay.

MINERAL RESOURCES OF MISSOURI.

BY PROF. G. C. SWALLOW,

FORMER STATE GEOLOGIST.

COLUMBIA Mo., *September 20, 1870.*

L. U. REAVIS, Esq.:

My Dear Sir: Your note requesting me to make out a chapter on the *Mineral Resources* of Missouri for the new edition of your work, was duly received. I have attempted to comply with your request; but numerous previous engagements have rendered it impossible for me to make it as perfect and complete as I would wish.

Permit me to suggest that your article on this subject, in the first edition, is too valuable to be omitted in the future editions. Our minerals and our soils are the foundations of the argument, and upon these you can scarcely say too much.

I heartily wish you entire success in your great work, hoping ere long to congratulate you in the Mound City, when it shall have become the *Business Metropolis* and the *Political Capital* of the nation.

Very truly, your obedient servant,

G. C. SWALLOW.

There is no territory of equal extent on the continent which contains so many and such large quantities of the most useful minerals as the State of Missouri. In making this remark there is no desire to underrate the mineral resources of other States or of the adjacent Territories, but to announce the fact that some good fortune has set the boundaries of this State around a portion of country filled with an unusual amount of the mineral substances useful in the arts and manufactures, and that several of those most useful are found in such quantities that the supply is virtually inexhaustible. There are some that no demand for home consumption or for foreign supplies can exhaust within the time allotted for the rise, progress, and decay of nations.

Only small portions of the precious metals have been discovered in Missouri; nor is it desirable there should be. It is true that deposits of silver and gold concentrate populations very rapidly and yield many large fortunes; but history does not show that countries producing silver and gold have been permanently prosperous. Gold built up California very rapidly, and it is now filled with a great and prosperous people; but gold does not keep them there, nor does it induce the present immigration. The beautiful climate and wonderful agricultural resources are its present attractions.

Mexico and Peru have large and numerous deposits of precious metals; but they have never secured permanent prosperity, though peopled by what were the best races of Europe.

Spain has had vast quantities of gold and silver, both at home and in her foreign possessions, from the earliest antiquity; but the most prosperous nations of ancient and modern times have imported nearly all the gold and silver they have used. Gold mining has yielded many colossal fortunes, as to Crœsus in ancient times, and to many familiar names of later date; still the great mass of those engaged in gold mining have lived poor and died poor. These results might be expected from the very nature of the business. Nine-tenths of all the labor spent in the search for and in mining gold meets with no reward, while some of it has been rewarded with signal success. All who engage in this business, therefore, have high expectations, and many spend their gains lavishly, live fast, and, if not successful, often become dissipated and worthless. Almost all other pursuits yield a reward which may be calculated with some degree of certainty, which gives stability and permanence and leads to regular habits and progress. These results become very marked in national character when examined in the light of history. Great Britain and Spain give a striking illustration. Scarcely three centuries have elapsed since the united crowns of Castile and Aragon ruled a more prosperous people than the thrones of Albion and Scotia. Spain extended her rule over the fairest portions of the New World and held the commerce of both hemispheres. Galleon after galleon, deeply laden with the precious metals from the mines of Mexico and Peru, filled the treasury of the government and the pockets of her people. England, on the other hand, was opening her mines of iron and coal and pushing her manufactories by all the appliances of science and art.

Spain has squandered her gold and become a mere pensioner on Cuba. But England now holds the commerce of both Indies, and the world pays a golden tribute to her iron and coal.

If Missouri will work up her iron and coal she may become as powerful and rich as England. She has more territory and better soil, more and better iron and quite as much coal.

People who work iron partake of its strong and hardy nature. They move the world and shape its destinies. The region tributary to St. Louis has far more of the very best varieties of iron ore than can be found available for any other locality in the known world; and the facilities for working these vast deposits are unsurpassed. The country is well watered; timber is abundant; and all is surrounded by inexhaustible coal beds. These facts alone will make St. Louis the great *iron mart* of the country.

SPECULAR OXIDE OF IRON.

This is one of the most abundant and valuable ores in the State. Iron Mountain is the largest mass observed. It is two hundred feet high and covers an area of five hundred acres, and is made up almost entirely of this ore in its purest form. The quantity above the surface of the valley is estimated at

200,000,00C tons. But this is only a fraction of the ore here, as it descends to unknown depths, and every foot of the descent will yield some 3,000,000 tons. Veins of this ore cut the porphyry at the shut-in, the location of the first iron furnace erected in this region. Fine beds of this ore were also found at the Buford ore-bed at the Big Bogy Mountains, at Russell Mountain, at the James iron-works, and other localities in Phelps county; and in sections two, three, ten, and eleven, of township thirty-five, range four, west, in Dent county, on the Southwest Pacific railroad, and in several other localities in that county There are several important deposits in Crawford, Phelps, and Pulaski counties.

SILICIOUS SPECULAR OXIDE

Is found in very large quantities in Pilot Knob, where it is interstratified with slates and porphyry, as in the famous Iron Mountain near Lake Superior. The iron of Pilot Knob has been worked for many years. Its quality is as good as its quantity is great.

MAGNETIC AND SPECULAR OXIDE

Exists in large veins in the porphyry of Shepherd Mountain. It is very pure, and large quantities have been worked.

There is iron enough, of the very best quality, within a few miles of Pilot Knob and Iron Mountain to furnish one million tons of manufactured iron per annum for the next two hundred years. All these ores are well adapted to the manufacture of pig metal, and the most of them are suitable for making blooms by the Catelau process, and steel by the Bessemer.

BOG ORE

Has been discovered in beds several miles in extent in the swamps and cypresses of Southeast Missouri — in Scott, Mississippi, Dunklin, Pemiscot, and New Madrid counties, in quantity sufficient in itself alone to make Missouri the *great Iron State.*

HEMATITE ORES

Of good quality are very generally distributed over the southern part of the State, where it is often found in very extensive beds. Large deposits have been discovered in Cooper, St. Clair, Green, Henry, Franklin, Benton, Dallas, Camden, Stone, Madison, Iron, Washington, Perry, St. Francois, Reynolds, Stoddard, Scott, and Dent counties. The beds discovered in Scott, Stoddard, and Perry counties are very extensive and of good quality. The beds in the tertiary rocks of Scott county are not so good. In these beds of hematite alone Misssouri has more iron than can be smelted in the present and succeeding generations.

SPATHIC ORE

Has been discovered in very extensive beds in the tertiary rocks of Scott county, where the ore is very pure. The coal measures of Missouri contain many beds of spathic ore; and it is found in greater or less quantities throughout the entire area of 27,000 square miles covered by these rocks. These beds of ore are similar to many worked extensively in England and Pennsylvania; and, in the absence of the vast beds of other ores of better quality, they would attract more attention and be made productive.

Were it possible to exhaust the more available deposits in the State, the spathic ores of the tertiary and coal rocks could supply all the demands for iron for a long period.

In a chapter so limited it is impossible to mention all the hundreds of localities already discovered, to say nothing of the areas not yet explored. There are already recorded in the reports of the geological survey fifty-six workable beds in Green, Phelps, Maries, and Crawford counties alone, and good ore is still more abundant in the counties of the Southeast.

In other States there are many very extensive iron deposits, which will naturally gravitate toward St. Louis. Among them there are some very valuable in the Indian Territory, which our railroads will make available.

But the most extensive iron bed yet observed is on the Missouri river, cropping out in the bluffs on both banks of the river for a distance of more than twenty-five miles. These beds are on the river, and many million tons could be mined and put on boats for less than one dollar per ton; and the expense of carrying to St. Louis, down stream, would be very small.

Other localities might be mentioned, but we have shown the position of enough of the various varieties of iron ore to supply any possible demand of any possible manufacturing city for the next thousand years, and all is so located as to be tributary to St. Louis.

The simple fact that such quantities of iron ore do exist so near and in places so accessible, will compel this young and vigorous city to become *the Iron Mart.* The iron furnaces at Iron Mountain, Pilot Knob, Irondale, Moselle works, James works, St. Louis, and Carondelet, fifteen in all, with a capacity of 130,000 tons, and two rolling mills with a capacity of 40,000 tons, and the numerous foundries and machine shops, are the growth of a few years — a mere beginning of the great work of utilizing our iron ores. These will increase in a rapid ratio until a hundred furnaces pour forth the molton metal, a score of mills roll it into rails and bars and plates, and a hundred foundries mold it into the ten thousand shapes and forms demanded by human industry. Then shall we see the millenium of iron men, and our people be prepared to appreciate the value of our iron beds; and they will appreciate the justice of your noble tribute *to the pioneers of iron in Missouri.*

COAL.

Mineral coal has done much to promote the rapid progress of the present century. Commerce and manufactures could not have reached their present unprecedented prosperity without its aid; and no people can expect success in those departments of human industry unless their territory furnishes an abundance of this useful mineral. Previous to the geological survey it was known that coal existed in many counties of the State, but there was no definite knowledge of the continuation of workable beds over any considerable areas; but since the geological survey commenced, the southeastern outcrop of the coal measures has been traced from the mouth of the Des Moines, through Clark, Lewis, Shelby, Monroe, Audrain, Boone, Cooper, Pettis, Henry, St. Clair, Bates, Vernon, and Barton, into the Indian Territory, and every county on the northwest of this line is known to contain more or less coal, giving us an area of over 26,000 square miles of coal beds in that part of the State. We have proved the existence of vast quantities of coal in Johnson, Pettis, Lafayette, Cass, Cooper, Chariton, Howard, Boone, Saline, Putnam, Adair, Macon, Carroll, Ray, Callaway, Audrain, and it is confidently expected that the counties to the northwest will prove to be as rich when fully examined. Outside of the coal-field as given above, the regular coal rocks also exist in Ralls, Montgomery, Warren, Callaway, St. Charles, and St. Louis, and local deposits of cannel and bituminous coal in Moniteau, Cole, Morgan, Crawford, Callaway, and probably other counties. Workable beds of good coal exist in nearly all places where the coal measures are developed, as some of the best beds are near their base, and must crop out on the borders of the coal-field. This is found to be the fact where examinations have been made. All of the little outliers along the border contain more or less coal, though the stratas are not more than forty or fifty feet thick. But, exclusive of these outliers and local deposits, we have an area of twenty-six thousand eight hundred square miles of the regular coal measures. If the average thickness of workable coal be one foot only, it will give 26,800,-000,000 tons for the whole area occupied by coal rocks. But in many places the thickness of the workable beds is over fifteen feet, and the least estimate that can be made for the whole area is five feet. This will give over 134,000,-000,000 tons of good available coal in our State. Such were our estimates of the coal in Missouri in 1855. Since then new beds have been opened in the area above designated and large tracts discovered in other parts of the State, along the whole line of the southeastern outcrop of the lower coal strata, from the mouth of the Des Moines to the Indian Territory. Along the lines of all the railroads in North Missouri, and along the western end of the Missouri Pacific, active and systematic mining has opened our coal beds in a thousand localities, and developed a series of facts which render it absolutely certain that our former estimate falls far below the real quantity in the State. Prior to 1855 no coal beds had been discovered on the Missouri river between Kansas City and Sioux City, save one or two thin beds in the upper coal measures, and practical men were slow to believe the geologist could detect the existence of coal beneath the surface. But some brave men at Leavenworth City have sunk a shaft to one of the lowest coal beds, 700 feet beneath their city, and more than 600 feet below the Missouri river at that point. The success of this enterprise proves the deductions of science that our lower coal beds, which crop out along the eastern boundary of our coal-field, from Clark county to Vernon, dip beneath the surface and extend to the west as far at least as Leavenworth, or beyond the western boundary of Missouri.

This and other similar developments prove to a moral certainty that our esti-

But granting that human power is moving westward, we must assume that somewhere in time it will be arrested, and culminate in the highest enfoldment of civil, social, and material life. Then, in its westward movement, will it be arrested in North America, or will it cross the Pacific to the inferior races of Asia, or will it reach and make a lodgment on the Pacific slope? We cannot so reason or apprehend. The vast arid and mountainous regions of the western half of the continent, and the unequaled extent of fertile lands on the eastern half of the continent, and adjacent to and on either side of the great river, fixes its location inevitably in the central plain of the continent; and in the center of its productive power, and with the development and complete organization of human power in the center of the productive power of the continent, will most certainly grow up the great city of the future—the great material, social, civil, and moral heart of the human race. The raw materials necessary to the artisan and the manufacturer, in the production of whatever ministers to comfort and elegance, are here. The bulkiness of food and raw materials makes it the interest of the artisan and the manufacturer to locate himself near the place of their production. It is this interest, constantly operating, which peoples our Western towns and cities with emigrants from the Eastern States and Europe. When food and raw materials for manufacture are no longer cheaper in the great valley than in the States of the Atlantic and the nations of Western Europe, then, and not till then, will it cease to be the interest of artisans and manufacturers, to prefer a location in Western towns and cities. This time will probably be about the period when the Mississippi shall flow toward its head.

The chief points for the exchange of the varied productions of industry in our Western valley will necessarily give employment to a great population. Indeed, the locations of our future great cities have been made with reference to their commercial capabilities. Commerce has laid the foundation on which manufactures have been, to a great extent, instrumental in rearing the superstructure. Together, these departments of labor are destined to build up in our fertile valley the greatest cities of the world.

It is something to us Americans that this great city, the great all-directing heart of the race, is to grow up in our land. Even to us of this generation a realization of the final fact is a proud thought to enjoy, in the present and coming conflicts of this progressive life. As we have already seen, St. Louis is substantially central to the Mississippi Valley, and no city on the continent can lay any just claim to become the future great city, and occupy a central position to so many valuable resources as she does. She is not only substantially in the center of the Mississippi Valley, but, allowing her to be nine hundred miles from New York City, she occupies the center of an area of 2,544,688 square miles, and within a circumference the outer line of which touches Chicago. She occupies the center of an area of country which, in fertility of soil, coal, iron, timber, stone, water, domestic navigation, and railways, cannot be equaled on the globe.

Cities, like individuals, have a law of growth that may be said to be constitutional and inherent, but the measure of that law of growth does not seem to be sufficiently understood to furnish a basis for calculating their growth to any considerable time in the future. In the development of a nation and country, new agencies are continually coming into the account of growth and work, either favorable or unfavorable. The growth of cities is somewhat analogous to the pursuits of business men: some move rapidly forward in the accumulation of wealth, to the end of life; others only for a time are able to keep even with the world. So, too, in the growth of cities; and thus it is difficult to calculate with exactness their future growth. Cities grow with greater rapidity than nations and States, and much sooner double their population; and, with the constantly increasing tendency of the people to live in cities, we can look with greater certainty to the early triumph of our inland cities over those of the seaboard; for, so surely as the population of the Valley States doubles that of the seaboard States, so surely will their cities be greater. The city of London, now the greatest in the world, having more than three million people, has only doubled its population every thirty years, while New York has doubled every fifteen years. According to Mr. J. W. Scott, London grows at an average annual rate, on a long time, of two per cent.; New York, at five; Chicago, at twelve and one-half; Toledo, twelve; Milwaukee, Detroit, Cleveland, Cincinnati, Buffalo, and St. Louis, at the rate of eight per cent. Mr. Scott gives these calculations as approximately true for long periods of time. They may be essentially true in the past, but cannot be relied on for the future; for, as I have already said, the growth of a city is as uncertain as a man's chance is in business—he may pass directly on to fortune, or may be kept back by the fluctuations of the markets, or greater hindrances interposed by wars. Touching the subject of climate, I shall not deem it of sufficient bearing upon this subject to enter into a nice discussion of the influence of heat and cold upon man in civilized life, in the north temperate zone of the North American continent. All experience teaches that there is not sufficient variation of the climate throughout the middle belt of our country to adversely affect the highest and greatest purposes of American industry and American civilization. The same rewards and the same destiny await all. The densest population of which we have any record is now, and has been for centuries, on the thirtieth degree of north latitude; and if such can be in China, why may it not be in America?

Again, returning to our first fundamental fact, that human power is moving westward from the city of London, we must calculate that that great city will be succeeded by a rival, one which will grow up in the new world, and that that new city will result in the final organization of human society in one complete whole, and the perfect development and systemization of the commerce of the world; will grow to such magnificent proportions, and be so perfectly organized and controlled in its municipal governmental character, as to constitute the most perfect and greatest city of the world—the all-directing head and heart of the great family of man. The new world is to be its home, and nature and civilization will fix its residence in the central plain of the continent, and in the center of the productive power of this great valley, and upon the Mississippi river, and where the city of St. Louis now stands. All arguments point to this one great fact of the future, and, with its perfect realization, will be attained the highest possibility in the material triumph of mankind.

Let us comprehend the inevitable causes which God and civilization have set to work to produce, in time, this final great city of the world in our own fair land; and, with prophetic conception, realizing its final coming, let us hail it as the master-work of all art and the home of consummated wisdom, the inheritance of organic liberty, and controlled by an all-pervading social order that will insure a competency to every member of the in-gathered family. The immense accommodation of railroads will, by rapid, cheap, and easy communication, draw to great centers from great distances around, and thus the great cities of the world will continue to grow until they reach a magnitude hitherto unknown; and, above them all, will St. Louis reap the rich rewards of modern discoveries and inventions, especially as regards steam and all its vast and varied influence.

Henceforth St. Louis must be viewed in the light of her future, her mightiness in the empire of the world, her sway in the rule of States and nations. Her destiny is fixed. Like a new-born empire, she is moving forward to conscious greatness, and will soon be the world's magnet of attraction. In her bosom all the extremes of the country are represented, and to her growth all parts of the country contribute. Mighty as are the possibilities of her people, still mightier are the hopes inspired. The city that she now is is only the germ of the city of the future that she will be, with her ten million souls occupying the vast area of her dominion. Her strength will be that of a nation, and, as she grows toward maturity, her institutions of learning and philosophy will correspondingly advance. If we but look forward, in imagination, to her consummated greatness, how grand is the conception! We can realize that here will be reared great halls and edifices for art and learning; here will congregate the great men and women of future ages; here will be represented, in the future, some Solon and Hamilton, giving laws for the higher and better government of the people; here will be represented some future great teachers of religion, teaching the ideal and spiritual unfolding of the race, and its allegiance to the angel world; here will live some future Plutarch, weighing the great men of his age; here some future "Mozart will thrill the strings of a more perfect lyre, and improvise grandest melodies" for the congregated people; here some future "Rembrandt, through his own ideal imagination, will picture for himself more perfect panoramic scenes of nature's lovely landscapes." May we not justly rejoice in the anticipation of the future greatness of the civil, social, industrial, intellectual, and moral elements which are destined to form a part of the future great city? And may we not realize that the millions who are yet to be its inhabitants will be a wiser and better people than those of this generation, and who, in more perfect life, will walk these streets, in the city of the future, with softer tread, and sing music with sweeter tones, be urged on by aspirations of higher aims, rejoice with fuller hearts, and adorn in beauty, with more tender hands, the final great city of the world?

THE RAILWAY SYSTEM OF ST. LOUIS.

To determine the importance of a State or city, its essential condition and advantages must be defined and understood, both in their immediate and approximate relations; and to ascertain their future greatness and controlling influence, their local and general relations must be considered in connection with the natural advantages which they possess for the civil and industrial pursuits of man, and their natural and artificial facilities for the exchange of the products of different lands and climates, and the intercommunication of one people with another. By these means the commercial and civil value of all States and cities can easily be determined, and their general values estimated in the march of civilization and progress. It is by these means that we propose to determine the commercial importance of St. Louis, and the place she will fill, and the influence she will exercise in the present continental strife for commercial supremacy.

The most important consideration of the subject is her system of railroads and navigable rivers, a full description of which we submit, in so far as the facts relate to the practicable purposes of commerce.

The Mississippi river is the continental stream of North America. It forms a line of unbroken navigation from New Orleans to Fort Snelling, a distance of 2,131 miles. No stream has ever served so valuable purposes to commerce and civilization, and no city upon its banks has ever or can ever share so largely in the commerce that floats upon its waters as St. Louis. In connection with its tributaries it affords more than ten thousand miles of inland navigation, and more than three-fourths of which bear directly upon the interests of St. Louis. More than ten thousand steamboats, together with a large number of barges, lighters, and similar crafts, used as auxiliaries in the carrying trade, are actively engaged in the commerce of these waters; the far greater part of which does now and will continue to bear upon the interests of St. Louis.

Besides the already navigable streams there are many smaller tributaries which will, when the country is older and more wealthy, be converted into canals, and thus furnish an extended western slack-water navigation.

Turning from the rivers, we now proceed to set forth her great system of railroads, as they are now completed; also those which are being built, and the most important of such lines as have been agitated.

1. The St. Louis and Cairo R. R. Projected.
2. Belleville and Southern R. R.
3. St. Louis and Evansville R. R. Building.
4. St. Louis and Southeastern Illinois R. R. Building.
5. New Albany and St. Louis R. R. Building.
6. The Ohio and Mississippi R. R.
7. The St. Louis, Vandalia and Terre Haute R. R.
8. The Indianapolis and St. Louis R. R.
9. Decatur and East St. Louis R. R.
10. Chicago, Alton and St. Louis R. R. This road will soon have a double steel track between Chicago and St. Louis.
11. St. Louis, Jacksonville and Bloomington R. R.
12. Rockford, Rock Island and St. Louis R. R.
    Peoria, Pekin and Jacksonville R. R.; a connection.
13. Quincy and St. Louis R. R. Prospective.
    Crossing the Mississippi river, north of St. Louis, the first road we meet is
14. The St. Louis and Keokuk R. R. Building.
15. The North Missouri R. R. North Branch.
16. The North Missouri R. R. West Branch.
17. The North Missouri and St. Joseph R. R., *via* Hannibal and St. Jo. R. R.
18. St. Louis, Chillicothe and Omaha R. R. Building.
19. Missouri Pacific R. R.
    Sedalia and Lexington Branch of Mo. Pacific.
    Sedalia and Ft. Scott Branch of Mo. Pacific.
20. St. Louis and Ft. Scott Air Line R. R. Prospective.
21. Southwest Pacific R. R.
22. Iron Mountain R. R. to Galveston and Mexico.
23. St. Louis and Springfield, Illinois. Projected.
24. Illinois Central R. R. Running through trains between Chicago and St. Louis and St. Louis and Dubuque, using the Vandalia line to come into St. Louis.

Thus we have twenty-four distinct trunk roads converging at St. Louis, nearly every one of which is built, or under way of construction, and not one will be abandoned. No other city on the continent or in the world has so many, nor is it likely that any rival place will ever be favored with so great a number. I have neglected to place on the list several local and connecting roads, which properly belong to the St. Louis system and are valuable feeders to other lines, but for their not being essentially trunk lines, were omitted. My object has been more especially to show that St. Louis stands in the center of a great system of railways and navigable rivers, which radiate from her as a focal point to almost every extremity of the country, touching oceans, lakes, and seas, and uniting the civil, social, and commercial interests of a continental people, as well as creating an easy exchange for the fish, fruits, and other products of antagonistic climates.

The following statement of distances will show how St. Louis stands in relation to some of the principal cities of the country, as well as to our seaboard markets.

Places.	Distance.	Places.	Distance.
From St. Louis to—	Miles.	From St. Louis to—	Miles.
Boston, via rail	1200	New Orleans, via rail	722
New York	1042	Galveston	787
Philadelphia	974	San Francisco	2353
Baltimore	929	Denver City	912
Washington City	951	Omaha	433
Richmond	1096	Leavenworth	296
Norfolk	1176	Chicago	280
Charleston	970	Cincinnati	340
Savannah	960	Louisville	302
Mobile	666	Indianapolis	238
Kansas City	272	Cairo	153
Buffalo	704	Detroit	564
Milwaukee	365	Pittsburgh	611

In submitting this statement of the railway system of St. Louis, its mighty frame-work and net-work which ramifies the entire Valley of the Mississippi, and extends its Briarean arms to each ocean, the gulf and the lakes, and holds in its grasp the empire of the continent, we also submit that in the most superlative degree does St. Louis occupy the center of the greatest productive power, as well as the greatest center of river navigation afforded on the globe; and thus uniting the greatest means with the greatest facilities that the world affords, who, with a just comprehension of the facts, does not see the truth of the argument in favor of the future great city so conclusively as to be convinced of its correctness, generations in advance of the actual existence of the city itself? But this vast contribution of productive power, this system of river navigation, as well as the ever-expanding railway system, has a primary meaning. They all mean and foreshadow generations of civil, industrial, and commercial progress, and these lead to a consideration of a new

RAILWAY POLICY FOR ST. LOUIS,

as well as for the entire West, and this new policy means nothing more nor less than a Western railway policy, and with its establishment will also be organized a political and commercial policy for the West. It is no longer the fact that the great States of the Mississippi Valley are commercial or political dependencies to the cities of the Atlantic seaboard. It is true they have political and commercial interest with those States and cities, and it is to be hoped ever will have. But the time is now and will continue henceforth, long as the waters run, that the commercial and political importance of the Valley States are greater than those of either seaboard, and therefore they must be the dictators of such political and commercial policies as their wisdom and welfare may demand. The political power and commerce of the American people have spanned the continent, and from the Pacific shore civilization re-acts to the center, where, like a great maelstrom, sweeping from the circumference to the center, will be the greatest power and activity of our people in their future growth and struggle for gain.

It therefore becomes the people of St. Louis, as well as of the West, to establish a railway policy that will best subserve their commercial interest—a policy that will create an exchange of Western products North and South, instead of allowing them to be carried away in less valuable channels, East and West. Nature has already dictated that the commerce of this great valley must follow the flow of the waters to the gulf, and there seek the markets of the world; and those of the West who do not already comprehend this truth will soon learn it through the impoverished railway policy that is rapidly binding them to the East, as the Philistines bound Samson.

St. Louis must make a bold stand for a railway policy that will cause the exchange of the products of the Valley States North and South—exchange them between the lakes and the gulf—between climates, and not along parallel lines of longitude. St. Louis wants the trade of the tropics and the trade of the North. She must have a railway policy that will establish this trade, and make her the point of exchange between the two climates.

By the new railway line now projected, *via* Iron Mountain, Fulton and Galveston Railroad, which is under way of construction, the gulf can be reached at a distance of 787 miles. When this road is completed it will be of vastly more value to St. Louis than any other road that reaches her, and its completion will open the way for that policy for North and South exchange which must be established in the interest of the trade of the Valley States.

In the interest of the especial climatic trade and postal service of the people between the lakes and the gulf, it is highly probable that a project will, in the course of ten years, be set on foot to construct a pneumatic tube from Chicago, *via* St. Louis, to New Orleans. The postal patronage, together with the fish and fruit trade, would well nigh, if not wholly, repay for its construction.

POPULATION CONSIDERED.

The material growth of St. Louis, from its foundation by Pierre Laclede Liguest, on the 15th day of February, 1764, will ever furnish a historical lesson of varied interest to those who now and henceforth enroll themselves among its inhabitants.

"In 1790 a St. Louis merchant was a man who, in the corner of his cabin, had a large chest which contained a few pounds of powder and shot, a few knives and hatchets, a little red paint, two or three rifles, some hunting shirts of buckskin, a few tin cups and iron pots, and perhaps a little tea, coffee, sugar and spice. There was no post-office, no ferry over the river, no newspaper." From its foundation to the date of the Louisiana purchase, in 1804, but little change was made in the character of its social society and industrial interests. The ruder and rougher forms of life were everywhere impressed upon the society of her people, and marked the growth of an infant city destined to be the future capital of the United States and the great city of the world. The Louisiana purchase at once fixed not only the destiny of the nation, but also of St. Louis. A change in the title of the land wrought a change in her material growth and prosperity. A newspaper was established in 1808; in 1809 fire companies were organized; in 1810 there were road-masters, who had power to compel the requisite labor on the highways; in 1811 two schools were established, one English, the other French; in the same year a market-house was built, and prosperity gradually awakened new life in the place, and pointed to a future full of hope.

A record of the population of St. Louis began to date in the year 1764, a little more than one hundred years ago, and the succeeding increase at different periods is shown by the following statement:

Years.	*Population.*	*Years.*	*Population.*
1764	120	1833	6,397
1780	687	1835	8,316
1785	897	1837	12,040
1788	1,197	1840	16,469
1799	925	1844	34,140
1811	1,400	1850	74,439
1820	4,928	1852	94,000
1828	5,000	1856	125,200
1830	5,852	1860	160,773
		1870	312,960

Dr. Scott, in fixing the annual average growth of cities, estimated that of St. Louis, previous to 1860, to be at an annual average rate of 8 per cent.

But by the rapid change which has so recently swept over the country—abolishing slavery and equalizing labor alike in all sections of the country, and founding our prosperity alone upon the advantages which God has fixed throughout the land—St. Louis, in spite of the terrible ravages of four years of devastating war, has grown into the ascendency, during the last ten years, at an annual average rate of a little more than nine per cent. But, if we allow a discount of two per cent. for decimations during the four years of war, we must, to attain to the present population of the city, have well nigh increased annually at the rate of twelve per cent. since the war. This would almost equal the increase of Chicago in the days of her precocious growth. In fact, St. Louis has to-day, notwithstanding the vigilance of the United States Marshal in taking the census, not less than 315,000 citizens within her corporate limits; and it requires but a slight analysis in the discussion to establish the fact that St. Louis is a much larger city than Chicago. Aside from the facts which the United States census has established for both cities, we have only to refer to the extent of area within the corporate limits of each of the cities to establish beyond a question of doubt the superiority of St. Louis over Chicago. The facts are these:

Incorporate limits.	*Area of square miles.*	*Pop. in 1870.*
St. Louis	19 9-10	312,960
Chicago	34½	297,718

These figures show Chicago to exceed St. Louis more than fourteen and one-half square miles in the area of her corporate limits---nearly double—and yet fall short in population about 15,000; and with an extension of the city of St. Louis so as to equal Chicago, St. Louis would contain at least 325,000, and 25,000 more than Chicago. Be it remembered that Carondelet, containing about five square miles, is included in the nineteen and nine-tenths square miles comprising the present city limits of St. Louis—the old city limits including only a fraction more than fourteen square miles. But there is still another view in the argument. St. Louis is a much older city than Chicago, and, as a consequence of her growth and wealth, far more of her business men, with their families, live in suburban places, as the facts will demonstrate. Kirkwood, of about 3,000 inhabitants, is made up wholly of citizens who in some way do business in St. Louis. Webster is the same way. Many live down the Iron Mountain railroad, at St. Charles, at Alton, at Lebanon, at Belleville, and East St. Louis—thus establishing, beyond any question of doubt, St. Louis to be the third city on the American continent, and the imperial city of the great States of the Mississippi Valley; and if Chicago would be a modern Carthage in industry and art, St. Louis will be a modern Babylon in commerce, skill and greatness, vieing for the rich trophies of the world.

In the discussion of this part of the subject, it must be borne in mind that, in the past, St. Louis, in establishing her increase at eight per cent. per annum, had many adverse interests to contend against, which impeded her growth and retarded her progress. She is now for the first time entering upon a new career of growth and prosperity. She is untrammeled. Advantages of every kind surround her with prodigal profuseness. Henceforth her future advance ment cannot be gauged or measured by the past, and instead of an annual growth of eight per cent., she will move forward at the rate of at least ten per cent. for the next decade. This we assume with the full assurance of being supported by the facts of the future, at least for twenty years to come. But, as it is well known that cities have a rapid or slower growth in the long run, varying according to the eras or transitions through which nations must inevitably pass, thereby rendering it impossible to fix a uniform standard of growth, we assume the following figures to be as near the range of a reasonable possibility, or at least for a few succeeding decades, as the best judgment could dictate in advance of the facts which time and other generations will demonstrate.

Starting with the present population, as given by the United States census, we submit the following figures as showing the probable prospective growth of St. Louis:

Population of St. Louis in 1870, per United States census							312,963
Population increased	at the rate	of	10	per cent	per annum	to 1880	811,742
"	"	"	9	"	"	1890	1,917,571
"	"	"	6	"	"	1900	3,464,079
"	"	"	4	"	"	1910	5,083,297
"	"	"	3	"	"	1920	6,831,502
"	"	"	3	"	"	1930	9,180,967
"	"	"	2	"	"	1940	11,192,633
"	"	"	2	"	"	1950	13,643,757
"	"	"	1	"	"	1960	15,071,194
"	"	"	1	"	"	1970	16,647,941

Notwithstanding the apparent correctness of the percentage of growth given above, it is not probable that either St. Louis or any other city of this earth will ever grow to such an enormous size as to contain at any time a population so numerous. We therefore submit the figures, and leave them for others to analyze and criticise. We, however, with confidence predict that St. Louis, in 1880, will not contain less than 800,000 inhabitants, and from 100,000 to 200,000 more than Chicago. Thus fixing her at that time the second city on the continent, and, in 1890, the first; and in less than one hundred years, the solution of our problem—the great city of the world. There are those, no doubt, who will regard the prediction for 1880 as reaching beyond the bounds of possibility; but not so. Let those object who are over-cautious and in ignorance of the under-life developments of our continental country, or envious of the prosperity of a rival city. There is no monopoly in progress, none in industry, none in intellect; they are gifts alike to all who, under the rule of God, toil in righteousness. Civilization in the nineteenth century is not walled in. It is the free heritage of the great family of man, continental, national and individual. Nations and States are born under its peaceful supervision as new heralds of man's rising and progressive life; and great cities, like stars that begem the skies, will adorn our republic under its higher administration, and be as fine jewels set in the crown of the imperial nation of the earth.

In considering the probabilities of the rapid growth of St. Louis in the future, it is well to consider how strongly the rapid growth of the great Valley States which surround her on every side, bear upon the subject. During the

accurate geological surveys are made. Tin ore from the Madison county lode has been smelted in several instances, and found to be very rich. In several cases, the smelting proved the ore to contain, at the lowest yield, six and one-half per cent. of pure tin. Other smelts, at the same time, yielded eight and one half per cent. of pure tin, this being the highest yield. Both together make an average yield of seven per cent. pure tin. This is understood to be by far the richest yield in the world, and the quantity of ore sufficient to supply the world with tin.

A joint-stock company, with a capital of $200,000, is now organized, under the name of the Missouri Tin Company, for the purpose of working the mines, and the company will proceed at once to erect furnaces and machinery, for the purpose of smelting tin. This enterprise will, without question, be a valuable contribution to the mineral development and industry of the State of Missouri.

VALUABLE STONES.

Notwithstanding the great variety of valuable stone in the State of Missouri for building and finishing purposes, there are but few of them, in comparison to the whole, that have entered into serviceable use in the State, and such as have, are only used in a too limited extent. It is time this negligent policy among our builders and stone-cutters were abolished. Why should we go abroad for stone when we cannot surpass in beauty and value that which belongs to our own State? Aside from the many valuable quarries of marble and hard and soft stone of the State, which are generally known, we have thought proper to mention two or more specimens which are not so well known to our citizens, and the use of which is improperly neglected by our builders and ornamental stone cutters. There is the

ROSS-ANTICO MARBLE OF CAPE GIRARDEAU.

This is a fine specimen, as well as quality, of variegated and somewhat chocolate-colored marble. Its texture is fine, and is susceptible of a superior polish. Its strength and specific gravity is nearly equal to that of granite. It will sustain a pressure of more than fifteen thousand pounds to the cubic inch. This valuable stone will supply a great want in our city and State for building purposes, as well as for tiling, for tablets, paneling, and various ornamental uses about the homes of the wealthy and tasteful of our people. Its similarity to the Etruscan highly befits it for such uses, while for monuments and out-door buildings it will hardly be surpassed in durability, for it has already been thoroughly tested by exposure in the cemetery at Cape Girardeau. It abounds in large quantities in Cape Girardeau county, and is easy of access, and can be put into market without difficulty. The quarry out of which this marble is now obtained is in the hands of a company, Colonel Charles Durfee & Co., who are making great efforts to bring it into commercial use

ST. LOUIS MARBLE.

Another fine quality of stone, known as the St. Louis marble, is found in great abundance in St. Louis county, about twenty-five miles west of St. Louis, near Glencoe station, on the Missouri Pacific railroad. This stone is of a beautiful greyish color, of fine texture, and susceptible of fine polish, and is known as a species of marble. It is of great strength, and well adapted for building purposes, as it weathers well. A company, the Messrs. Terrys, are using every effort to bring this valuable stone into market and practical use, in supplying a choice material for many of the new buildings of our city. It is more properly defined as a light, variegated, fossiliferous marble. The bed is compact, without lines of stratification, and favorable for getting out slabs or columns of large dimensions.

MISSOURI BLUE GRANITE.

This granite is found in St. Francois county, on the line of the Iron Mountain road, at Knob Lick. Its complexion is a hue between the Quincy and New Hampshire, and sustains the great pressure of 18,444 pounds to the cubic inch. It is remarkably fine-grained and uniform, and will undoubtedly be extensively used where strength and durability are required in building.

Other valuable marbles are found in different parts of the State, but not having the necessary facts, a special description of them must be omitted.

QUEENSWARE.

It is well known to those familiar with the resources of Missouri, that there are to be found in different parts of the State quite a number of the most valuable clays used in the manufacture of queensware; and although no home effort has been made to convert these raw materials into useful articles, large quantities have been exported from the State, and made into wares and returned to our market, to be distributed to the trade, which ought to be supplied from the hands of our own industry. Kaolin, out of which the finest wares are made, is found in Cape Girardeau county in inexhaustible quantities. And why it is not converted into wares, of an innumerable variety and value, is a standing marvel to those who are familiar with the fact of its existence and quality. Why there may not be built a new Staffordshire in that county, supplying to the continent wares for every kind of domestic use, we cannot understand. Enterprise, capital, and skilled labor must be organized and applied. One company is already organizing, and without question will meet with great success, but there is room for many more. How often must it be published abroad that Missouri has many resources sufficient to supply the people of this great valley with many of the most important materials required in civilized life? and yet they remain undeveloped. Will those who have capital unoccupied accept of the advantages? Let us have a Staffordshire in America, a workshop equal to that of the Old World, whose labor will supply valuable wares to the millions of people belonging to those great States which surround us.

MISSOURI AS A WINE-PRODUCING STATE.

BY L. D. MORSE, M.D.,

PRESIDENT MISSISSIPPI VALLEY GRAPE GROWERS' ASSOCIATION.

It is a little over twenty years since grape culture was commenced as a business in Missouri, since which it has steadily increased, and rapidly so within the latter half of the period. During the last five years the increase has been at the rate of about 300 acres per year. Within the period last named, several companies have been formed for producing wine on a large scale. The Cliff Cave Wine Company, in the south part of St. Louis county, has about twenty-five acres of vines, sold a large quantity of grapes last year, and made 3,000 gallons of wine. The Augusta Wine Company, of St. Charles county, has 22,775 vines, and made last year 8,000 gallons of wine. The Bluffton Wine Company, of Montgomery county, has 59,834 vines, and made last year from the portion in bearing 13,490 gallons of wine. The Missouri Smelting and Mineral Land Company, of Stanton, Franklin county, is engaged in grape growing as a portion of its business, and has about seventy acres of vines planted, nearly all of which are in bearing this year.

In addition to the foregoing, we have the American Wine Company, of St. Louis, started several years earlier. It does not depend upon raising grapes for wine, but buys largely, and claims to have made last year over 100,000 gallons of still wines, and half a million bottles of champagne.

The vineyards of the town of Hermann yielded last year over 150,000 gallons of wine, and about 85,500 pounds of grapes sold, the total value of both being estimated at $157,557.

In the Report of the Department of Agriculture for 1868, partial reports from nineteen counties are given, the average footing to 1,508. Statistics obtained last year by the Mississippi Valley Grape Growers' Association, entirely reliable so far as they go, indicate that there are about 3,000 acres of vineyards in the State, and the entire value of the grape product of the State this year will not be less than $3,000,000.

SUPERIORITY OF MISSOURI GRAPES AND WINES.

It is not so much, however, the *number* of acres planted during the last few years, as it is the more or less favorable results from those in bearing, and the comparative quality of the fruit and wines produced therefrom, which tend to determine the question of superiority of our State above most others.

What little statistical information has been gathered thus far on this subject, and the very imperfect statements and incorrect figures given in the various reports, including that of the U. S. Agricultural Department, make it impossible to give reliable comparisons; but even this last named report shows that the average produced per acre in Ohio was 3,745 lbs. grapes, or 320 gallons wine; it was in New York 4,571 lbs. grapes, or 416 gallons wine; and in Missouri 6,900 lbs. grapes, or 483⅓ gallons wine. A more reliable proof of the superiority of Missouri's grapes over all others, we find by comparing the strength of the must by Oechsle's must-scale, which always comes out in favor of Missouri, even against the most celebrated wine localities of the Union. This is due to climate and soil. Rev. Chas. Peabody, who has given much attention to the investigation of this subject, says: "The two important natural conditions demanded by the grape are climate and soil. Given these two, all the rest will eventually follow from the application of the skilled industry of the vine-dresser. In this portion of the Valley of the Mississippi, we find these two elementary conditions, climate and soil, existing together. That the soil and climate of Missouri and the adjacent parts of other States, especially those on its eastern and western boundaries (Illinois and Kansas), are eminently adapted to the growth of the grape, is a point too well established to need discussion here. The fact is well known and universally acknowledged throughout the entire district, and perhaps I may venture to add, throughout the United States. Compared with other sections of the United States (at least all those east of the Rocky Mountains), so far as their capabilities have been tested, our advantages for the production of wine are certainly superior."

We have not the space to show by the isothermal lines, ascertained by years of actual observation, that our mean temperature during the various seasons comes nearest to those most celebrated places in France where the grape is known to succeed, and must confine ourselves to but few data, of which the following tables, extracted from essays read before the Mississippi Valley Grape Growers' Association, will afford a ready comparison:

Place.	*Aug. deg.*	*Sept. deg.*	*Oct. deg.*	*Av'ge deg.*
Cleveland	70.3	64.0	51.3	61.68
Cincinnati	74.2	66.0	53.2	64.47
St. Louis	76.5	68.7	55.4	66.86

For the highest development of the wine properties of the grape a mean temperature of no less than 65° Fahrenheit is demanded during the season of ripening. In the tables above alluded to we find the following:

	Average of—					
	April, May and June.		*July, Aug. and Sept.*		*Six months.*	
	deg.	*in.*	*deg.*	*in.*	*deg.*	*in.*
Kelly's Island, O., 1867	57.3	3.18	72.0	1.54	64.6	2.36
St. Louis, Mo.	63.7	3.95	75.1	1.65	69.4	2.80
Marseilles, France	63.4		72.1		67.7	

Besides the high temperature, a diminished rain-fall during the same season is essential to the perfection of the grape. Dr. Stayman, of Leavenworth,

Kansas, in an able discussion of these meteorological influences, comparing the averages of Illinois, Missouri and Kansas with those of New York, New Jersey and Pennsylvania, for 1867, finds a difference of 4.14° more heat and 6.45 inches less rain for the months of July, August and September, and for the whole period 7.20° more heat and 10.38 inches less rain in favor of the Western States.

Wherever Missouri wines have been tested, in comparison with those of other States, either at home or abroad, they have almost invariably taken the highest rank. At the meeting of the American Pomological Society, held in St. Louis in September, 1867, there was a large exhibition of American wines, including twenty varieties, from various States. The committee on Catawba wines, using a scale of 100 to designate degrees of excellence, rated the best Missouri sample at 95, and other samples from this State at 90, 84, &c. The highest from any other State was Illinois, 83; the best, from Ohio, was rated at 70. These were still wines. The sparkling Catawba of the American Wine Company, of St. Louis, were rated one and two degrees higher than samples from the celebrated Longworth Wine House, of Cincinnati. The committee was composed of two gentlemen from Ohio and one from Washington.

At the Paris Exposition, the American Wine Company's champagne was awarded honorable mention, and diploma sent them on account of its fine flavor, although the French jurors remarked it had *too much* of the fruity taste. The German jurors, accustomed to wines of high bouquet and flavor, were very much pleased with the American wines which possessed these qualities. The American committee, consisting of the Hon. Marshall P. Wilder, Alexander Thompson, William J. Flagg, and Patrick Barry, said: "From what comparison we have been able to make between the better samples of American wines, on exhibition at the Paris Exposition, with foreign wines of similar character, as well as from the experience of many European wine-tasters, we have formed a higher estimate of our own ability to produce good wines than we had heretofore." Wines which have since repeatedly been sent to Germany from Missouri have been highly spoken of, and were pronounced very superior wines by the best connoisseurs. It is also a notable fact that the trade in native wines has assumed such proportions in *St. Louis,* that even her importers of foreign wines, who have heretofore strongly disfavored any others, feel now compelled to buy and keep always on hand the Catawba, Concord, and Norton's Virginia.

There are several other varieties that are destined to take high rank, but have not yet been made in sufficiently large quantities to become well known. There are about seventy-five varieties of native grapes in cultivation and on trial in the State. About one-third of this number may be considered as well tested, and more or less successful.

Our Concord wine is becoming more and more popular, and should take the place of imported clarets. It suits the uncultivated taste better than either claret or Catawba. The Norton's Virginia, as it becomes better known, is more and more esteemed for its valuable tonic and astringent qualities. As a medicinal wine, it is not excelled probably by any wine, native or imported.

Catawba has generally been considered too acid by those unaccustomed to it, but it makes an exceedingly wholesome and palatable summer drink, and is especially admired in the form of Catawba cobblers. When made into sparkling wine or champagne, it has a very agreeable bouquet, and is preferred by those who become accustomed to it to the best imported champagne. It is purer, contains less alcohol, and is rapidly superseding them.

WINE CONDUCIVE TO HEALTH AND TEMPERANCE.

Taking into consideration the fact that the manufacture of wine is yet in its infancy in this country, the above results indicate that it is rapidly attaining a prominent place among the leading industrial pursuits, and materially aiding the cause of temperance by decreasing the consumption of distilled and fortified liquors. On this point an intelligent writer says:

"Of the good or evil effects of drinking pure wine, Americans have small means of judging. The dogmas of total abstinence have been built upon facts existing in two countries where pure wine is an almost unknown thing—upon British and American facts. Not in France, not in Spain, or Portugal, or Italy, or Switzerland, or South Germany, are gathered the awful statistics of the temperance lecturer; but from Britain, from America, and other countries where a kind of necessity, or at least a controlling fatality, has led to the using as a beverage what in grape-growing countries is hardly known save as medicine.

"The advocates of abstinence, having made out their case against distilled spirits, demand judgment against wine also. Having shown that drinking whisky or rum tends in a dangerous degree to make men drunkards, they jump to the conclusion that wine drinking must also tend in a like degree to the same calamitous result. By such reasoners it is assumed:

"*First*, that alcohol as found in distilled spirits, and alcohol as found in wine that has not been distilled, exists in both cases under identically the same conditions, and has on the drinker the same effects.

"*Secondly*, that foreign wines which are usually consumed in America and Britain are the same as what the people of the countries which produce them drink at home, and the same as what we should drink in case we grew our own wines at home.

"But distilled and undistilled alcohol exist under very different conditions and have very different effects. And to reason from Port, Sherry, and Madeira, and other liquors that come to us in ships, to the wines that will spring from our own soil, if our vine culture be blessed, is by no means admissible. Simple alcohol is not a drink at all. It is never taken without a large admixture of water, and usually of other substances. Brandy, whisky and rum contain nearly as much water as they do of alcohol, even before being diluted for drinking; while wine is in its nature a very delicate combination of various ingredients, with all of which we are not yet fully acquainted. Alcoholic drinks, then, being essentially compounds either naturally or artificially formed, they cannot be fairly judged without considering the properties of the substances which compose them, the proportions they bear to each other, and the manner in which they combine. And to assert that the alcohol which condenses in the worm of the still from the vapor of boiling wine is the very same thing to the drinker of it—to his stomach, brain and nerves—that it would have been if it had remained united with all those other constituents, with the sugar, acids, tannin, resin, salts and ethers which were its companions in the vine sap, were elaborated with it in the leaf, and ripened with it in the grape, is to say what requires the strongest proof to sustain it. But no such proof exists, while the contrary can be abundantly shown."

As conducive to health, our light wines possess a special value deserving of more general appreciation. It has been said, with too much truth, that we are a nation of dyspeptics. For the cause of the frequency of dyspepsia, we may rationally look to the habit of eating fast, bolting the food in a half-masticated condition, drinking too largely of water and other liquids, the too common use of salt meat, particularly salt fat pork, among the hard-working classes, &c. There is a large portion of our population who, although not confirmed dyspeptics, are yet persons of feeble digestive powers—a condition sometimes brought upon themselves by their own improprieties or bad habits, and quite as often inherited from parents, for the progeny of such people are sure to inherit the "family failing." Now it generally happens that this class of people are under the necessity of accomplishing more work, either bodily or mental, than they are physically capable of doing without loss of vigor. Their powers of assimilation are unequal to the task of appropriating of each meal sufficient to meet the interstitial destruction or necessary out-goings of the system. Hence, they are always overworked, and live a life of fatigue. Their muscles are soft and flabby, and their vessels deficient in tonicity. They are liable to disease from various causes; the circulation in the extreme vessels being weak, they are unable to resist the effects of cold, and are hence liable to congestions. They have no power to resist malaria or contagious diseases. Under a feeling of relaxation and fatigue, they often resort to distilled spirits to their injury.

It is certain that the habitual daily use of a small allowance of such a stimulus as our pure wines afford, would bestow upon such persons the nervous energy necessary to enable them to digest more food — to economize the waste of the system — to perform the duties of life with more ease and comfort, and would make them more useful members of society instead of the mere drones they often are and must continue to be under a total abstinence regimen. It would also better enable them to resist disease, which is an important consideration in malarious districts. When moderately taken with a regular meal, the small amount of stimulus contained in the light wines is very little felt; no unnatural appetite is created for such stimulus, but rather a feeling of satiety is produced, digestion is aided, the wants of the system are better supplied, and there is less inclination or craving for stimulus between meals. This would be particularly the case with the class referred to, who need "wine for the stomach's sake." As wine would enable the body to appropriate more food and gain strength, the feeling of fatigue, with the instinctive craving for stimulus, would be removed.

While people continue to drink for the sake of drinking, by all means give them the least dangerous article. Let it be more abundant and cheaper than the more fiery and maddening compounds.

NOTE.—The American Wine Company has made during the present year 100,000 gallons of wine, and from the vintage of 1870 will put up about 750,000 bottles of Imperial champagne. The increased production by other companies furnishes the most favorable showing, for the rapid growth and increase of the grape and wine business of the State of Missour'

THE CIVIL AND INDUSTRIAL MISSION OF THE AMERICAN PEOPLE.

I feel more deeply than ever before, that there is nothing in human history which can compare in interest with the condition of the American continent on the eve of its discovery and colonization, and its transition into the sphere of civilized and Christian culture, looking back from our present point of view upon the various stages of this transition, as one great operation in the order of Providence.

Consider it a moment: there it lay upon the surface of the globe, a hemisphere unknown to the rest of the world, in all its vast extent, with all its boundless undeveloped resources, not seen as yet by the eye of civilized men, unpossessed but by the simple children of the forest. There stretched the iron chain of its mountain barriers, not yet the boundary of political communities; there rolled its mighty rivers unprofitably to the sea; there spread out the measureless but as yet wasteful fertility of its uncultivated fields; there towered the gloomy majesty of its unsubdued primeval forests; there glittered in the secret caves of the earth the priceless treasures of its unsunned gold; and more than all that pertains to material wealth, there existed the undeveloped capacity of a hundred embryo States; of an imperial confederacy of republics, the future abode of intelligent millions, unrevealed as yet to the "earnest" but unconscious "expectation" of the elder families of man, darkly hid by the impenetrable veil of waters. There is to my mind an overwhelming sadness in this long insulation of America from the brotherhood of humanity, not inappropriately reflected in the melancholy expression of the native races. The boldest keels of Phœnicia and Carthage had not approached its shores. From the footsteps of the ancient nations along the highways of time and fortune—the embattled millions of the old Asiatic despotisms, the iron phalanx of Macedonia, the living crushing machinery of the Roman legion, which ground the world to powder—the heavy tramp of barbarous nations from "the populous north;" not the faintest echo had aroused the slumbering West in the cradle of her existence. Not a thrill of sympathy had shot across the Atlantic from the heroic adventure, the intellectual and artistic vitality, the convulsive struggles for freedom, the calamitous downfalls of empire, and the strange new regenerations which fill the pages of ancient and mediæval history. Alike when the Oriental myriads, Assyrian, Chaldean, Median, Persian, Bactrian, from the snows of Syria to the Gulf of Ormus, from the Halys to the Indus, poured like a deluge upon Greece, and beat themselves to idle foam on the sea-girt rock of Salamis and the lowly plain of Marathon; when all the kingdoms of the earth went down with her own liberties, in Rome's imperial mælstrom of blood and fire, and when the banded powers of the West, beneath the ensign of the cross — as the pendulum of conquest swung backward — marched in scarcely intermitted procession for three centuries to the subjugation of Palestine — the American continent lay undiscovered, lonely and waste. That mighty action and reaction upon each other of Europe and America — the grand systole and diastole of the heart of the nations — and which now constitutes so much of the organized life of both, had not yet begun to pulsate. The unconscious child and heir of the ages lay, wrapped in the mantle of futurity, upon the broad and nurturing bosom of Divine Providence, and slumbered serenely, like the infant of Danæ, through the storms of fifty centuries.—EDWARD EVERETT.

Ninety-four years ago — when the fifty-two signers of the Declaration of Independence, appealing to the Supreme Judge of the world for the rectitude of their intentions, declared that the united colonies are, and of right ought to be, free and independent States — but few of the most sanguine of that day dreamed of the extent and greatness which this country would attain in the comparatively brief space of a century. But before our Independence was achieved, the thought of continental empire had already entered the minds of many far-seeing persons in this and other lands. "Prophetic Voices about America" were not wanting in numbers to foretell the triumphs of that spirit of adventure which, in the fifteenth century, carried Vasco di Gama around the

Cape of Good Hope, and Columbus to America. Even the age seemed to be instinctive with a better life, and prophets of one land and heroes of another were unqualifiedly pointing to America as the place for the future empire of the world.

As early as 1755, John Adams, but twenty years old, and the future statesman of Massachusetts, wrote to a friend in the following words: "Soon after the reformation a few people came over into this new world for conscience sake. Perhaps this apparently trivial incident *may transfer the great seat of empire into America. It looks likely to me;* for if we can remove the turbulent Gallics, our people, according to the most exact computations, will in another century become more numerous than in England itself. Should this be the case, since we have, I may say, all the naval stores of the nation in our hands, it will be easy to obtain a mastery of the seas, and the united force of all Europe will not be able to subdue us."

This was the expression of a young school-teacher twenty-one years before the Declaration of Independence was made by the colonies. John Adams lived to see a system of government founded which, with broad and comprehensive policies, was destined to bring forth upon the American continent a nation of grander proportions and greater triumphs in civilization than his most enlarged understanding could comprehend.

His son, John Quincy Adams, at a later day, remarked of his father's letter: "Had the political part of it been written by the minister of state of a European monarchy, at the close of a long life spent in the government of nations, it would have been pronounced worthy of the united wisdom of a Burleigh, a Sully, or an Oxenstiern. *In one bold outline he has exhibited by anticipation a long succession of prophetic history, the fulfillment of which is barely yet in progress, responding exactly hitherto to his foresight,* but the full accomplishment of which is reserved for after ages."

Next to John Adams stands Mr. Jefferson, with clear conceptions of the future of the American nation. Soon after the treaty with the Kaskaskia Indians, by which was acquired a broad belt of territory extending from the mouth of the Illinois river to and up the Ohio, Mr. Jefferson first began to look with serious consideration to the future greatness of the nation; and that treaty, together with the Louisiana purchase, led him to say that he "would not give one inch of the waters of the Mississippi river to any nation." And with prophetic conception he was again led to say: "When we shall be full on this side the Mississippi river we may lay off a range of States on the western bank, from the head to the mouth, and so, range after range, advancing compactly as we multiply."

In addition to the Louisiana purchase, Texas was annexed in 1845. New Mexico, California, and all the territory between the Mississippi river and the Pacific ocean has been added within the present century; and in rapid succession has State after State come into the Union, and the telegraph, the railroad, the steamboat, the printing-press, and the school-house, have followed on in this great march of empire, and taken the place of the Indian trail, the wigwam, the hunting-ground, and the home of the buffalo.

Turn which way we will, upon this "vast, wide continent," and we see the chain of empire being made complete under one all-embracing Constitution. Climates of every character, minerals of every quality and value, rivers stretching in great lengths and uniting every zone, all combine to give greatness and destiny to this nation, made of the wisdom and excellences of all nations, and this people, made of the commingled and regenerated blood of all people. Sublime thought! Grandest and broadest of our age; that which energizes the individual and regales the future with royal promise.

At the beginning there were thirteen sparsely populated colonies; now we have thirty-seven powerful States, and ten large Territories on the threshold of membership. The following statistics, showing the means and degrees by which the great Empire of the West has been regarded, will be read with thrilling interest by every American citizen:

New States and Territories—When Admitted.—Under President Washington's administration, the following new States were admitted: Vermont, in the year 1791; Kentucky, in 1794; Tennessee, in 1796.

Under President Jefferson's administration, the following new States and Territories were added to the Union: Ohio, in the year 1802; Louisiana, purchased in 1804. This purchase contained space enough for fifty new States. It gave to the United States the entire control of the Mississippi, the outlets of which had hitherto been in the hands of a foreign power. Territorial governments were organized in Mississippi, Indiana and Louisiana.

Under President Madison's administration, the following addition was made to the Union: Indiana, in the year 1816.

During the administration of President Monroe, the following States were added to the Union: Mississippi, in the year 1817; Illinois, in 1818; Missouri, in 1821; Maine, in 1820; Florida, purchased in 1821.

Under the administration of President Jackson, the following States were admitted: Michigan, in the year 1837; Arkansas, in 1836.

During the administration of President Polk, the following new States were admitted: Texas, in the year 1845; Iowa, in 1845; Florida, in 1845; Wisconsin, in 1847; California, New Mexico and Utah were bought.

Under the administrations of Presidents Taylor and Fillmore, the following State was admitted: California, in the year 1850. The following new Territories were organized: New Mexico and Utah, in the year 1850; Washington in 1853.

Under President Pierce's administration, Arizona was purchased.

Under the administration of President Buchanan, the following States were admitted: Minnesota, in the year 1857; Oregon, in 1859; Kansas, in 1861; Dakotah Territory organized in 1861.

During the administration of President Lincoln, the following States were admitted: West Virginia, in the year 1862; Nevada, in 1864. The following Territories were also organized: Arizona, in the year 1863; Idaho, in 1863; Montana, in 1864.

Under the administration of President Johnson, the Territory of Wyoming was organized in 1868; Northwestern America, or Alaska, was purchased, by treaty of May 28, in the year 1867.

Thus stands the record to-day of the American nation, with a population running from 3,000,000 in the year 1776, up to 42,000,000 in the year 1870. Our commerce, in the year 1791, was valued at $52,000,000 imports and $19,000,000 exports. Now the imports of merchandise to our country are, at gold value, $286,519,344, and our national wealth estimated at $23,400,000,000, at an annual increase of $921,700,000.

Our principal agricultural products are estimated at $3,282,950,000, and our entire industrial resources are valued at $4,223,000,000.

How marvelous the progress of our people! and with us, instead of colonies as with Britain, we acquire strength and greatness by effacing the boundary lines of conterminous countries by treaty, and absorb the new regions into the Federal family, thereby consolidating whenever we extend our national domain and power. Turning, then, from the mightiness of the American nation at the present time, and looking forward to the future, we are to inquire what will be its civil mission, and what the industrial career of its people. What are to be the future honors and the glory of the Republic? Over what lands is her flag yet to float? To what people are her laws yet to give protection? What grand victories is she yet to achieve in the future empire of the world? These are questions now being inspired by the loftiest patriotism of the American statesman, and everywhere is growing up in the hearts of the people the thought of a transcendent national destiny for the great Republic of the world.

But before we consider this branch of the subject, let us consider the essential industrial mission of our people, their future commerce, their accumulation of wealth, and their future great field of labor. These things are held as being pertinent to the subject of the future great city of the world.

It is already evident that the industrial mission of our people will, at least, be continental; that, since the landing of the Pilgrims upon the narrow belt of the Atlantic, and their career in that land which De Tocqueville called an "inhospitable clime," there has been one steady march of the American people from the Atlantic toward the Pacific. Commerce was the incentive that urged on the civil conquest of the continent; that spread the fleet of boats upon our Western waters, directed the ships around Cape Horn and to our Pacific coast, and drove the hundreds of thousands of wagons across the arid plains of our continent.

The civil conquest of our own land is about to be accomplished by the meeting of the Eastern and Western columns of American civilization in the central plain of the continent, and the advance of the North and South flanking columns, which are now rapidly tending to the center. But this civil conquest accomplished, what remains for the restless, pioneering, and homeless Americans to do? They cannot stay within the boundary lines of our great Republic when other lands furnish a field for adventure, speculation, and skill. Then it is we are to look beyond to the higher aspects of the industrial mission of our people. To our continent belong five systems of water navigation: First, the Atlantic Ocean system; second, the River system; third, the Lake system; fourth, the Gulf system; and fifth, the Pacific Ocean system. The canal system is only auxiliary. Nature gave these systems.

After them comes a mightier system of commercial facilities—the railways civilization has given to man. This system supersedes oceans, lakes and rivers, and this system must control, in the future, the higher commercial and industrial destines of all people; while the ocean systems of commerce are destined to become the most obsolete of all these facilities afforded to man. Of the five water systems of navigation belonging to our continent, the river system is by far the most valuable, and, with the Gulf, is destined to control the foreign commerce of our continent; and both, united to our railway system, fix the industrial mission of our people henceforth to the far-off years of the future.

Civilization is rapidly reversing the order of nature. To the barbarian and semi-barbarian nations, the oceans were facilities for exchanging their commerce, the land an obstacle; but civilization is about to reverse the order, and transform the land into a facility and the oceans into obstacles. The car will take the place of the ship, and the land of the ocean, and commerce will find its goal in continental development; and not, as heretofore, beyond distant oceans and among the islands of the sea. The railway systems of continents and the world are soon to be the great rule of commerce, while ships will be the exception. Already the maritime nations of the earth foresee their doom in the coming reversal of the order of things, and are struggling to hold the seas supreme over the land, the ships over the cars; hence their aggressions upon the land in their haste to sever continents, that the ships may pass through and speed on to the uttermost parts of the earth.

But before we further consider the railway system as destined to control and direct the future industry of the world, let us go back and consider for one moment the commerce of the globe, which the nations are now striving to control. Since the discovery of America, perhaps there has been no artificial improvement to which so much importance has been attached in its bearing upon the future commerce of the world as the construction of the Pacific railway, and no man better vindicated the importance of such a facility across the continent than the Hon. Thomas H. Benton, in the many speeches he made from time to time in favor of its construction, and from one we make the following pointed quotation touching the great importance of the road in its bearing upon the commerce of the world. Hear his plea: "I enforce another advantage, not so immediate, but obvious to the thinking mind, and important to America, Europe, and Asia; and which, in changing a channel of rich commerce, may have its effect upon the wealth and power of nations, and operate a change in the maritime branch of national wars. I allude to the East India trade, already incidentally touched upon, and the change of its channel from the water to the land, and the effect of that change in nullifying the maritime supremacy of naval powers by making continents, instead of oceans, the great theaters of international commerce. No events in the history of nations have had a greater effect on the relative wealth and power of nations than the changes which have been going on for near three thousand years in the channels of Asiatic commerce. During that time nations have risen and fallen, as they possessed or lost that commerce. Events announce the forthcoming of a new change. The land becoming a facility and the ocean an obstacle to foreign trade, must have an effect upon Europe, conterminous upon Asia, and upon America, separated from it by a western sea over which no European power can dominate. I confine myself to the American branch of the question, and glance at the past to get an insight into the future. I look to former channels of this Asiatic commerce—their changes, the effects of the changes—and infer from what has been, what may be—from what is, to what will be.

"I. *The Phœnician Route.*—Tyre, queen of cities, was its first emporium. The commerce of the East centered there before the captivity of the Jews in Babylon, upwards of six hundred years before the coming of Christ. Nebuchadnezzar, King of Babylon, conquered Tyre and razed it to its foundations; but he was no statesman—merely a destroyer—and did not found a rival city; and the continuance of the India trade quickly restored the queen of cities to all her former degree of prominence and power. Alexander the Great conquered her again. He was a statesman, and knew how to build up, as well as how to pull down, and looked to commerce for exalting and enriching that magnificent empire which his war genius was conquering. He founded a rival city on the coast of Egypt, better adapted to the trade; and the prophecy of Ezekiel became fulfilled on Tyre: she became a place for fishermen to dry their nets.

"II. *The Jewish Route.*—In the time of Solomon and David, the Jews succeeded to the East India trade, made it a leading subject of their policy, and became rich and powerful upon it. Jerusalem rivaled Nineveh and Babylon; and Palmyra, a mere thoroughfare in the trade in the midst of a desert, became the seat of power and opulence, of oriental magnificence, and the center of the arts and sciences. The Jews lost that trade, and Jerusalem became as a widow in the wilderness, and Palmyra a den for foxes and Arabs.

"III. *The Alexandrian Route.*—This was opened by Alexander the Great; its course along the canal of Alexandria to the Nile, up that river to Coptus; thence across the desert with camels to the Dead Sea, and down that sea to the neighboring coasts of Asia and Africa—a route chosen with so much judgment that it made Alexandria and Egypt the seats of wealth, power, learning, the arts and sciences, and continued to be the channel of trade for a period of eighteen hundred years—from three hundred years before Christ to the close of the fifteenth century—when the Portuguese discovery of the passage by the Cape of Good Hope annihilated the Egyptian route, and transferred to Lisbon the glories of Alexandria. But not without a great contest. Solyman the Magnificent, then Sultan of the Turkish Empire, fought the Portuguese for the dominion of routes—carried on long and bloody wars to break up the Cape of Good Hope route, assisted by the Venetians, because of their interest in the Egyptian route, and menacing Christendom—this alliance of Christian and Saracen against Christians—according to the Abbe Raynal, indorsed by the philosophic historian Robertson, with the 'most illiberal and humiliating servitude that ever oppressed polished nations.' From this calamity Christendom was saved by the valor of the Portuguese and the talents of their renowned commander, Albuquerque; but the contest shows the value which all nations placed on the possession of this trade, and the reversed conditions of Alexandria and Lisbon, of Egypt and Portugal, upon the defeat of the Turks and Venetians, shows that that value was not ever-estimated.

"IV. *The Constantinoplitan Route.*—This became fully established in the time of the Greek Empire, and during the two hundred years of the Crusade irruptions, and to which the enlightened part of the Crusaders greatly contributed. For, while a religious frenzy operated upon the masses, the extension of their trade with India was the systematic, persevering, and successful policy of all liberal and enlightened minds, availing themselves of that frenzy to promote and establish the commerce upon the possession of which the supremacy of nations depended. It was fully established; and the long and tedious transit across the Black Sea to the mouth of the Phases, up that river to a portage of five days to the Cyrus, down that river to the Caspian Sea, across it to the mouth of the Oxus, up it nine hundred miles to Samarcand, once Alexandria, the limit of Alexander's march to the northeast; and after this long travel, an overland journey of ninety days on the Bactrian camel to the confines of China, commenced. Such was this extended route. Yet it was upon this route, so extended and perilous, that Europe was supplied with East India goods for several centuries; the profits of the trade being so great that after its arrival at Constantinople, it could still come on to Italy, and even round to Bruges (Brussels) and to Antwerp. It was upon this route that the Genoese established their great commerce, gaining permanent establishments with great privileges at Constantinople (its suburb Pera) and in that Crimea, then resplendent with wealth, since impoverished, now the scene of bloody strife; and of which the issue would be fortunate, if it restored the Crimea to what it was when Caffa was as celebrated as Sebastopol is now, and celebrated for streams of commerce instead of streams of blood. But to this route of Constantinople the Cape of Good Hope passage became as fatal as it was to that of Alexandria.

"V. *The Ocean Route.*—It has been the line of the East India trade since the close of the fifteenth century, and must have continued to be so forever if a marvel had not been wrought, and the land become the facility—the ocean the obstacle—to commerce. All the powers that have land for distant communications must now betake themselves to the steam car. Why contend with ships for the dominion of the sea, when both the ships and the sea are to be superseded? Take the case of Russia. She has been one hundred and fifty years building up a navy—to become useless the first day it is wanted. Not only useless, but an encumbrance and a burden, requiring impregnable posts, and vast armies, and murderous battles to protect and save it—save it from going to swell the enemy's fleet, and be turned against its builders. Why build any more ships when there is the land to carry commerce, without protection, to every part of Europe, and to America by Behring's Straits, rendering fleets inoperative and harmless? But I confine myself to our own commerce and our own land. There is the road to India, pointing west, half the way upon our own land, and the rest upon a peaceable sea washing our shores, but separated from Europe by the whole diameter of the earth. Can we not cease wrangling over an odious subject of domestic contention, and go to work upon the road which is to exalt us to the highest rank among nations, and make us mistress of the richest gem in the diadem of commerce? Can we not cease contention, and seize the supreme prize which is glittering before us? Make the road; and, in its making, make our America the thoroughfare of Orient commerce—throw back the Cape and the Horn routes to what Tyre became when Alexandria was founded, and what Alexandria became when the Cape of Good Hope was doubled, making Europe submissive and tributary to us for a transit upon this route, and dispensing us from the maintenance of the fleets which the ocean commerce demands for its protection."

The railway is built, and what in Benton's day was an extended wilderness of country, from the Mississippi river to the Pacific ocean, is now States and populous Territories, with rapidly growing cities, rich in wealth. Yet the road is not the wonderful thoroughfare for the commerce of distant nations that earlier enterprise anticipated. Nor will it ever be. Every foot of railway built the more and more confirms the continental destiny of the American people; and by the business of this road being absorbed by the local interests of the people at each end and along its line, and the failure to revolutionize the commerce of the world, the spirit of adventure has gone again to the ocean, and seeks new channels through the isthmuses of Suez and Darien. By these highways the commerce of the world is again sought to be controlled. In this contest America again has the advantage, in climate, ocean and distance, as the following testimony of Mr. Nourse, of the United States navy, given in his pamphlet on the *Maritime Canal of Suez*, will assure: "for while Suez is the center of the old continent, Darien is the center of the great ocean — the Atlantic-Pacific of the water as well as of the land of our globe. For this fact is to be remembered—

"From the Gulf of Mexico all the great commercial markets of the world are down hill. A vessel bound from that Gulf to Europe places herself in the current of the Gulf Stream and drifts along with it at the rate, for part of the way, of eighty or a hundred miles a day. If her destination be Rio or India, or California, her course is the same as far north as the island of Bermuda.

"And when there shall be established a commercial thoroughfare across the Isthmus, the trade winds of the Pacific will place China, India, New Holland, and all the islands of that ocean, down hill also from this sea of ours. In that case Europe must pass by our very doors on the great highway to the markets both of the East and the West Indies. This beautiful Mesopotamian sea is in a position to occupy the summit level of navigation, and to become the great commercial receptacle of the world. Our rivers run into it, and float down with their currents the surplus articles of merchandise that are produced upon their banks. Arrived with them upon the bosom of this grand marine basin, there are the currents of the sea and the winds of heaven, so arranged by nature that they drift it and waft it down hill and down stream to the great market-places of the world."

THE ISTHMUS OF SUEZ COMPARED WITH THAT OF DARIEN.

Before taking up our journey, then, to Suez, let us look for a moment at the two isthmuses, side by side. Whoever casts the eye on a map of the great continents will hardly fail to mark some striking peculiarities common to both. One of these is the peninsular form of each, and its tending southward, either in a mass, as Africa and South America, or in broken peninsulas, as Southern Asia and Europe. A second peculiarity is the existence of island groups on the right hand of the southern limits of each continent; as the West Indies and the Falkland group, southeast of America and Australasia, southeast of the various peninsulas into which Asia is broken. A third and equally noticeable common mark appears in that narrow neck of land which, in each continent, joins the land masses and separates great seas — the two isthmuses which we are considering. In the Eastern hemisphere, the land mass of Asia and Europe is thus joined to Africa by a neck of less than a hundred miles in extent. In the West, the great American Isthmus — of about fourteen hundred miles in its full extent from Tehauntepec to the Atrato river — at one point narrows itself to even a less breadth than Suez. In the country of Darien proper it is scarcely more than thirty miles wide. And this further point of interest may be again noted on the world-map, that the Isthmus of Suez is but the center of the old continents, Asia, Europe, and Africa, while the American Isthmus is the center of oceans as well as of countries. The commercial value of this will be seen at a glance, and it belongs to the Isthmus of Darien.

The chief practical point of difference, in considering the American Isthmus and the African, with the view of opening up communication across each, is their opposite geological formation. Suez is an arid, sandy, longitudinal depression, of which more than one-half is on a level with or below the Red Sea and the Mediterranean. The American Isthmus strikingly contrasts itself, in its being chiefly a ridge of the Great Cordilleras. Its counter-slope toward the Pacific is not in most places found to be extended. To cross the Isthmus of Suez is to encounter its drift sands, but scarcely an elevation whose mean height is above fifty feet. To cross Central America is to encounter, in Honduras, elevations of at least two thousand nine hundred feet; or, in Panama, the line of the lowest level as yet found, with any certainty, elevations from four hundred and fifty to two hundred and seventy feet. The summit ridge, on the Panama railroad, is two hundred and eighty-seven feet above the mean tide-level of the Atlantic.

The contrast between the two isthmuses is as marked from a historic point of view. Suez has witnessed the tramp of many armies, and the noise of busy trade around cities now wholly lost beneath the sands. The narrow neck of Darien has scarcely a historic record. M. de Lesseps, the engineer of the Suez canal, remarks: "We cannot approach history without touching upon Suez; the Bible gives its early record; Abraham, Isaac and Jacob, and the patriarchs, crossed it; Moses was rescued from a branch of the Nile running through it. Afterward the third station of his rescued people was Ethan, which still keeps its name. 'Pihahiroth,' one of their encampments, meaning in Hebrew the 'Bay of Reeds,' has its name preserved by the Arabs in the track near Lake Timsah. Tradition points to the same locality as a resting-place for the Holy Family when fleeing from Herod. The Persians fought upon the plains around Pelusium, near the modern Port Said. Alexander's troops thronged the isthmus; Cæsar disembarked on this coast; Pompey was there assassinated."

Alongside of such a record the American Isthmus has, as yet, but little to show; but little of any record of the races within it before the Spanish occupancy, and but little even since that date except the heroic crossing of Balboa, the murderous visits of the Buccaneers, and the struggle for colonization by such noble men as Paterson and Campbell. Yet may not this isthmus, when she shall have become the highway of nations, more than compensate for the past by her greater instrumentality in promoting peaceful intercourse, in civilizing and christianizing her neighboring districts and the East? There seems surely a common point as regards both isthmuses, vitally affecting the future of each hemisphere, centering in the opening up of world-intercourse across each. There seems also some natural indications that each will permit such opening. Their very narrowness suggests it.

Certainly the great interests of civilization loudly call for such open and easy intercourse. For to say that these narrow necks *join* two land masses is to use language commonly held and expressive of a physical or geological fact. But, commercially, the opposite is true. They *separate* men. They are the *bar* to the world's trade, and to the fuller extending of the accompanying blessings of civilization.

The Isthmus of Darien, now crossed by the Panama railroad, proves, by her busy throng from the two sides of the great Pacific and from distant New Zealand and Australia, what she will be, and what more successfully she can do for humanity, when a yet readier water passage shall be opened.

The Isthmus of Suez, until fully opened for heavy freighting, will continue to make necessary the hundred-day voyage around the stormy cape. For, however readily the traveler bears the heavy expense of a shorter overland route by the railroad from Alexandria to the Red Sea, the freights of commerce bear neither this nor the yet greater disadvantages of transhipments. The bulk of trade still follows the route discovered nearly four centuries ago. It awaits the completion in full of the maritime canal which shall in fact join Asia to Africa and to Europe. Let us compare two distance-saving tables on this point.

Distance-saving Tables, or Comparison of Routes, (A) by Suez Canal with Route by Cape of Good Hope, (B) by Darien Canal with Route by Cape Horn.

The distances are in most cases taken either from a table prepared by the Bureau of Navigation, Navy Department; or from Berghaus' Chart, or the tables of the Pacific Mail Steamship Company.

A.—Table *of the Saving in Distances for Trade passing through the Suez Cana to Bombay, a central point in the Indian Ocean.*

PORTS.	*Distances in marine leagues.*		*Saving in leagues. (A league is about 3.45 miles.)*	*Calling the distance from Liverpool to Bombay 100 miles.*	
	By Cape.	*By Canal.*		*By Cape.*	*By Canal.*
St. Petersburg	6,550	3,700	2,850	111	62¾
Amsterdam	5,950	3,100	2,850	100	52
Liverpool	5,900	3,050	2,850	100	52
London	5,950	3,100	2,850	100	52
Cadiz	5,200	2,224	2,976	88	37¾
Lisbon	5,350	2,500	2,850	90	42
Havre	5,800	2,824	2,976	98	48
Marseilles	5,650	2,374	3,276	95	40
Trieste	5,960	2,340	3,620	100	39⅛
Constantinople	6,100	1,800	4,300	103	30½
New York	6,200	3,761	2,439	104	63
New Orleans	6,450	3,724	2,720	109	63

(*a*) The saving between London and the ports on the east coast of Asia may be stated at about 4,800 miles; the saving from London to Melbourne, Australia, at about 3,000 miles.

(*b*) Lesseps, in his original memoir (1855), estimates the saving between the East and West to be an average of 3,000 leagues.

(*c*) The French engineers, in 1801, estimated that the Suez Canal would save one-third of the distance and one-fifth of the time in navigating from France to India.

(*d*) The saving between England and India may be stated at 49 per cent.; between France, Southern Russia, Italy, Greece, and Turkey, at 52 per cent.

B. — TABLE *showing the Saving in Distance for Trade passing through the Darien Canal.*

PORTS.	DISTANCE.		Saving.
	By Cape Horn.	By Darien Canal.	
New York to Valparaiso	8,720	4,800	3,920
Liverpool to Valparaiso	9,100	7,500	1,600
New York to Callao	10,020	3,550	6,470
Liverpool to Callao	10,400	6,200	4,200
New York to Honolulu	13,530	6,850	6,280
Liverpool to Honolulu	13,780	9,500	4,280
New York to San Francisco	13,610	5,310	8,300
Liverpool to San Francisco	13,665	7,960	5,705
New York to Jeddo	16,700	10,200	6,500
New York to Shanghai	14,500	11,100	3,400
New York to Hong Kong	17,420	11,850	5,570
New York to Hong Kong by Cape of Good Hope	14,015	....	....
New York to Melbourne	12,720	10,400	2,320
Liverpool to Melbourne	13,350	12,600	750
New York to Sydney	12,870	9,950	2,920
Liverpool to Sydney	12,850	12,400	450
Havre to San Francisco	13,640	7,900	5,740

Those estimates, which are best understood by having the eye either on a globe, or upon the world, on Mercator's projection, will suffice at present as points of comparison in proof of the interest which for so many years has held many of the ablest minds to the problem of canalizing both isthmuses. Among these the late Henry Wheaton, United States Minister to the Court of Berlin in 1845, deserves high place. In the midst of his official duties he found time for the study of the subject in its widest range, and addressed an elaborate dispatch to our Secretary of State, discussing with marked ability the canalizing of each of the isthmuses, and developing the results to be expected therefrom. This was before the foundation of the Pacific States had been laid. (See Lawrence's foot-notes, Wheaton's International Law, and Ex. Doc. 29th Congress, 21st session.)

The following additional tables, kindly furnished by Mr. F. A. Walker, Chief of the Statistical Bureau, United States Treasury Department, will be found in place here.

(A corresponding table made by the friends of the Suez Canal would claim, in brief, an annual tonnage of 6,000,000, from almost the outset of the opening of navigation, with a steady increase.)

Table *showing the Trade of England that would pass through the Darien Canal if now finished, taken from the Official Returns for the year 1867.*

Countries Traded with.	*Exports and Imports.*	*Tonnage.*
Half of Mexico	$ 3,014,005	22,401
Half of Central America	2,642,650	7,652
Half of New Granada	8,613,995	11,019
Chili	35,004,090	220,771
Peru	25,926,110	209,401
Ecuador	775,715	2,725
China	85,975,900	197,288
Java	6,812,765	30,703
Singapore	17,813,505	123,436
Australia and New Zealand	67,475,780	264,815
Islands of the Pacific	236,730	2,762
California	14,239,970	127,086
	$268,531,115	1,219,762
Value of ships, $50 per ton	60,988,100	
Total value	$329,519,215	

Table *showing the Trade of France that would pass through the Darien Canal if now finished, taken from the Official Returns for the year 1865.*

Countries Traded with.	*Exports and Imports.*	*Tonnage.*
Half of Mexico	$ 7,641,470	34,672
Half of Central America	2,612,162	10,721
Half of New Granada	1,905,260	6,703
Chili	10,994,595	25,263
Peru	11,870,240	49,201
Ecuador	556,923	2,283
China	13,618,446	18,863
Java	860,227	3,749
Singapore	....	......
Australia	908,933	5,217
Islands of the Pacific	....	......
California	1,607,929	8,587
Value of cargoes	$52,576,185	165,259
Value of ships, at $50 per ton	8,262,950	
Total value	$60,839,135	

Table *showing the Trade of the United States that would pass through the Darien Canal.*

Countries Traded with.	*Imports and Exports. 1869.*	*Tonnage. 1868.*
Dutch East Indies	$ 2,080,031	13,283
British Australia and New Zealand	809,037	44,624
British East Indies	9,432,214	107,977
Half of Mexico	5,999,967	72,930
Half of Central America	2,109,778	41,520
Chili	3,272,467	49,078
Peru	3,059,755	78,429
Sandwich Islands	2,083,484	56,603
China	25,584,853	107,884
Half of New Granada	5,186,025	308,220
Value of cargoes	$59,617,611	880,548
Value of ships, at $50 per ton	44,027,400	
Total value of ships and cargoes	$103.645.011	

The foregoing tables show what would probably be the amount and direction of the commerce passing through the Darien Canal when first completed, but in this there would be an immediate and rapidly increasing change inuring to the benefit of the United States. At present the balance of trade is so decidedly against Europe and America, and in favor of the East Indies and China, that vessels sailing from the ports of the former are never half laden, but bring full cargoes on their return passages of the products of the East. This condition of the trade is not owing to a want of market in Eastern and Southern Asia for the products of the United States, but to the present great cost of getting those products to that market, and the nearer but greatly less demand we find for them in Europe. A canal through the Isthmus of Darien or Tehuantepec would so materially shorten the distance and lessen the expense of the transit to Asia and Australia that, in less than three years, the breadstuffs and other products sent from our ports to these countries would not only change the balance of trade in our favor, but would also rebuild the commercial marine which the late war so completely destroyed; and the magnificent harbors of the West India islands and our Gulf coast, of which Tampa Bay, Appalachicola, Pensacola, Mobile, New Orleans and Galveston are the principal belonging to us, would, as the receptacles for shipment of the vast products of the Southern States and the Valley of the Mississippi, soon make the Gulf of Mexico the grandest center of commercial activity that the world has ever witnessed.

This brief comparison of the isthmuses will at present suffice. The tables have been brought side by side, with the design of enlisting deeper interest in the proposed survey for our own Darien Canal. Its importance can scarcely be over-estimated; and the interest in it, and effort to be enlisted for its construction, may be quickened by such comparisons as we are now making.

For it is to be kept steadily before the eye, that the termini of the *two great transit routes,* in the two hemispheres, are the radiant points for the great trunk lines of the world's commerce, viz: (1) From the Persian Gulf, or Suez, east to Bombay, Calcutta and Australia, and from Port Said west to all parts of Europe, North and South America; and (2) from Darien east to Europe, and west to Asia, South American west coast, and Australia.

We now turn from these comparisons of the American route, as yet unsurveyed, but challenging the genius of exploration and of engineering, to the record of the present finished route in the East; again saying, "*May the Suez Canal secure our own.*"

That the English are beginning to comprehend the state of the case, may be inferred from an article on the Suez Canal in a recent number of *Once a Week,* from which we extract the following passages:

"That the Suez Canal will bring about a revolution in the commercial world is certain; the extent of the revolution must be left to future times to decide.

"With the new direct passage to the East, is there not every probability of the ports of North Africa and of South Europe becoming the great commercial emporiums of the future? The way is now clear from North America to Hindostan and with the exception of the *detour* made by the Red Sea, the course is a direct one. The Mediterranean lies in the line between East and West, and may be said to connect both. What an enviable position! On the one hand America, flourishing, young, and active; on the other India, surpassingly wealthy, and itself the connecting link whose shores, abounding with good ports, are almost everywhere the fringes of good and largely-yielding soil. Now is the time for Trieste and Marseilles to bestir themselves. The golden opportunity is offered, and the earliest bidder will obtain the greatest bargains. Who knows where will be the London, the pre-eminent commercial city of future times? It would be odd, indeed, if, contrary to all modern anticipations, it should *not* be in North America, but in one of the oldest districts of the Old World. The Old World is very much larger than the New, is as rich, or richer, in minerals, and contains a greater proportion of richly-productive soil. After consideration, then, it would not be surprising if the commercial supremacy which successively left Tyre, Rome, and Venice, should desert London — not for New York, but for some place on the ancient coast of the Mediterranean. Should this really happen (of course, it is at present a mere speculation, and a few years will decide the probability or improbability of its ultimate occurrence), there can be no doubt that the Suez Canal will have been the great, if not the sole, cause of the regeneration of the world of the ancients.

"Let England not be blind to the probable influences of the Suez Canal. It behooves her particularly, of all the nations of the world, to be on the alert, even for events which it may take centuries to culminate, for she has the greatest interests at stake. She is now on the top of the pinnacle of glory, supported by the richest possessions, the most flourishing colonies, and the greatest commerce of the world.

"The greatness of England may be said to have had its foundation in the discovery of the Cape route to India. This event developed the energies of the nations of Western Europe, and its effects were almost immediately felt in the rapid rise of Spain, then of Portugal, next of Holland, and lastly of England. They are all nations possessing extensive coasts open to the Atlantic, and therefore received the benefits of the newly-found way to the large world. The discovery converted the Mediterranean into a comparatively small expanse of water, shut out of the wider world; and, ever since, the countries on its shores have gradually lessened in importance; England has become rich, while Eastern Spain, and Italy, and Greece have become poor—because, by the Cape route, she is nearer to China and the East Indies. The fact stands on adamant. The inference is as true. The Cape route is, or will be in a few years, worthless for communication with the East, the way by Suez being the nearer and the safer. Our Eastern commerce must decline, as assuredly as that of South Europe will increase. Such must be the case, even should we continue our hold on India and we cannot hope to preserve an ascendency over three hundred millions of foreigners if we begin to lose *prestige* in the world.

"Regarding Eastern commerce, a vigorous activity on the part of the Mediterranean States will be accompanied by a comparative decline on that of England; in other words the salvation of the Mediterranean will be the ruin of England. But, some people will very naturally remark, we shall still have the American commerce in our hands, and the resources and wealth of America are worthy of comparison with those of the East. Granted; but the retention of half a possession is no recompense for the loss of the other half. We may, however, cull some consolation from the philosophic reflection that half a good thing is better than none at all; and in that light we should be thankful for our own fortune. *America is now our last resource, and will be the friend to save us from utter bankruptcy and ruin.*

"If the Suez Canal had been completed a century or more ago, before the resources of the New World had been known and appreciated, there is much ground of probability in the supposition that our country would have sunk into respectable insignificance, and that the progress of America in civilization and prosperity would have been far less rapid than it has been under existing circumstances. So widely different must have been the course of events, and so gigantic are the interests concerned, that the subject fills the mind with amazement. Whole countries, nay, continents, would have been materially affected, and not merely a British colony at the Cape of Good Hope, as many persons erroneously suppose. We have, indeed, as Englishmen, much cause for congratulation upon the long delay in removing the barrier between European and Asiatic seas, until the present hour, when the productions of America have been so generally and so abundantly developed. *We cling to America as to the last hope of a sinking man.*

"These are gloomy forebodings for the future of our country. They will undoubtedly prove true in the end, unless England shakes off the foolish apathy with regard to foreign affairs which seems to have taken possession of her during these last three or four years. She must not be content to confine her whole attention to her own island home, if she has the ambition still to be a power in the world. She must not selfishly withdraw her support from her young colonies, who need her assistance now, but who will be her strong defenders or aiders in the future. She must not allow France or any other power again to undertake the grandest enterprise of the day. On the contrary, she must be ever bold and fearless—active and energetic in every quarter of the globe—resentful of every injury, and foremost in every great work. She has been overreached by the latest French movement. Let her apply a lesson from it, and avert the dangers now threatening her, by excavating a channel across the Isthmus of Panama. Let her begin this great work immediately—not a moment should be lost—and the rich Eastern and Southeastern lands of Asia will be within easy distance of her by a new route in a direct line across the united Atlantic and Pacific oceans.

"By this means only is the speedy destruction of our commercial interests and of our existence as a great independent nation to be prevented. The Panama Canal is the natural sequence of the successful piercing of the Isthmus of Suez. Nay, more — it is absolutely necessary for the safety of England. Apart from its necessity to this country particularly, it will be extremely beneficial to the whole world in general, by reason of its inspiring a fresh enterprising spirit of energy in men, and engendering emulations and instincts of progressive activity in nations. There is every reason, every necessity in the world, for the work to be commenced, and that quickly. The present is the golden opportunity—procrastination may snatch it away."

Then is it not manifest from this general consideration of the subject that we, too, of the New World have a Mediterranean Sea in our Gulf of Mexico and Carribean Sea? And in the future growth and organization of the world's commerce, can we not reasonably expect that thousands of ships from the Atlantic and Pacific—from the combined fleets of the nations of the earth—will associate in *rendezvous* in that world's commercial place which those two waters are destined to afford? Every consideration in our geography and resources, as well as the rapid tendency to a complete organization of the world's commerce, point to this one great fact. The Mediterranean of the New World is just as surely to supersede, in commercial importance, the Mediterranean of the Old World, as does the civilization of the New World supersede the civilization of the Old. Our Mediterranean will yet have its Suez Canal. It has its new Rome, its Constantinople, its Genoa and its Venice, its Smyrna and Palermo. In short, to the Mediterranean of the Old World belongs scarcely anything of nature or civilization that does not belong to the Mediterranean of the New World. Whether in oceans East and West, or whether in continents North and South; or whether in islands and cities, in climates and peoples, we may turn to the long line of historic scenes which have been enacted upon the shores of the Mediterranean of the Old World through thousands of years of man's history, growth, and the rise and fall of nations, the commercial greatness, and the diffusion of the arts and sciences—and there seems to be reserved in the future, and to be enacted upon the shores of the Mediterranean of the New World, still mightier deeds in commerce, in art, in PEACE! Why may we not anticipate a superior and more advanced rehearsal of history? Even now it is being enacted, and must go on.

Having pointed out the routes over which the controlling commerce of the world has passed for nearly three thousand years, and considered the probable influence which the use of the Suez and Darien canals will exert in the control and direction of the future commerce of the distant nations and peoples of the earth, and considered our advantage upon the ocean, and the certainty of the world's commerce seeking our markets through the Gulf of Mexico, and from thence to the great cities in the central plain, where it will be exchanged, distributed, and consumed, we return to the railway system, and consider the special industrial mission of our people. We have already said that the railway systems, in their more mature development, will be dominant over the water systems in affording commercial facilities, and will, in the future, control the industry of the world, and therefore the industrial mission of all considerable peoples who build for themselves these most useful agencies that the arts have produced.

America is destined to be the great railway continent of the world and the essential industrial mission of the American people will conform to their great railway system. Hence their mission must be essentially continental; and now that the continent, from East to West, has been spanned by a great trunk line, and an entire line of battle formed from ocean to ocean in the civil conquest of the continent, a new movement is already begun which is destined to extend our railway system to the Gulf, west of the Mississippi river, and into Mexico, and from thence through Central to South America; and thus will be indicated the industrial mission of our people. They will go forth, as from the beginning, following the track of the ancient civilization across the continent in a southwesterly direction, and thus continue on in their mission, carrying their arts and their arms into Mexico, and from thence to Central and South America — ever marching in unity and order with the railways, as the great vitalizers of their industry and commerce.

A glance at the elaborate and carefully prepared tables on the two following pages will show that nearly half of all the railroads in the world are within the boundaries of the United States of America. The Anglo-Saxon race first put their mark on the western continent at Plymouth and Jamestown, and now they have compassed it with bands of iron. Reference to other tables will show that this vast work of building more than fifty thousand miles of railway has been accomplished within forty years.

In 1830 there were twenty-three miles of railroad built and in actual operation within the boundaries of the United States. In 1870 the completed railroads of this great country have reached nearly fifty-one thousand miles. The present annual increase of railroads in the United States is about five thousand miles, nor is it likely that this ratio of augmentation will decrease for years to come. Wherever a railroad will add the amount of its cost to the value of the country through which it passes, it is certain to be built. In the infancy of our railroad experience there were thousands of obstacles and difficulties to be overcome: the lack of capital, the want of engineering skill, the absence of that experimental knowledge which makes every blow and every dollar tell its whole value, were serious drawbacks upon railroad building. Warily and wearily the companies went on, adding a few miles from year to year, until their roads were completed. But the same indomitable spirit of energy and enterprise which had settled a wilderness, felling forests, fencing fields, and fighting savages, in its onward course, was equal to the emergency of building railroads. And it will soon happen that the American Union will be covered with a grand network of railways, penetrating not only every State, but almost every county and township in this vast territory.

No continent of the globe is so well adapted, in its topographical character, for a vast system of railways as ours; and whereas we now have 50,000 miles in operation, the child is born that will see on this continent well nigh 150,000 miles, diverging from the center to all parts of our national domain; thus rendering the nation more powerful for good in peace than army and navy can accomplish.

The following table, already referred to, is the most wonderful exhibit of human progress that the genius of man has thus far been able to develop. It spreads out before the understanding an art, world-wide in its use, and the most powerful of all man's works for the promotion of a unity of human civilization.

RAILROADS OF THE WORLD.

Statement showing the extent and population of all countries in which Railroads have been constructed, the length and cost of these works, and the extent of mileage to area and population. Compiled from the most recent information.

COUNTRIES AND STATES.	Extent and Population.			Railroads.			Sq. mile to each mile of Railroad.	No. of Inhabitants to each mile of Railroad.
	Area in sq. miles.	Population, absolute.	Popul'n per mile.	Length in miles.	Cost in dollars, absolute.	Cost per mile.		
NORTH AMERICA.								
United States of America	3,001,002	38,315,000	12.76	47,254	$2,041,225,770	$44,255	63.51	810.83
Dominion of Canada. Ontario	147,832	1,962,067	13.27	1,407	107,815,774	76,344	104.98	1,394.51
Dominion of Canada. Quebec	209,990	1,354,067	6.45	575	43,016,519	74,811	365.20	2,354.90
Dominion of Canada. New Brunswick	27,037	319,027	11.79	226	6,954,232	30,771	119.63	1,411.62
Dominion of Canada. Nova Scotia	18,671	382,365	20.47	145	6,955,178	47,969	128.79	2,637.00
United States of Mexico	772,672	8,259,080	10.69	202	11,093,840	54,920	2,825.14	40,886.53
WEST INDIA ISLANDS.								
Island of Cuba	47,278	1,449,264	30.63	431	22,458,548	52,108	109.69	3,362.59
Island of Jamaica	6,250	441,264	70.60	14	391,174	27,941	446.43	3,151.85
SOUTH AMERICA.								
United States of Colombia	521,912	2,797,473	5.36	48	8,000,000	166,667	10,873.33	58,280.68
Republic of Venezuela	426,706	1,565,310	3.67	32	2,758,784	86,212	13,334.56	32,589.79
British Guiana	96,300	155 026	1.64	60	5,539,140	92,319	1,605.00	2,583.77
Empire of Brazil	2,973,400	10,045,000	3.31	512	102,992,384	201,157	5,807.42	19,619.14
Republic of Paraguay	86,206	1,000,000	11.60	46	4,130,340	89,790	1,874.08	21.739.13
Republic of Peru	498,703	2,513,901	6.04	101	5,697,410	56,410	4,937.65	24,890.19
Republic of Chili	249,798	1,704,931	6.96	394	24,155,746	61,309	634.01	4,327.23
Argentine Republic	1,126,430	1,259,355	1.11	231	12,455,058	53,918	486.32	5,451.75
EUROPE.								
United Kingdom of Great Britain and Ireland	122,519	29,293,319	239.09	14,247	2,511,314,435	176,269	8.60	2,056.10
French Empire	211,160	37,382,225	177.03	9,934	1,576,664.892	158,714	21.26	3,763.06
Kingdom of Spain	182,713	16,031,267	87.74	3,429	367,437,924	107,156	53.29	4,675.20
Kingdom of Portugal	36,476	3,987,861	109.33	522	52,887,474	101,317	69.89	7,639.59
Swiss Republic	15,272	2,524,240	165.28	897	78,157,928	87,132	17.02	2,814.09
Kingdom of Italy	109,783	24,896,801	226.78	4,109	382,580,772	93,108	26.72	6,059.09
Roman States	4,548	692,606	152.28	216	18,643,472	86,317	21.06	3,206.51
Kingdom of Prussia	139,499	23,595,543	169.14	5,926	747,689,346	126,171	23.54	3,981.70

North German States (other)	24,352	5,657,791	227.77	1,311	117,107,697	89,327	18.57	4,315.68
South German States	44,519	8,524,460	191.47	2,681	234,914,279	87,659	16.53	3,179.59
Austrian Empire	240,252	82,573,002	135.53	4,429	327,369,535	73,915	54.24	7,354.39
Kingdom of Belgium	11,403	4,940,570	442.92	1,703	182,198,861	106,987	6.69	2,901.33
Kingdom of Holland	13,621	3,735,682	274.26	881	85,634,081	97,201	15.46	4,240.27
Kingdom of Sweden	170,552	4,114,141	24.12	1,194	74,539,032	62,438	142.89	3,445.69
Kingdom of Norway	123,228	1,701,478	13.81	44	4,055,656	92,174	2,800.63	38,669.95
Kingdom of Denmark	14,726	1,608,095	109.20	401	22,902,714	57,114	36.72	4,010.21
Empire of Russia (in Europe)	1,965,730	65,902,267	33.53	8,700	1,448,356,214	166,477	225.94	7,574.92
Ottoman Empire (in Europe)	200,000	15,725,367	78.31	319	14,936,551	46,729	629.50	49,295.82
Kingdom of Greece	20,166	1,325,340	65.72	100	5,000,000	50,000	201.66	13,253.40
ASIA.								
Turkey in Asia	673,300	16,050,000	23.84	143	6,964,243	48,701	4,708.40	112,237.76
Persia	526,000	10,000,000	19.01	100	6,000,000	60,000	5,260.00	100,000.00
British India	1,402,200	179,492,000	128.01	4,092	391,888,791	95,769	342.67	43,864.12
Java	52,000	13,917,000	267.63	102	7,650,000	75,000	509.80	136,441.17
Ceylon	24,700	1,791,000	72.51	37	2,280,530	61,636	667.57	48,405.13
AFRICA.								
Egypt	178,000	2,500,000	14.04	468	45,163,879	96,504	380.34	5,341.88
Algeria	214,000	2,500,000	11.68	28	1,825,824	65,208	7,367.31	351,428.55
Cape Colony	120,000	300,000	2.50	85	7,828,792	92,103	1,411.76	3,529.86
Natal	20,000	150,000	7.50	2	119,422	59,711	10,000.00	75,000.00
AUSTRALIA.								
Victoria	86,800	574,331	6.62	409	46,549,268	113,812	212.22	1,404.23
New South Wales	323,400	378,935	1.17	174	14,007,522	80,502	1,858.62	2,177.79
Queensland	678,000	59,712	.89	102	10,161,519	99,622	6,647.06	585.41
South Australia	383,300	140,416	.37	87	5,142,427	59,108	4,405.75	1,613.97
New Zealand	106,500	175,357	1.64	17	1,491,402	87,729	6,264.70	10,315.12

RECAPITULATION.

North America	4,177,204	50,591,606	12.11	49,801	$2,267,061,313	$45,523	83.88	1,116.00
West India Islands	53,528	1,890,528	35.32	445	22,849,722	50,348	120.29	4,248.38
South America	5,979,455	21,040,997	3.52	1,424	165,728,862	116,382	4,128.83	14,775.98
Europe	3,651,331	284,212,055	77.83	61,043	8,252,390,863	135,189	59.82	4,655.93
Asia (containing railroads)	2,978,200	221,250,000	77.98	4,474	414,783,564	92,709	666.67	49,452.39
Africa	532,000	5,450,000	10.24	583	54,937,917	94,233	912.52	10,639.11
Australia	1,578,000	1,328,751	.85	789	77,352,138	98,038	2,000.00	1,684.09

Let us turn now to a final consideration of the civil mission of our people, for this, too, cannot be regarded otherwise than a great consideration in the world's civilization. Are we to remain one people — the great republican nation of the world? What civil mission through the national life is our people yet to fulfill? What beneficent influences are they yet to extend upon the nations and the people of the earth?

In the consideration of the civil and industrial mission of our people, we must not forget that all the future greatness and glory of each depend as well upon the maintenance of fundamental principles of civilization over this entire continent. We must have one race, one language, one law, and one religion, and the entire life of our people tempered by cardinal principles of justice and morality. Sad and trying experience has long since taught mankind the absolute necessity of these essentials. We look over the history of all races of men that have lived in Western Asia and Europe, and we find that the antagonism of races, of religions, and of language has been the bane of all national development and high civilization. But few of the nations have escaped bloody wars produced by collisions between races, religions, laws and languages; wars that have been destructive of the best productions of civilization. We look further East to find an exception to the general experience. In the far East we find China spread over with a single race, a single law, a single language, a single religion, and a common civilization, all tempered with the highest principles of honor and morality. Through thousands of years have they perpetuated themselves, and this example we find nowhere else on the globe. Turning from the far East, it is in the far West that we would imitate, on a higher scale, that grand experience of man in history. We have every advantage to do so. We have a continent at our command. Its topography and natural advantages and resources are in every way fitted for man's highest use and civilization. We have all the essential elements of one race, diverse from every other, and peculiar to the country. So, too, have we of law, of language, of religion, and of civilization. It therefore remains for our people to be faithful to the highest use of what they possess. The theory of our government is correct. Let us labor to progress from the theory, TRANSITIONAL REPUBLICANISM, to the practice, ORGANIC LIBERTY.

With the knowledge of the grand possibilities which our nation and people can yet attain, let us pray for a coming statesman, a law-giver, who will herald the rising glory of the Republic. A man of mighty, wide, grasping, reasoning, calculating, poetic mind, who, though born in a manger, the kings of the earth will bow before his simple grandeur and majesty. A statesman too lofty in his bearing to deceive his people, and too pure in his nature to usurp their rights and bounties; a man whose life-example is a source of perpetual admiration for all his people; a man, in short, who in every way is a statesman which the necessities of the Republic demand to point the way to its future greatness and honor. The birth of such a man is not impossible. God gives to the necessities of men and nations, and while we hope for the future, let us fully realize the present, and vindicate the Republic, its national life and character.

Said Carnot, the great French statesman, when speaking of Republics: "*One* only has been the work of philosophy, and that is the United States." The universal judgment of enlightened mankind corroborates the truth of this statement. When our fathers appealed to the Universal Judge of the world in vindication of the rights and independence of the colonies, they opened a way that no man can shut — a way for the free exercise of the inherent rights of all mankind, through the rolling ages of the future. They established a government that interposed "no restraint but those laws which are the same to all, and no distinction but that which a man's merit may originate." They established a union of independent colonies, which, yielding to an irresistible national attraction, sought a new life in becoming a part of the great whole.

Then realizing the character of a nation just born, we can readily apprehend what good it is destined to subserve in the civil interests of mankind, and over what lands its laws will seek dominion. Said the Hon. Charles Sumner, in speaking of the final supremacy of our constitution over all of North America: "The end is certain; nor shall we wait long for its mighty fulfillment. Its beginning is the establishment of peace at home, through which the national unity shall become manifest. This is the first step. The rest will follow. In the procession of events it is now at hand, and he is blind who does not discern it. From the frozen sea to the tepid waters of the Mexican Gulf, from the Atlantic to the Pacific, the whole vast continent, smiling with outstretched prairies, where the coal-fields below vie with the infinite corn-fields above—teeming with iron, copper, silver, and gold—filling fast with a free people, to whom the telegraph and steam are constant servants — breathing already with schools, colleges, and libraries—interlaced by rivers which are great highways—studded with inland seas where fleets are sailing, and 'poured round old ocean's' constant tides, with tributary commerce and still expanding domain. Such will be the great Republic, one and indivisible, with a common Constitution, a common Liberty, and a common Glory."

Said the Hon. William H. Seward: "This Union has not yet accomplished what good for mankind was manifestly designed by Him who appoints the seasons, and prescribes the duties of States and Empires. It shall continue and endure. No other government can exist here."

With these eloquent declarations we at once ascend to the grandeur of the subject, and behold the great Republic, actuated by the inevitable tendency of power and profit, moving forward to complete dominion over North America. The boundary lines of Canada and those of Mexico will soon be effaced, and the new regions absorbed into the Federal family. Beyond this will follow Central America, the West India and Sandwich Islands, and still beyond, South America will furnish a new field of industry and civil government for the redundant population of our Continental Republic; and, strengthened by the universality of one language and one law, the power and civil mission of our people will go forth from one people to another, until Old England, "proud and potent as she now appears," shorn of her colonies, will, like a widowed mother, kindred in language and religion, but weak like the shorn Samson, supplicate the young child, America, for sustenance and protection. Thus will America move forward until, in political power and prestige, she becomes the New Rome of the world, and in industry and civilization the Chinese or Celestial Empire of the earth—uniting at once, in universal relationship and in the highest possible order of development, and under one constitution, the representative characters of the two mightiest historic nations of the earth.

In the gift of empire, dominion will be hers, and her flag will yet wave in amity over the most ancient capitals of the world. Her art and industry will yet make the earth bloom as a universal Eden. In Epopæia America will yet have greater poets than have ever walked upon the earth. In classics she will have her Salamis and Lepanto, her Alhambra and Parthenon; and with a universal recognition of the principles of the golden rule by all, who will not with prayerful hearts

"Hail the dawn of the coming day"?

The universality of one language, one law, and one religion over all this continent, will be invulnerable to the powers of the world. Europe and Asia, distracted with their many languages, nationalities, and religions, will continue for centuries to struggle with all the adversities produced by discordant elements among nations; hence the civil mission of our people will be universal and beneficent to all parts of the world. Intervening between the two great oceans of the globe, ours cannot fail to be the great representative nation of the earth in its population, its laws, and its commerce.

In its bosom all the extremes of the earth will be represented, and to its growth all parts of the world will contribute. We look around, East, West, North and South, and in every land foreign powers watch our progress with awe, and seek favor from our institutions. After all, it is America that will inherit the earth.

India with its 200,000,000, China with its 400,000,000, Polynesia with its 26,006,000 — more than two-thirds of the whole human race—are only now for the first time really open to our enterprise and commerce; and "no matter in what region a desirable product is bestowed on man by a liberal Providence, or fabricated by human skill — it may clothe the hills of China with its fragrant foliage — it may glitter in the golden sands of California — it may wallow in the depths of the Arctic Seas — it may ripen and whiten in the fertile plains of the sunny South — it may spring forth from the flying shuttles of Manchester in England, or Manchester in America—the great world-magnet of commerce will attract it alike," and to us will be given sumptuously from the bountiful supply, as it is "all gathered up for the service of man." Then, conscious of a transcendent destiny for the Great Republic of the world, and the co-equal industrial mission of the American people, the hopes and motives of all are made doubly strong as they go forward in the battle of life.

Already the nation is in a great transition; its very life is epical and unencumbered. From its crucifixion between the two thieves, slavery and rebellion, it triumphantly rides over the billowy waves of sad and desolating war into the haven of peace, hope, and prosperity. But the subject must not be dismissed without its appropriate lesson of patriotism—a plea for an unchanging devotion of the citizen to the Union of the States, as an absolute necessity for the perpetuity of the life of the Republic. The truest and broadest sense of filial love is understood to be a love of country — loyalty, patriotism. The necessity of this devotional sentiment or principle, by the citizen to the government, is just as important to the welfare of mankind as the devotion of the individual to society. Each citizen is a part of the whole; the whole a union of States and individuals for common defense and common interest. The one complements the other. In all ages of the world, patriotism has given to the citizen the qualities of the hero, and furnished the orator, the statesman, and the poet with themes of unequaled magnitude and grandeur.

"Our country!—'tis a glorious land!
With broad arms stretched from shore to shore.
The proud Pacific chafes her strand,
She hears the dark Atlantic roar."
* * * * * * *
"Great God! we thank Thee for this home—
This bounteous birthland of the free;
Where wanderers from afar may come,
And breathe the air of liberty.
Still may her flowers untrampled spring,
Her harvests wave, her cities rise;
And yet, till time shall fold his wing,
Remain earth's loveliest paradise."

The revolution of '76 sowed in the hearts of the American people the seeds of an imperishable devotion to the Union of these States—a devotion which nought but the foulest hand, moved by the most corrupt heart, would dare to reach forth to destroy; and though we are now in the midst of a transition, such as comes in the life of nations, when the event and the struggle vastly overawes the individual comprehension and convictions, and thus leads for a time to an unhappy condition and dire results, it needs no prophetic eye to see beyond to the new unfoldment, when union and patriotism will again walk together all over this broad land, as Enoch walked with God. But such a result will not be the fruit of a miracle; it will only come as the result of earnest and devoted toil, thus cultivating in the hearts of the American people a deep and fervent attachment to Union.

What man—what woman—what citizen—conscious of being either sire or descendant in this nation, and among this people, is not willing to share even the meanest part in so grand a mission? The destiny is alike to the State and the citizen; the growth and prosperity of the one contributes to the welfare of the other, and everywhere under the shield of the Constitution, freedom is the same to all. What land affords greater opportunities? What people are more equal?

Turning, then, from this hopeful consideration, "and beholding my country at last redeemed and fixed in history, the Columbus of nations, once in chains, but now hailed as benefactor and discoverer, who gave a new liberty to mankind," let us anticipate the consummation of the future, and with the eyes of Cassandra, behold "one vast confederation stretching from the frozen North in one unbroken line to the glowing South, and from the wild billows of the

Atlantic westward to the calmer waters of the Pacific, and over all this vast continent one people, one law, one language, and one faith; and in the full fruition of our arms and arts, our industry and dominion, this whole land begemmed with mighty cities of civilization; then, with eyes lifted toward heaven, behold upon the starry scroll of the future Columbia's name recorded, her future honors and happiness inscribed. Then, closing the vision, let us turn to man, and with a voice that will reach all hearts and consciences, bid him go forth in peace to the great mission of the higher and better conquest of the world; and—

"Thou, too, sail on, O Ship of State;
Sail on, O Union, strong and great;
Humanity, with all its fears,
With all the hope of future years,
Is hanging breathless on thy fate.
We know what Master laid thy keel,
What Workman wrought thy ribs of steel;
Who made each mast, and sail, and rope,
What anvils rang, what hammers beat,
In what a forge, and what a heat
Were shaped the anchors of thy hope.
Fear not each sudden sound and shock—
'Tis of the wave, and not the rock,
'Tis but the flapping of the sail,
And not a rent made by the gale.
In spite of rock and tempest's roar,
In spite of false lights on the shore;
Sail on, nor fear to breast the sea—
Our hearts, our hopes, are all with thee;
Our hearts, our hopes, our prayers, our tears,
Our faith triumphant o'er our fears,
Are all with thee—are all with thee!"

AMERICA.

"Melodia rules thy destiny, O Land
Of coming years; O Empire wise and grand,
America! and thou at last shall be
The consecrated home of Poetry—
The fairer Greece, adorned with noblest art,
And bathed in sacred love from God's creative heart.
For thee, for thee, the wise Melodians throng
Even now, and chant in Heaven their morning song.
For thee and for thy sons methinks they sing;
They come, and angel songs as offerings bring.
For thee and for thy race methinks they cry,
'Love, Wisdom, Inspiration, Liberty,
The four great Angels of the coming time,
To their Olympian goal lead on thy race sublime.'
Thou art that rock-built Pharos that above
Earth's ocean lifts the immortal flame of love.
E'en now thou shinest like a beacon-star,
Leading Earth's myriads o'er the deep afar.
Thou art the lost Atlantides that lay,
To ancient thought, beyond the waves away;
The New Jerusalem the ancient Seer
Of Patmos saw, descending white and clear
From highest heaven; the rich and wise Cathay
Columbus sought, faith-guided, on his way.
The Old, the New, the Future, and the Past,
Meet and embrace, complete in thee at last.
Thou art the crowning flower of Earth and Time,
The destined Eden of Mankind divine."

THE GREAT BRIDGE NOW BEING BUILT OVER THE MISSISSIPPI, AT ST. LOUIS.

"What a glorious future may we not anticipate for our own St. Louis! Why, sir, I imagine I can see the Oriental traveler, on his brief excursion round the world, pause upon the central span of the Eads Bridge, and, amid a prodigality of gigantic achievements of science and progressive effort, still read in the distant future developments of equal or greater magnitude. He stands upon a structure which rests upon the deep foundations of the earth itself, and presents in its strength and massive grandeur, in its piers of granite and arches of steel, fit emblems of our moral as well as physicals tructures, the steadfastness and wisdom of our institutions, and the solidity of our industries. Beneath him flows the great Father of Waters, bearing on its bosom the argosies of an empire, while on every hand the evidences of triumphant art command his attention. A city of 1,000,000 inhabitants lies before him, and it may be on one of its ascending steppes the capital of the nation rears its peerless dome. Strange wonders, these, of Time's begetting, and of progressive revolutions! The providential mystery which hid this continent from the knowledge of the civilized world for thousands of years, begins to clear away under the sunshine of facts which surrounds him, and the grand revelation is made that it was reserved for a period when mankind should aim to be fraternal, and the victories of peace should be acknowledged the crowning glories of ambition."—B. R. BONNER.

Each age and each nation produces its great works in some phase of human progress. The early Jews built the tower of Babel; Egypt had the pyramids and Catacombs; Greece her Parthenon and unequaled temples of worship; Rome had her Coliseum; the middle ages their walled cities. But modern civilization, passing beyond the age of selfishness, ambition, and idolatry, gives to mankind magnificent structures of greater use as the triumphs of the genius of the race.

The greatest work of mechanical art that the world has yet beheld is the Crystal Palace of the nineteenth century. It combines in one grand masterpiece of art, and one glow of associated beauty, the highest civilization and progress of man.

The leading feature of the present age is the strife for commercial dominion. In this department of civilization is enlisted more capital, talent, and men than in any other. All the rapid strides of the race are made in its interest—whether in the achievement of art, of science, or of genius. The wild billows of the Atlantic have been defied by steam and electricity, and the two great continents of kindred shores united by these subtle agents; and now with one steady grand march does civilization, carried by the tides of men, continue its journey to the West—to the high mountains, and the broad and calmer waters of the wide Pacific Ocean. With these great movements come the masterworks of mechanics and arts.

Since the invention of the steam engine, the railway system may be regarded as the greatest aid to civilization the arts have produced, on account of the rapid intercommunion of men and ideas, and the exchange of products. But a great and valuable railway system without bridges to cross the inland streams would be an impossibility; hence the remarkable development of genius and art, and the concentration of capital, to construct in ample proportions these master-fabrics for commercial use. Nor are they constructed as the easy work common to the ordinary routine of life. But rather are they, who project great works in advance of the resistless moving times, compelled to contend against a vast array of ignorance, prejudice, and selfishness. Yes, there is one thing common in the history of all great undertakings that have to break a new path: they have to combat against frivolous objections and contempt, and, even in the best cases, against the unsympathetic attitude of the masses. At the same time it must be confessed that these opposing elements have never failed to pass into their opposites, as soon as perseverance, talent, and business energy on the part of individuals have, in spite of them, realized what has once been acknowledged as possible and necessary. In all such cases contempt has been exchanged for admiration, doubt has been compelled to give way; and the more rapidly and victoriously the enterprise, which was once so strongly doubted or even assailed, progresses, the more surprisingly does the number of those increase who would fain have it believed that they stood as prophets of good by its cradle. Such was the case—to confine our examples to American soil—with the Erie canal, with the leveling of Chicago, with the Pacific railroads, and finally with that immense structure which, before the face of St. Louis, is soon destined to span the Father of Waters. This one circumstance might be sufficient to secure the work its proper place among the great feats of humanity in modern times. But such is no longer necessary as an argument; the structure has its days of combat behind it—already its creators can point with silent finger to the actual progress which it has made, and to the point which it has at this moment attained, and allow that which has already been accomplished to speak for that which is yet to be accomplished. And it speaks irresistibly; it tells us not only that the completion of a work which in its line has no peer, is certain, but it tells us also that, as in the case of the Pacific railways, the goal will be reached many a day sooner than the original calculations and pre-suppositions led us to expect.

That the trade of the central portion of the Mississippi Valley, which centers in St. Louis, and advances every year with such gigantic strides, was not sufficiently provided for by the present arrangements for transportation across the broad stream which separates Missouri and Illinois, or, to speak more correctly, the true East and West of the United States, has been known and seen by every one for many years.

Passing from this general allusion to the struggle which enterprise is compelled to wage against established conditions, we at once submit a general statement of the great Bridge under consideration.

The plan of the Bridge, as it is now being built, is quite original in many particulars, and when completed will, in all probability, be superior to any structure of the kind in the world. So great and important is the structure, that a complete description of its main work will not be uninteresting to the general reader; for the work itself has its lesson as well as its value, and therefore its manner of building, as well as its style of structure, will be of great public interest.

THE PIERS OF THE BRIDGE.

The locality at the river chosen for the bridge is a scene of the strangest and most exciting kind. Along the banks are extensive workshops, heaps of hewn stone, beams, iron-work and cement barrels, forges, offices and sheds for supplies, derricks and other arrangements for hoisting, and pile-drivers, whose construction alone is a sort of miracle, and finally the lofty bridge-scaffoldings, composed of thousands of beams, arms, and parts of iron machines over the shore piers, which are in progress of construction inside of strong caissons. In the midst of the river, 500 feet from either shore, and 520 feet distant from each other, we see the same scaffoldings, only more complicated and more lofty, and, notwithstanding their colossal size, affording an almost elegant spectacle in their wonderful symmetry. Structures of all kinds, and palisades that go down a hundred feet into the river, intended to break the current, and more particularly the floating ice in winter, surround these wonderful constructions that rise from the bosom of the river.

Like the building yards on shore, and even more than these, they are crowded with a perfect bee-hive of engineers and workmen, whose self-conscious ability is infinitely increased by the enormous mechanical powers which stand here ready for use at every step, in the form of floating derricks, steam engines, pumps, and hydraulic jacks. These are the building yards of the two piers. Under these scaffoldings and iron constructions the heavy masses of stone which are intended to carry and hold the three arches of the bridge mostly counterparts of the ponderous structures of the ancient Egyptians, are put together. But how much easier was the task of those ancients, who piled up their edifices in the familiar element of atmospheric air! In our case they had to penetrate into the deeps, but not, like the miner, into the solid element of the earth; they had to break through a volume of water thirty feet deep, and, after arriving at the bottom, to burrow through the sixty and ninety-feet thick layers of treacherous, ever-changing Mississippi sand, in order to rest the basis of the piers upon the eternal ribs of the earth itself, on the rocks of primeval worlds.

The investigations of years in regard to the undercurrent of the Mississippi have shown that no river in the world changes its sand-bed so rapidly and to such an extent; and more particularly the soundings that were made near St. Louis showed that at times, when the river overflows, its sand-layers may be carried away to the depth of forty feet, and, under extraordinary circumstances, scoured down to the very rock itself. Thus was demonstrated the necessity of laying the basis of the piers upon the rock itself, which under one pier is ninety feet, under the other one hundred and twenty feet, under the ordinary high-water line. Inasmuch, on the other hand, as the law of Congress, made in the interest of navigation, prescribes that the height of the arches shall be fifty feet above the city directrix, or ordinary high-water line of the river, it results that the entire height of the piers must reach 165 and 194 feet respectively.

The system by which the base is laid upon the rock is that of sinking. On colossal iron caissons (open below and resting upon the sand itself), which, with the increasing weight of the piers built on top of them, and as the sand under them is removed to the upper world, sink deeper and deeper, this lowering is effected. In order, however, to render the caissons—which, in spite of the thickness of their iron walls and their solid construction, might not be able to withstand the pressure of the growing masonry and the masses of sand that press against their side walls — capable of resistance, the atmosphere, by means of enormous air-pumps, is compressed in them in such a manner that their power of resistance can be increased to meet any exigency. When the caisson or air chamber, as it is called with propriety, strikes upon the rock—that is, when the sand-pumps working it have removed the gigantic layers of sand through which it had to penetrate, and when the pier that rests on the caisson is separated only by the air-chamber from the rock—then it (the caisson) is filled with concrete, which completes the indissoluble connection between pier and rock. When the last particle of compressed air in the air-chamber has given place to this indestructible compound of cement and stone, all that remains to be done is to fill up in a similar manner the perpendicular shafts which communicate between the air-chamber and the upper world, and the whole structure of the pier in solid compactness, incorporated with the rock far below, stands aloft, bathing high above its colossal and yet elegant form in the rays of the sun, out of the floods of the river.

IN THE AIR-CHAMBER.

During the last few months a visit to one of the air-chambers under the piers was one of the principal attractions that St. Louis had to show to visitors. The further the piers themselves advanced—that is, the deeper the air-chamber sunk with its burden—the greater was the compression of the air necessary to render them capable of supporting the immense weight which increased with every inch of sinking, and all the harder was the work inside the caisson. When the air-chamber of the east pier, on the 28th of February last, reached the depth of ninety-five feet under the bed of the river, with a weight of 20,000 tons upon it, the workman who removed the last of the sand had to work under the pressure of three atmospheres; and it was not possible so entirely to avoid all kinds of mischances, as has hitherto been the case, without changing the workmen as frequently as possible. In order to afford a more complete understanding of the matter, we must remark that the introduction of the compressed air into the caisson can be measured with such wonderful accuracy that the sinking can be regulated to an inch. This sinking is accurately calculated according to the quantity of the sand removed from beneath the air-chamber, which is nine feet high. The sand itself is removed by means of powerful pumps, which pump up the sand in great streams after it has been softened and brought in the condition of drifting sand by means of water supplied from a hose, and then driven back to the river from whose depths it had been taken.

As we have already said, a number of shafts passing vertically down the pier effect a chimney kind of a communication between the air-chamber and the upper world. In the central and widest of these was a winding stair-case, which was lengthened as the pier reached downward, and was used for people to pass up and down. The smaller shafts, which also passed down the pier perpendicularly, contained the pipes which serve to introduce the compressed air, the hose for moistening the sand, the pump which removes it, machines for the introduction of materials, and a telegraphic arrangement by means of which the workmen from beneath, "where all things hideous are," are able to correspond every moment with "those that breathe in the rosy light."

The entrance into the caisson itself was effected by means of an air-lock at the bottom of the winding stair-case—a lock which, like the caisson, is constructed of thick iron, and is an integral part of it. As soon as the chamber was entered, which was capable of holding six or eight persons, the current of air admitted rushed round with such impetuosity that even strong organizations entering this kingdom of darkness and night for the first time could not disembarrass themselves of a certain feeling of uneasiness. The iron door that led to the outer world pressed firmer against its frame, by the force of the air streaming in, than could be done by a lock or any other contrivance. The stop-cock through which the air streamed in was not closed until the atmosphere in the air-lock had reached the same density as that in the main part of the caisson. As soon as this was the case the door leading into the caisson opened of itself, and we were ready to enter this subterraneous workshop, where even the clearest voice loses its sound, and where, deep under the echo of human speech—yea, deep under the water's undermost depths—busy workmen pave the way for the sinking pier.

For a while one felt perfectly comfortable in this underworld — a world such as no mythology and no superstition ever dreamed of. The transition, indeed, became apparent by pain in the ears, bleeding at the nose, or a feeling of suffocation; but these inconveniences and seeming dangers, inevitable upon such a visit to hell, were insignificant in comparison with the interest which it offered. It was undertaken by hundreds and hundreds of visitors, including many ladies, and none returned from that depth without carrying along with them one of the most remarkable reminiscences of their whole life. Shrouded in a mantle of vapor labor the workmen there, loosening the sand; dim flicker the flames of the lamps, and the air had such a strange density and moisture that one wandered about almost as if he were in a dream. For a short time all this was extremely interesting and delightful, but it was not long before the wish to escape again from this strange situation gained the upper hand over the charm which it exercised. Gladly did the visitor, after a quarter of an hour, re-enter the air-lock, with an unfeigned feeling of relief, to watch the air beginning to escape from this chamber. At once the door behind him leading from the caisson closed by the denser air, and fastened as firmly as if there was a mountain behind it. The compressed element escaped whistling from the air-lock; the air within was more and more equalized with the air without;

a few minutes, and they were of equal density; then the door, no longer pressed against its frame by the dense atmosphere, opened to the winding stairs, and the visitor came forth taking a long breath, and, to use Schiller's words, once more "greets the heavenly light" which shone from far above down the shaft.

THE BRIDGE WHEN COMPLETED.

At present both the piers may be considered as finished. The east pier has been resting with its caisson on the rock since the 28th of February, and the filling of the chambers was then rapidly accomplished. Its western companion had then only three feet more to sink, and this it might have done in a very short time, but the supply of granite failed to arrive in time, and so interrupted the building itself. It is laid down in the plan that the portion of the piers above water, and exposed to the action of the air, shall be built of the strongest granite, while the parts extending from the rock to a certain point under the lowest water shall be built from limestone blocks from Grafton quarry, in Illinois. When the expected granite arrived, the construction of the piers above the surface of the water made rapid progress, and in a few weeks they will have reached the prescribed height of fifty feet above the water level. Their total height, or, if you prefer it, their total depth, will then, as stated above, be 194 and 165 feet respectively—the east pier being the highest, because the rock on the Illinois side of the river lies deeper than it does on the Missouri side. The hexagonal foundation of the piers is 82 feet in length; their weight amounts to from 28,000 to 33,000 tons. No less solid and massive is the construction of the abutments. In their case, likewise, they had to go down to the rocks. Upon the Missouri side of the river this presented little difficulty, which, however, will be made up for on the Illinois side, on account of the nature of the American bottom. On this side the works are already advancing, inside a gigantic coffer-dam, towards the surface. On the other side they are just being begun. We know, however, that in the character of this work a beginning is the beginning of a certain, and particularly of an early, termination. It will therefore not be long before the Illinois abutment will rapidly follow its *vis-a-vis* and the two piers.

These four piers will form the substructure which now approaches its termination with rapid strides. Upon the masses thereof, which are put together to last for an eternity, the bridge itself will rest, which is destined to facilitate the proudest inland commerce over the proudest of streams. They will carry three arches, which, as was already remarked, will measure—those extending from the abutments to the piers 500 feet each, and the span of the principal arch between the two piers 520 feet. The possibility of erecting such long spans, considering the enormous weight which they will have to bear, was at first strongly doubted, and still more strongly contested. Captain Eads, however, sustained on the one side by his calculations, on the other by the example of the arched bridge at Kulinburg, in Holland, which spans the Leck with a span of 500 feet, as well as by the plans of the English bridge-engineer

Telford, which were made in the beginning of this century, was enabled to invalidate and set aside all these objections. Cast-steel is selected as the material of these arches. Each of them will be double, that is to say, will consist of two concentric arches 12 feet apart, and joined together by a network of the most massive steel braces. Such double arches will be stretched four in each span, running parallel with each other from pier to pier. Upon their iron necks will be laid the real bridge in two stories. The lower of these stories is intended for the railways; the upper belongs to vehicles and foot passengers. Being fifty feet wide, both will afford space enough to satisfy the demands of the liveliest traffic. Meanwhile, underneath, the largest steamers, even when the water is at its highest, may dash along; and while over them the East and West exchange their riches, they may, unimpeded, perform the exchange between the North and the South. St. Louis, however, will not only have the boldest arch bridge in the world, but it will also have the first structure of the kind built of steel, the true noble metal of our times. Let us leave to Europe her Krupp and her arsenal full of cast-steel cannon—the one steel bridge over the Mississippi casts into the shade all that equivocal wealth of the old world.

It remains to say a few words in regard to the shore structures, or, more properly, to the approaches to the bridge. The street leading directly to the bridge—Washington avenue—is one of the broadest and finest in St. Louis. Like the whole of the St. Louis shore, it slopes rapidly when it approaches the river. It will be sufficient, therefore, to prolong the bridge, which rises about fifty feet above the shore, a comparatively short distance—three blocks—1,049 feet into the city, in order that its level may equal that of Washington avenue. A viaduct of five arches, of twenty-seven feet span each, under which the traffic of the cross streets below may be carried on unobstructedly, will form the continuation of the bridge, and of course will be of the same height and breadth. At the end of it the high level road will pass into Washington avenue, which still continues to rise, whereas the low level road, with its railways, will run into a tunnel, 4,800 feet in length, which passes under a large portion of the city, and terminates at the spot where the great St. Louis Central Railroad Depot will be erected—where at present the Pacific railroad crosses Eleventh street. The tunnel will be fifteen feet wide and seventeen feet high. By means of soundings and borings it has been ascertained that there are only layers of clay to be tunneled through, and therefore the latter portion of the enterprise will offer no particular difficulties. With the approach to the bridge over the flat marshy ground on the Illinois shore, the company itself has nothing whatever to do. Dykes and trestles, branching off according to the convenience of the different railroad companies to north, south, or east, will complete the connection with the bridge. The upper carriage-way will be carried out upon solid constructions as far as Fourth street in East St. Louis, from which point the Missouri traffic will divide up in all directions.

And now, what will this gigantic work—measuring from the Illinois abutment to Washington avenue, in St. Louis, 2,230 feet—cost? We put down the estimates for the different parts, as well as for the whole structure:

Superstructure (piers and abutments)	$1,540,080 00
Superstructure (arches and roads for traffic)	1,460,418 30
Approaches	520,397 24
Tunnel	410,477 55
Expropriations	539,900 00
Railroad	25,680 00
Total expense of bridge	$4,496,953 09

Of this capital, three millions ($1,200,000 in St. Louis, the rest in New York) have already been subscribed, and the outlay up to the present moment is $1,700,000. At the same time the financial management has hitherto been so successful, and the different contracts made so advantageously, that the progress of the bridge will certainly not be interrupted by any pecuniary difficulties. No less certain is it that advantage will be taken of the work as soon as it is completed. The data which have been made and collected with extreme care in regard to this point by one of the directors, Dr. William Taussig—who must be considered one of the most energetic promoters and patrons of the great national enterprise—lead to the following results:

At least thirteen railroads will have their terminus on the Illinois shore of the Mississippi in East St. Louis. And at least eleven railways will soon leave St. Louis itself, cutting the State of Missouri in all directions. Of only three of all these have we any statistical reports, and these relate only to the freight traffic of the year 1867. They show that during that year 767,400 tons of freight were carried over these lines. The most modest estimate of the traffic of twelve railways, which will be the total number finished and in operation before the completion of the bridge, cannot place it below a million of tons. The contracts already made with the different railway companies, and those still to be negotiated, secure to the Bridge Company an average tariff of 65 cents a ton, which would yield a yearly revenue from freight alone of $550,500. The remaining traffic (horse-cars, coal carts, farmers' wagons, and other freight conveyances, along with cattle transport), according to present estimates, may be reckoned at $129,647, and passengers on the railways $112,000, so that altogether the total revenue would amount to $892,147. From this sum $40,000 must be subtracted for annual incidental expenses, and there will remain over a sum equal to eight and a half per cent. on a capital of ten millions.

It is expected that the bridge will be inaugurated in the last days of next year. However, if we may draw a conclusion from the past favors of fortune upon the work, the latter part of the summer of 1871 will see the first train of cars pass over the steel and granite structures of this unrivaled bridge. Then it will not only be a source of pride to every Missourian in particular and every American in general, but its massive and yet magnificently elegant forms will be a source of astonishment to the ordinary spectator and of admiring appreciation to the professional engineer. Then likewise will be brilliantly verified the words with which the architect closed the report which he laid before the company in the spring of 1868, and which are as follows:

"It is safe in stating that rarely has an enterprise been inaugurated which appeals so strongly to the support of our citizens of all classes, which promises so much to add to the welfare and prosperity of the city, and which offers such a safe and remunerative return for the labor and capital invested in it."

At the present time the west pier is sunk to the rock, and the air-chambers of both piers, and the shafts in them, have been filled up with concrete; and the masonry has been carried up to about six feet above low-water lines. The caisson for the east abutment is being built at Carondelet, and will be launched about August 10th of this year.

The west abutment has also been built up to about twelve feet above low-water, and by February 1st of next year all the masonry of the piers will be ready for the superstructure. The contract for the superstructure has been awarded to the Kingston Bridge Company, of Pittsburg, Pa., and that company is now working in the most urgent manner to fill their contract, which obliges them to furnish and raise the superstructure of the bridge within seventeen months. A notable feature of this contract consists in the fact that it has been let at prices below those estimated by the Chief Engineer.

This constitutes a brief outline description of the great St. Louis Railway and Passenger Bridge, which is now in process of construction.

A very brief classification of the approved bridges of the day, and an allusion to specimens of the various kinds, will, perhaps, enable the casual reader to receive a better impression of the magnitude of the St. Louis bridge. There are four prominent styles of bridges, which are generally adopted by the engineering profession when they aim to erect something that will endure to remote generations—the tubular, the suspension, the lattice, and the arch—all constructed of iron, in one or more of its forms. The tubular, invented by Robert Stephenson, although materially aided by Fairbairn, will always, we think, be regarded as one of the great ideas of the nineteenth century. It is a straight, hollow, rectangular tube. The Britannia bridge is the grandest specimen; for its longest span or reach, between supports, is 459 feet. But long as it is, it was lifted in one piece 100 feet high, to its present postion. The Victoria bridge has no span of equal length, nor was it elevated in the same way.

The suspension, in its crude forms, is of ancient date. It is found in all lands, but until later years it has never received the indorsement of engineers as the reliable support of railway trains; and in this respect it can hardly be said to have thoroughly disarmed sound criticism, when we claim we are building something that is truly permanent. It possesses some qualities that will always render it popular. It can be constructed more easily in many positions. A much greater span can be obtained than by any other known method, and the cost is comparatively less. Perhaps this last feature can be understood when we remember that the Niagara bridge, with a span of 821 feet, was built for less than the yearly interest on the sum expended on the Britannia bridge. Its general construction is well known. In Europe, the prominent specimens are the Menai, by Telford, with a span of 580 feet, and the Freyburg, in Switzerland, with a span of 870 feet. In this country, Ellet and Roebling have identified themselves with the Wheeling, Niagara, Cincinnati, and other bridges. Ellet constructed the Wheeling bridge, 1,000 feet span, which failed to withstand the winds; yet Mr. Ellet was a great man. Mr. Roebling may be regarded as the great exponent of the suspension bridge in this country. His reputation may well be envied; for while the great engineers of Europe were declaring it was impossible, he went on with the Niagara bridge; and now, after eighteen years' successful usage, it has caused the engineers of the old world to reverse their theories.

He built the Cincinnati bridge, and if, in future times, the suspension shall have become recognized as a thoroughly safe, permanent structure for railway trains, to Mr. Roebling, more than any other, will the credit belong.

The lattice bridge has been and is now a very popular type of bridge. The name will readily convey a correct impression of its general construction. In some respects it is preferable to the tubular. It is less costly and is less rigid, which some claim to be an advantage. As fine a specimen of this kind, perhaps, as can be seen anywhere, is at Cologne, over the Rhine. Its longest reach is 330 feet. It is, however, liable to oscillation.

But yielding everything to the suspension and the lattice that can with reason be claimed for them, it is questionable whether they possess the elements of perpetuity equally with the arch. We know arch bridges have endured for centuries; we do not yet know how long a railway suspension, tubular, or lattice bridge will continue.

The first cast-iron arch bridge was built in 1779, with a span of 100 feet. Many other iron arch bridges have been successfully constructed. They have always been highly esteemed for their strength and durability. The great drawback, perhaps, has been an inability to construct them with a span so wide as to compare favorably with those of other styles. In England, the largest is the Southwark, with a span of 240 feet and a rise of 24 feet. Note this fact, and remember the length of the Britannia, 459 feet, and the length of the Cologne, 330 feet, and then the importance of the St. Louis bridge, with its span of 520 feet, will appear.

Its form is as enduring as any tested by the experience of ages. Its size surpasses that of any, when we consider the true comparison, the length of span. Its material, cast-steel, is the best in the world, ranking with wrought-iron in the ratio of two to one.

The importance of the St. Louis bridge is still further increased when we consider its foundations, their depth, their mode of construction, and the attendant difficulties.

Other engineers of great eminence have proposed the erection of bridges of greater span than this, but it rarely occurs that the location and conditions of the case justify, as in this one, such bold grasp of mind on the part of the engineer, with the no less accompaniment of a proper manifestation of public spirit on the part of capitalists to carry out his design.

Mr. Latrobe, a noted engineer of Baltimore, has expressed his opinion upon the construction of a bridge at St. Louis. He favored the use of piers higher than those of the present plan, requiring a stationary engine to draw the cars from either side to the center in passing over. He also advocated the use of spans 400 and 500 feet in length.

That modern engineers are anticipating something altogether superior to the past achievements, the following remarks of Mr. Roebling are evidence. He says:

"It was left to modern engineering, by the application of the principle of suspension, and by the use of wrought-iron, to solve the problem of spanning large rivers without intermediate supports. Cast and wrought-iron arches, of 100 feet and more, have been quite successful. Nor can it be said the limit of arching has been reached. Timber arches of much greater span have stood for years, and have rendered good service in this country as well as on the continent of Europe. It is worthy of notice, however, and to be cited as a curious professional circumstance, that the best form of material, so profusely applied by nature in her elaborate constructions, has never been used in arching, although proposed on several occasions. This form is unquestionably the cylindrical, combined in small sections, as is illustrated by vegetable and animal structures. Where strength is to be combined with lightness and elegance, nature never wastes heavy, cumbrous masses. The architects of the middle ages fully illustrated this by their beautiful buttresses and flying arches, combinations of strength and stability, executed with the least amount of material.

"The wrought-iron pipe, now manufactured of all sizes and in such great perfection, offers to the engineer a material for arching which cannot be excelled. A wire cable, composed of an assemblage of wires, constitutes the best catenary arch for the suspension of great weights; and, as a parallel to this, if the catenary is reversed, the best upright arch for the support of a bridge may be formed by an assemblage of wrought-iron pipes, of one and a half or two inches diameter or more. Arches of 1,000 feet span and more may be rendered practicable and safe upon this system. I venture to predict that the two great rival systems of future bridge engineering will be the inverted and upright arch—the former made of wire, and the latter of pipe, both systems rendered stable by the assistance of lattice work, or by stays, trusses, and girders."

It has already been stated that the bridge to be built at St. Louis is to be made of cast-steel; and in the meantime, extensive experiments have been going on to thoroughly test the strength of the metal, and no possible precaution will be neglected or effort omitted to make this bridge a complete and perfect success. Although not so great in length as the Victoria bridge over the St. Lawrence, which is nearly two miles long, nor the bridge over the Nebudda, in India, which is one and a half miles long, nor the bridge from Bassein to the main land, which is over three miles long, yet its magnificent spans and stately piers place it far above these bridges in character and structure. And when once built it will be grander than the Colossus at Rhodes, grander than the Pharos at Alexandria. It will vitalize the commerce of the Mississippi Valley, and unite the great railway chains between New York and San Francisco, the Lakes and the Gulf. When completed, it will place the name of its builder, Capt. James B. Eads, with those of Telford, Smeaton, Stephenson, and other distinguished engineers of the world. Mr. Eads already stands prominent as one of the most enterprising and public-spirited citizens of St. Louis; and should this bridge enterprise, in which he is more prominent than any other, prove successful, his character and reputation will become the public property of the country, even as the bridge itself will be. Almost proverbial for the invariable success attending everything he undertakes, and with a world-wide reputation for practical ingenuity and indomitable energy, we hail his prominent identification with this work as an assurance of its successful completion. To him, and to the enlightened, public-spirited citizens who have pledged their capital and influence to sustain the enterprise, will justly belong the glory that will surely attach to the St. Louis Bridge.

PROPOSED UNION DEPOT.

Cotemporaneous with the completion of the great bridge will be the necessity for a grand Union Passenger Depot in St. Louis, where all the railroads leading into the city could receive, deposit, and exchange their passengers with comfort and convenience to the traveling public as well as with economy and dispatch to the different railroad companies. Every day the need of such a building is more and more apparent to the leading railroad interests and the community, as the bridge now constructing approaches its completion.

Acting, therefore, at the suggestion of some of the most prominent and controlling representatives of the railroads leading into this city, and at their request, the Executive Committee of the Bridge Company have selected a site and prepared plans for a proposed structure, which, through their chairman, William Taussig, Esq., they have already submitted to railroad companies and the public.

After examining the whole line of the tunnel, from the end of the bridge to its terminus near the Pacific Railroad track, with a view to a grand Central Depot, the *site* has been selected, convenient for all the railroads, and central to the business of the bridge.

The *buildings* have been devised with a view to furnishing all the necessary office rooms for the different railroad companies, and their necessary adjuncts, express and fast freight lines, telegraph, &c., &c., thus combining everything to secure the prompt dispatch of business, and offer all possible inducements to trade and traffic.

The business of the railroads will require at least twelve tracks under the streets and in the depot. The offices for the different railroad, including express and freight companies, can be accommodated above the track, and communicate with it by flights of steps and by elevators.

DESCRIPTION OF DEPOT BUILDINGS AND TRACKS.

The depot buildings will occupy the three blocks from Fifth to Eighth street, between Washington avenue and Green street.

The "track-floor," which will be 20 feet below the level of the streets, will be 297 feet wide, and in length extending from Fifth to Eighth street, with the necessary space east of Fifth street and west of Eighth street to enter the tunnel at either end.

There will be ten tracks between Washington avenue and Green street, and four tracks under Washington avenue. There well be six platforms from 20 to 24 feet wide, with broad stairs from the platforms to the waiting-rooms above.

The ten tracks under the three blocks will be inclosed by arched walls three feet thick, and heavy retaining walls on the south side of Washington avenue, and under the curb of the southern sidewalk on Green street.

The streets—namely, Washington avenue, Sixth and Seventh streets—will be supported on iron columns, girders, and joists, and covered with Nicholson pavement.

The interior walls of the building will be supported on iron columns and girders.

The entire three blocks will be covered with buildings, the exterior walls of which will be built of cast-iron, and the interior walls of brick.

The group of buildings covering the block from Fifth to Sixth street will be four stories high, with French roof above; in the first story, and in the west end of the block, six baggage rooms for the railroads, with elevators for baggage from the platforms below, and track to distribute baggage from room to room.

On the lower story of this building will be the office, reading-room, billiard and bar room, table-d'hote, barber shop, wash room, &c., &c., of the hotel. There will be an open court in the interior of this building, which will be entered from Sixth street, with a large light-shaft in the same to track-floor below, also an entrance on Fifth street.

The third and fourth stories of the building to be appropriated to guests' rooms, and the fifth story, or French roof, to the kitchen, laundry, and general stores, boilers, machinery, and the general working departments of the hotel. This fifth story to be reached by four large elevators: one to serve the ordinary on second floor, and table-d'hote on first floor; one for passengers, and one for baggage; and one for general use, elevating of stores, fuel, &c. On the first floor, in Green street, will be a yard in connection with the elevator for the reception of stores, fuel, &c. Also in the yard will be contained the receptacle for the kitchen refuse, &c., conveyed from thence by large iron pipes. The water and soil from laundry, &c., to be conveyed to sewers beneath the track-floor.

In the first story of the block between Sixth and Seventh streets will be the ladies' and gentlemen's waiting-rooms, ticket and telegraph offices, with stairs from the waiting-rooms to the tracks below. These waiting-rooms will be provided with ample accommodations for washing, &c., and with stairs from the eastern ladies' waiting-room to the hotel above.

There will be room for seven large offices on Washington avenue, and seven on Green street — eight of them 23 by 46 feet; two, 30 by 40 feet; two, 35 by 46, and two 18 by 46 feet.

In the first story, from Seventh to Eighth street, there will be fourteen offices on Washington avenue and Green street: twelve, 23 by 46 feet, and two 18 by 46 feet. On Eighth street, Washington avenue, and Green street, there will be three large express offices. Those on Washington avenue and Green street will be 113 by 46 feet, and that on Eighth street 132 by 45 feet.

The express offices will be furnished with every convenience, as elevators for raising and lowering goods from platforms on track-floor below.

In the second, third, and fourth stories of these buildings will be 330 large and commodious offices and rooms, independent of those designed for guests' rooms in the hotel. These rooms will be furnished with all modern conveniences, and will be accessible by commodious stairs at proper intervals, and have communication to same from balconies around the court, over track-floors.

The whole space between the buildings on Washington avenue and Green street, from the east side of Sixth street to the rear of buildings on Eighth street, will be covered by a dome-shaped glass roof, and will be 700 feet long by 135 feet wide.

The track-floor, besides being lighted by the glass roof, will be illuminated from the sidewalk, by Hyatt's patent lights, all around the building.

It is proposed to make the building practically fire-proof, by the substitution of iron for beams, girders, joists, partitions, etc.

The general style of the exterior will be Franco-Italian, and, being of iron, will necessarily be ornate.

RAILROADS.

The following roads will use the Passenger Depot—all of them, except those marked *, having their lines now running into the city:

1. The Missouri Pacific.
2. The North Missouri.
   a. The St. Louis, Council Bluffs and Omaha;*
   b. The St. Louis and Keokuk;* both coming in on the North Missouri Railroad track.
3. The South Pacific.
4. The Iron Mountain.
5. The St. Louis and Indianapolis.
6. The St. Louis, Vandalia and Terre Haute.
7. The St. Louis and Chicago.
8. The Ohio and Mississippi.
9. The Decatur and East St. Louis.
10. The Rockford, Rock Island and St. Louis.
11. The St. Louis and Belleville, and its Eastern connections.
12. The St. Louis and South-Eastern.

It is proposed to use smoke-consuming engines for the purpose of bringing trains into and out of the tunnel and depot. By deadening the floors and operating the trains with signals, no noise will be created, and the occupants and guests above will suffer no inconvenience from that cause.

This is a gigantic scheme involving a large expenditure, but it is more comprehensive in its objects, more thorough in its arrangements, and will command greater capabilities than any passenger depot ever before devised; and now is the fitting time for all the important interests concerned to secure its manifold advantages.

Before the buildings included in the design can be finished, the bridge across the Mississippi, opposite Washington avenue, will be completed, and the twelve railroads enumerated will be pouring into the city a vast amount of trade and travel, which will require corresponding facilities for their proper accommodation.

From the opening of the bridge will date the most rapid growth of railroad business consequent upon the continuity of the tracks across the river, and the disappearance forever of all the annoyances and expenses of ferrying, which are now unavoidable. At all hours of the day and night trains will then arrive and depart from the Union Passenger Depot, in every direction, without impediment, with perfect convenience to the traveling public. St. Louis will then at once take rank in public estimation as the most attractive railroad city of the interior.

No railroad now constructed, or that may hereafter be constructed, across the continent can fail to contribute its share of trade and travel to this point.

A city thus situated, which in fifteen years, with its railroad system yet in its infancy, has grown from a population of 80,000 to more than 300,000, may with certainty anticipate a further rapid augmentation of population and business, demanding extraordinary efforts on the part of her enterprising citizens. St. Louis will soon be one of the largest, if not the largest, iron and steel manufacturing points in the United States, which will add immensely both to the river and railroad traffic, and demand greater facilities for its commercial exchange. In fact, the entire business interests of the city demand a great Union Depot as an adjunct or complete provision for the business of the bridge.

APPENDIX.

HISTORICAL AND COMMERCIAL REVIEW OF ST. LOUIS.

In the preceding volume we have endeavored to present the facts and circumstances which foreshadow the destiny of St. Louis — a destiny so important that not only the people of the Mississippi Valley but of this nation, and even of the world, are interested.

The spirit of modern civilization is different in its operation and character from the social forces of by-gone eras. It is more catholic in its objects, more active and concentrated in its energy, and has wonderfully abridged the time formerly necessary for historical events to work out their accomplishment. Under the singular velocity it has imparted, the scenes and changes of the human drama are enacted so swiftly that the prophecy of to-day is either authenticated or disproven by the developments of to-morrow. It is this fact which gives us confidence in proclaiming the destiny of St. Louis as we have represented it in this book. Already the currents of our civic and political progress are shaping towards its development, and it will not require many years to make it more clearly evident. There are many now who believe in the future of St. Louis as the leading city of the continent and the Capital of United States, who two years ago looked with incredulity upon such prognostications, and regarded them as mere dreams of ardent minds. The agitation of the question has also spread abroad the fame of our stately and expanding city, and a conviction of the glorious future before her is growing rapidly, not only among our own citizens, but among those disconnected in every way with our municipal interests.

Believing earnestly as we do in this future, our object is to foster an intelligent anticipation of it in the public mind; and if our volume assists towards this end it will not have been written in vain, and the time and labor necessary to group and present the facts and argument it contains will be amply repaid.

We cannot consider our work complete without some review of the history of St. Louis. The Past often interprets the Future, and is always interesting in connection with it; and, as an appropriate appendix, we present the following historical review, with which is incorporated some valuable and significant statistics illustrating our present social and commercial condition.

POLITICAL CONDITION OF NORTH AMERICA PRIOR TO THE FOUNDING OF ST. LOUIS.

The 15th of February, 1764, may be accepted as the exact date of the first settlement on the site of St. Louis, and the name of Pierre Ligueste Laclede may justly appear in history as the founder of the city.* It is difficult to realize that scarce a century has elapsed since the solitude and silence of the forest primeval reigned over a scene now covered with the countless buildings of a stately city and pulsating with the life of busy thousands. There is, however, no doubt as to the date given, as it is a matter, if not of official record, yet so authenticated by collateral circumstances as to eliminate nearly all uncertainty. At the time of the event the political condition (if we may so speak of a vast territory for the most part *terra incognita*) of the North American continent was somewhat confused as to ownership and boundary. England, France and Spain held nominal possession of vast regions, but with so little certainty of title or jurisdiction that their rival claims would probably have remained an endless source of dispute and conflict had they not been in a measure decided by the treaty of Aix-la-Chapelle in 1748. This treaty, however, embraced no adjustment of boundaries, which was practically impossible at the time, but provided for the restitution of conquests made from each other by the powers named, and it was not many years after followed by war between France and England. The leading cause of the conflict was the action of the former power in establishing a line of military posts along the lakes and the Ohio and Mississippi rivers, for the purpose of connecting her Canadian possessions with the country bordering the Mississippi river southwardly, over which she also claimed jurisdiction. The bitter and sanguinary hostilities which ensued were terminated by the treaty of Paris, consummated on the 16th of February, 1763, and which closed the celebrated seven years' war on the European continent. The result of this treaty practically left England and Spain the possession of North America. The former retained the Atlantic seaboard colonies, and acquired the Canadas and Louisiana, lying east of the Mississippi, except the town of New Orleans and its territory. She also obtained the Floridas from Spain, by restoring to that power Havana and the greater part of the island of Cuba. By a secret treaty of the same date France ceded the country west of the Mississippi, and known by the general designation of Louisiana, to Spain, but of this illimitable territory little if anything was then definitely known.

When we remember the tardy means of communication at this period between the Old and New Worlds, it is easy to understand the delay and difficulty in giving any practical effect to the terms of this treaty. It does not appear that Spain exercised any general jurisdiction over the territory acquired until the year 1768, although in the spring of 1764 D'Abadie, the Spanish Governor-General, was instructed to formally promulgate the transfer made

* Notwithstanding the apparently conclusive reasons for believing that the true family name of the founder of St. Louis was Ligueste rather than Laclede, we have adopted the latter in this sketch as the more popular and familiar to the majority of readers.

under the treaty. The immense territory of Louisiana, the upper portion of which bore the name of "The Illinois," consequently remained under French laws and jurisdiction throughout its scant and widely separated settlements until 1768. The English were more prompt in claiming actual control of the territory ceded by the treaty of 1763, and vigorous measures were taken in various directions to obliterate the evidence of French domination. In the vicinity of St. Louis, east of the Mississippi, Fort de Chartres, one of the military posts established by France along the line of her frontier, was surrendered to Capt. Sterling, of the English army, in 1765, under the treaty of Paris. This fort was situated in the American Bottom, a short distance above Kaskaskia, and the French commander at the time of the surrender, St. Ange de Bellerive, removed with his troops to the west side of the Mississippi, on the 17th of July, 1765, to the settlement on the site of the present city of St. Louis, which had been made about seventeen months before. Without going into the details of English and Spanish occupancy, we will proceed to the history of St. Louis proper.

THE LACLEDE EXPEDITION — ITS OBJECT AND CHARACTER.

Pierre Ligueste Laclede has left but faint traces in history prior to the time when his name becomes identified with the founding of St. Louis. He was born in one of the French provinces bordering on the Pyrenees, and appears to have emigrated to Southern Louisiana with the design of trading with the Indians, bringing with him credentials from the Court of France that secured him the consideration of the authorities. The New World then offered an exciting field for adventurous minds, and many young men crossed the Atlantic to its shores, impelled either by that thirst for gold which at one time created the dream of an El Dorado beyond the Western Ocean, or the desire to explore the vast continent whose mighty natural features astonished Europe. It is probable Laclede was in part actuated by both these motives, but he was neither a mere gold-hunter nor a reckless adventurer. Although little is known of his history, except during the period embraced between the years 1763, the year before the founding of St. Louis, and 1778, the year of his death, we can clearly gather the prominent traits of his character. He was brave, self-reliant, and resolute, and his idea of fortune-making in the New World was based on the sober expectation that there was ample opportunity for energy and enterprise in developing the trade in peltries and other articles with the native tribes that roamed over the boundless country of forest and prairie. How long he remained in New Orleans prior to engaging in his famous expedition northward is not ascertainable, but it appears probable that he was there for a considerable time.

In 1762 D'Abadie, Governor-General, granted to Laclede, in connection with other associates, a charter under the name of "The Louisiana Fur Company," which conferred the exclusive privilege of trading "with the Indians of the Missouri, and those west of the Mississippi above the Missouri, as far north as the River St. Peters." Antoine Maxent and others were interested equally with Laclede in the franchises acquired, but he appears to have been the active and leading spirit of the association. Before entering upon some account of the first expedition organized under the auspices of this chartered company, and which resulted in the founding of St. Louis, it is necessary to glance at the progress made at the time in the settlement and exploration of Upper Louisiana.

The town or city of New Orleans was the capital of the Louisianas, being in fact the only place of any size or importance in the valley of the Mississippi. The immense territory on either side of the great river northward was very imperfectly known, for although partially explored by Marquette, Hennepin, La Salle, Cartier and others, but little accurate information had been gained as to its topography and inhabitants. The great Valley, the destiny of which, as the center of our nation's wealth and prosperity, is now so rapidly developing, was then in its primitive condition, with the exception of a few scattered settlements whose people struggled for an existence amid the unfriendly influences of a trying climate and an unsubdued wilderness. Above New Orleans there was a settlement of some consequence in the vicinity of the present city of Natchez, but from that point to Ste. Genevieve there were but few traces of human occupation. On the eastern side of the Mississippi a few settlements had been formed at Fort de Chartres and vicinity, St. Phillips, Kaskaskia, Cahokia and some other points, but they were comparatively insignificant and had sprung up under the fostering influences of French military protection. The trade in lead, oils and peltries had concentrated at Ste. Genevieve, then a post of some importance, with several small settlements in its vicinity, and which bore the name of La Poste de Ste. Genevieve. The settlers at the places named were nearly all of that adventurous type of character usually to be found among the pioneers of civilization in a wild continent peopled only by barbaric and nomadic tribes. They included, however, many persons of refinement and education who had come from France or Spain to seek their fortunes in the New World, and were as a body of men consequently different from the more reckless and uncouth pioneers of a later date who have pushed westward the boundaries of the Union against the ineffectual struggles of the Indian tribes.

The only inducement at this period for any persons to penetrate Occidental Louisiana or "The Illinois," was the prospect of trade in furs or minerals, or the love of exploration and adventure, and it is only the daring and resolute who are willing to embark in such pursuits; but notwithstanding this, these pioneers appear to have managed the fierce aborigines with more discretion than their successors, who inaugurated an unextinguishable war.

Such was the condition of the Mississippi Valley as to settlement at the period indicated. The rule of the red man had been impinged upon but not broken, and the active and aggressive foreigners had as yet wrought little change upon the face of nature. Notwithstanding the time that had elapsed since De Soto discovered the Mississippi to the South and Marquette and Joliet to the North, the explorations of the river and its tributaries and the region through which it flowed had not been of an accurate or exhaustive character, and the development even of the fur trade was insignificant. Beyond the mouth of the Missouri the white man had made little or no progress, and whatever trade was carried on between New Orleans and the country north of the mouth of the Ohio originated south of the present site of St. Louis.

THE FOUNDING OF ST. LOUIS.

In the summer of 1763, an expedition was organized in New Orleans for the purpose of carrying into operation the powers conferred in the charter granted by Governor D'Abadie to Laclede and his associates. The immediate object in view was the establishing of a permanent trading post and settlement on some advantageous place north of the settlements then existing. Laclede was the prominent personage in organizing the expedition, and it left New Orleans under his command on the 3d day of August, 1763. It is impossible to procure accurate information respecting the size and character of the party participating in the expedition, but it was probably not very numerous and was composed mainly of hunters and trappers accustomed to the hardships and dangers of such enterprises. The means of transportation were the strong heavily-fashioned boats then in use, in which was stored a large quantity of such merchandise as was necessary for trade with the Indians.

The voyage up the Mississippi was a tedious one, and three months after the departure from New Orleans, or on the 3d of October, the expedition reached Ste. Genevieve. This town, which was founded about 1755, and is perhaps the oldest settlement in Missouri, was then a place of some consequence and the only French post on the west bank of the river. The intention of Laclede was to seek a place further north, and after a short stop at Ste. Genevieve the party continued their course, their destination now being Fort de Chartres, to which place Laclede had an invitation from the military commander, and where he determined to rest and store his goods while exploring the country for a suitable location for the proposed trading post. At the time of the arrival of the expedition the fort was commanded by M. de Neyon de Villiers, who, although of a haughty disposition, appears to have welcomed the party with kindness and hospitality. The energetic spirit of Laclede did not permit him to remain inactive for any length of time while the object of the expedition was unaccomplished, and a few weeks after his arrival at Fort de Chartres he started with a portion of his party towards the mouth of the Missouri. Among those who accompanied him were two brothers, Pierre and Auguste Chouteau, whose family name is thoroughly identified with the history of St. Louis. The prospecting party started in the beginning of February, 1764, and they went as far as the mouth of the Missouri, but without fixing upon a site for the post. On their return along the western shore, Laclede landed at the sweeping curve of the river on which now stands the city of St. Louis, and impressed by its pleasant aspect of woodland and prairie swelling westward from the river, he determined to establish here the settlement and post he desired. This memorable event occurred on the 15th of February, 1764, and Laclede having selected the site immediately proceeded to clear away trees and mark out the lines of a town, which he named St. Louis in honor of Louis XV of France, evidently ignorant at the time that this monarch had transferred to Spain the whole country west of the Mississippi.

When Laclede and his men selected their trading station, the marvels of its future development were undreamed of. Around them lay a limitless and untrodden wilderness, peopled only by tribes of savage and unfriendly Indians, and in which subsistence could only be obtained by the chase. It is only when we thus contemplate our ancestors struggling with unconquerable energy and daring, amid innumerable dangers and hardships, that we properly estimate their worth and character. It is only then that we realize that the natural advantages of the location chosen formed only one element in the colossal result of their work. The others are to be found in those motives and heroic qualities which give stability and nobleness to human actions. It is pleasant and inspiring to see in the historical perspective of our city samples of frugality, fortitude and self-reliance, for these are the only foundations for a community upon which prosperity can be immutably erected.

SUCCEEDING HISTORICAL EVENTS.

Laclede's party had been increased somewhat in numbers by volunteers from Ste. Genevieve, Fort de Chartres and Cahokia, then called "Notre Dames des Kahokias," but still numerically it was but a small band, and could have made no sustained resistance to Indians had they disputed their right to settlement. It does not appear, however, that the pioneers encountered any hostility from the natives. Not long after their arrival a large body of Missouri Indians visited the vicinity, but without unfriendly intent. They did not belong to the more war-like tribes, and being in an impoverished condition all they wanted was provisions and other necessaries. The settlers were in no condition to support their visitors, but as they were equally unprepared to provoke their hostility their arrival caused no small uneasiness, and it is said a few of Laclede's party apprehending trouble, recrossed the river and returned to Fort de Chartres or Cahokia. By judicious management and by announcing the anticipated arrival of French troops from the fort, Laclede finally succeeded in inducing the Indians to depart, very much to the satisfaction of his people. After some progress had been made in the actual establishment of a settlement, Laclede returned to Fort de Chartres to make arrangements for the removal to St. Louis of the goods left there, as it was expected that the fort would soon be surrendered to the English. During the ensuing year this event took place as before stated, and Louis St. Ange de Bellerive, the French commander, removed with his officers and troops, numbering about fifty men, to St. Louis on the 17th of July, 1765; and from this date the new settlement was considered the capital of Upper Louisiana. At this time M. Aubrey was Commandant-General at New Orleans, M. D'Abadie having died during the preceding year, as stated in Marbois' History of Louisiana, from the effects of grief at the transfer to Spain of the French possessions.

St. Ange, on arriving at St. Louis, at once assumed supreme control of affairs, contrary to the treaty of Paris. There was indeed no person who could have conferred upon him this authority, but there was none to dispute it. Nearly all of the settlers at St. Louis and other posts in the valley of the Mississippi were of French nationality or accustomed to the rule of France. In Lower Louisiana the promulgation of the terms of the treaty was received with intense dissatisfaction, which was also the case at St. Louis when the intelligence was subsequently announced there. The authority of Spain could not at this time be practically enforced, and the inhabitants of St. Louis not only submitted to the authority of St. Ange, but appear to have welcomed his arrival with satisfaction. He proved a mild and politic Governor, fostering the growth and development of the new settlement and ingratiating himself with the people. He maintained friendly relations with the Indians, and was instrumental in inducing Pontiac, the famous chief of the Ottawas, to abandon his fierce crusade against the English. Between Laclede and St. Ange the most friendly relations existed. An important act of the latter was the formal issuing of land grants to citizens of St. Louis, the recording of which in the "Livre Terrien" conferred titles to land granted them by the former, and formed the basis of a simple land system.

ST. LOUIS IN EARLY DAYS.

The extent of the town in its early days, if it did not form some faint prophecy of future development, still clearly proves that more than a mere trading post was intended by the founders. The principal street (La Rue Principale) ran along the line of Main street of to-day, extending from about Almond to Morgan street. The next west was about the same length, and corresponded to the present Second street, and, after the erection of a church in the vicinity of the present site of the Catholic Cathedral, received the name of Church street (La Rue de l'Eglise). The next street, now Third, was originally known as Barn street from the number of buildings on it of the character indicated. In mentioning these streets, however, we speak of a time many years subsequent to the arrival of Laclede. Before the topographical features of the present site of our city were altered by the course of improvements they were materially different from the present. Most of our citizens will find it hard to realize that originally a rocky bluff extended on the river front from about Walnut to Vine street with a precipitous descent in many places. As building progressed this bluff was cut away, and the appearance of a sharp but tolerably even incline to the river from Main street was gained. At the corner of Commercial alley and Chestnut street and at several other places there are at present palpable evidences of this rocky ridge, portions of it yet remaining. At first it is probable the Laclede settlement bore the appearance of a rude and scattered hamlet in the wilderness, and it required the growth of several years before the semblance of streets was formed by even imperfect lines of buildings of the most primitive character. Immediately west of the bluff mentioned was a nearly level strip of land protected by gentle elevations westward, and here was the site of the Laclede settlement. The river front was covered with a growth of timber, in the rear of which was a large and gently rolling prairie with scattered groves of heavy forest trees, which received the title of "Le Grande Prairie," and it is not difficult to believe that if the selection of the spot was not made because of its adaptability as the site of a great city it was because of its natural pleasantness and beauty.

THE YEARS OF SPANISH CONTROL.

In 1766 an effort was made by Spain to assume control of the territory ceded to her by the treaty of Paris, and General Don Antonio D'Ulloa arrived at New Orleans with Spanish troops, but owing to the hostile feeling of the inhabitants he finally departed without attempting to exercise the powers of Governor. The rule of France was maintained in Lower Louisiana until the arrival of Count O'Reilly in 1769, who took possession of the Territory and New Orleans, obliterating forcibly French supremacy and strengthening his authority by severe measures towards the more active adherents of France.

The scattered settlements of Upper Louisiana, although equally opposed to Spanish authority, had no adequate means of resistance; and when Rios, a Spanish officer, arrived at St. Louis with a small body of troops, on the 11th of August, 1768, he only encountered a passive hostility. He took possession of the country in the name of his Catholic Majesty, but does not appear to have exercised any civil authority, as the archives show that St. Ange acted as Governor until the beginning of 1770. On the 17th of July, 1769, Rios and his troops departed and returned to New Orleans to co-operate with Count O'Reilly in enforcing Spanish authority in the lower Province.

During the same year Pontiac, the Ottawa chief, arrived at St. Louis for the purpose of visiting his former friend, St. Ange de Bellerive, by whom he was cordially received. The visit was fatal to the Indian warrior, for, while on an excursion to the English territory on the other side of the river, he was killed by a Kaskaskia Indian.

In the latter part of 1770, Count O'Reilly having acquired full control of Lower Louisiana, determined to bring the upper Province into equal subjection. He appointed Don Pedro Piernas as Lieutenant-Governor and Military Commandant of the province, and dispatched him with troops to St. Louis, where he arrived on November 29th of the same year. He did not enter on the exercise of executive functions until the beginning of the following year, but the delay was not occasioned by any active hostility on the part of the people. From this event we may date the commencement of Spanish domination in Upper Louisiana.

The new Governor, fortunately, proved an excellent administrative officer; and as his measures were mild and judicious, he soon conciliated the people. He made no abrupt changes in the laws, and improved the tenure of property by ordering accurate surveys and determining the lines of the land grants previously made. Under the liberal policy of the Spanish Governor St. Louis prospered rapidly, while immigration constantly added to the population. In 1774 St. Ange de Bellerive, who had accepted military service under Piernas, died, and was buried in the Catholic cemetery with every mark of public esteem and respect. In his will he commended his soul "to God, the blessed Virgin, and the Saints of the Celestial Court," and appointed Laclede his executor.

Emigration from the Canadas and the lower Province increased rapidly under the benignant policy of Spain, and settlements sprang up at different points along the Mississippi and Missouri rivers, some of which, however, date from a few years earlier. In 1767 Carondelet was founded by Delor de Tregette, and appears at first to have been known as Louisburgh, and at a different period as *Vide Poche*, but finally received its present name in honor of the Baron de Carondelet. In 1769 Les Petites Cotes, subsequently St. Andrews, and now St. Charles, was founded by Blanchette Chasseur. The first settlement at Florissant, afterwards called St. Ferdinand, was made by Beaurosier Dunegant in 1776; and so the career of growth and prosperity was inaugurated in this portion of the Mississippi Valley.

The successor of Piernas was Don Francisco Cruzat, who assumed office in 1775, and was succeeded by Don Fernando de Leyba in 1778. It was during the administration of the latter that the death of Laclede took place, while on his way to New Orleans, at the age of fifty-four. He was buried near the mouth of the Arkansas river, June 20, 1778, amid the wild solitude of a region in which he had acted as the pioneer of civilization.

The war which was now raging between Great Britain and her American colonies could hardly be unfelt on the far western shores of the Mississippi. Many of the inhabitants of St. Louis, and other places on the same side of the river, were persons who had changed their residence from the opposite shore when it passed under English rule. They were influenced by a hereditary hostility to that power; and although enjoying a mild government under Spanish rulers, their independent spirit, apart even from their feeling towards England, enlisted their sympathies in behalf of their colonial brethren in the East struggling for freedom. Their great distance did not secure their prosperity from the disastrous influences of war. It was known that Spain sympathized with the colonies, and this speedily endangered their security; for the ferocity of many of the Indian tribes was directed against them by the English.

In the early part of 1779 Col. Rogers Clark, under the authority of Virginia, visited the settlements of Cahokia, Kaskaskia, and other places, for the purpose of endeavoring to enlist men for an expedition against St. Vincents, now Vincennes, then held by the English under Governor Hamilton.

THE ATTACK ON ST. LOUIS BY INDIANS.

About this time an alarming rumor became prevalent that an attack on St. Louis was being organized under British influence. Actuated by a spirit of generous chivalry, Clark offered the assistance of himself and men to Lieut.-

Gov. Leyba for the protection of the town, but his offer was declined on the ground that the danger was not imminent. (There seems to be some uncertainty as to this incident, but it is supported by the excellent authority of Judge Wilson Primm, and is corroborated by Stoddard in his historical sketch of Louisiana.) Whatever was the ground of the fancied security, the sequel proves either that he was an execrable traitor or shamefully incompetent to meet the exigencies of the time. Apprehensions, however, began to disturb the people, and the defenseless condition of the town induced them to undertake some means of fortification. Although they numbered little more than one hundred men, they proceeded to build a wall of logs and earth about five or six feet high, inclosing the dwellings of the settlement. It formed a semicircular line, with its ends terminating at the river, and supplied with three gates, at each of which a heavy piece of ordnance was placed and kept in constant readiness. For some months after this work was completed, nothing occurred to indicate an Indian attack. Winter passed away, and the inhabitants finally began to consider their apprehensions groundless, which conclusion was assisted by the assurances of the Governor that there was no cause for anxiety. In reality, however, the long pending attack was now being secretly organized. Numerous bands of Indians, composed of Ojibways, Winnebagos, Sioux, and other tribes, with some Canadians, numbering in all nearly 1500, had gathered on the eastern shore of the river, a little above St. Louis, and arrangements were consummated for a general attack on the settlement on the 26th of May.

The 25th of May, 1780, was the festival of Corpus Christi, which was celebrated by the Catholic inhabitants with religious ceremonies and rejoicing. There was no feeling of apprehension abroad just at this time, notwithstanding that an event calculated to arouse alarm had occurred but a few days before. An old citizen named Quenelle had crossed the river to Cahokia creek on a fishing excursion. While watching his lines he was startled to see on the opposite shore of the creek a man named Ducharme, who had formerly lived in St. Louis and who had fled to escape punishment for some crime committed. He endeavored to induce Quenelle to come over to him, but the latter thought he detected the presence of Indians in the bushes opposite, and refused, returning hastily in his canoe to the town, where he reported what had occurred. The Commandant ridiculed his story, and it did not create any general fear among the inhabitants. Corpus Christi was celebrated with unusual animation, and a large number of the citizens left the inclosure of the town and were scattered about the prairie — men, women, and children — gathering strawberries. A portion of the Indians crossed the river on the same day, but fortunately did not make the attack, owing, probably, to their not knowing how many of the men had remained in the town. Had they done so, the result would surely have been fatal to the young settlement. On the following day the whole body of the attacking force crossed, directing their course to the fields over which they had seen the inhabitants scattered the day before. It fortunately happened that only a few of them were outside the town, and these, seeing the approach of the Indians, hastily retreated towards the upper gate, which course led them nearly through a portion of the hostile force. Rapid volleys were fired at the fleeing citizens, and the reports speedily spread the alarm in the town. Arms were hastily seized, and the men rushed bravely towards the wall, opening the gate to their defenseless comrades. There was a body of militia in the town from Ste. Genevieve, which had been sent up, under the command of Silvia Francisco Cartabona, some time before, when apprehensions of an attack prevailed. This company, however, behaved shamefully and did not participate in the defense, many of them concealing themselves in the houses while the fight was in progress. The Indians approached the line of defense rapidly, and when at a short distance, opened an irregular fire, to which the inhabitants responded with light arms and discharges of grape-shot from their pieces of artillery. The resistance made was energetic and resolute, and the savage assailants seeing the strength of the fortifications and dismayed by the artillery, to which they were unaccustomed, finally retired, and the fight came to a close.

Commandant Leyba appeared upon the scene at this juncture, having been started from a carouse to some idea of the situation by the sound of the artillery. His conduct was extraordinary; he immediately ordered several pieces of ordnance which had been placed near the Government house to be *spiked,* and was then, as it is chronicled, rolled to the immediate scene of action "*in a wheelbarrow.*" He ordered the inhabitants to cease firing and return to their houses. Those stationed near the lower gate not hearing the command paid no attention to it, and he directed a cannon to be fired at them. This barbarous order was carried out, and the citizens only escaped the volley of grape by throwing themselves on the ground, and the shot struck down a portion of the wall. The unparalleled treachery of the Commandant was fortunately exhibited too late to be of assistance to the Indians, who had been beaten back by the determined valor of the settlers, and the attack was not renewed. When they had left the vicinity, search was made for the bodies of the citizens who had been killed on the prairie, and between twenty and thirty lives were ascertained to have been lost. Several old men, women and children were among the victims, and all the bodies had been horribly mutilated by their murderers.

The traitorous conduct of the Commandant, which so nearly imperiled the existence of the town, had been obvious to the people generally; and justly indignant at his cruel rascality, means were at once taken to transmit a full report of his proceedings to Galvez, then Governor of Lower Louisiana. This resulted in the prompt removal of Leyba, and the settlement was again placed under the authority of Cruzat. Leyba died the same year from the effects, it is said, of poison administered by his own hand; universal obloquy and reproach having rendered his life unendurable. He was buried in the village church, "in front of the right-hand balustrade, having received all the sacraments of our mother the Holy Church," as is set forth in the burial certificate of Father Bernard, a "Catholic Priest, Apostolic Missionary Curate of St. Louis, country of Illinois, Province of Louisiana, Bishopric of Cuba." The year 1780, rendered so memorable by this Indian attack, was afterwards known as "*L'anne du grande coup,*" or "year of the great blow."

There is no doubt but this assault on St. Louis had for its object the destruction of the settlement, and was only frustrated by the gallantry of the people, that it was partially instigated by English influence is almost unquestionable. The Indians accepted their defeat and departed without attempting any other demonstration. It is said their retreat was occasioned by the appearance of Col. George Rogers Clark with four or five hundred Americans from Kaskaskia, but this is not substantiated. Pending the arrival of Cruzat, Cartabona, before mentioned, exercised the functions of Lieutenant-Governor, but, however, for only a short period. One of the first works undertaken by Cruzat was the strengthening of the fortifications; he established half a dozen or more stone forts, nearly circular in shape, about fifty feet in diameter and twenty feet high, connected by a stout stockade of posts. The fortifications, as extended and improved by Cruzat, were quite pretentious for so small a settlement. On the river bank, near the spot formerly occupied by the Floating Docks, was a stone tower called the "Half Moon" from its shape, and westwardly of it, near the present intersection of Broadway and Cherry street, was erected a square building called "The Bastion;" south of this, on the line of Olive street, a circular stone fort was situated. A similar building was built on Walnut street intended for service both as a fort and prison. There was also a fort near Mill Creek, and east of this another circular fort near the river. The strong stockade of cedar posts connecting these forts was pierced with loop-holes for small arms. This well-devised line of defenses was not subjected to the test of another Indian attack, for although during the continuance of the Revolutionary war other settlements on the Mississippi and Missouri rivers had to contend against the savages, St. Louis was not again molested.

From this period the progress of St. Louis was slow but satisfactory under the liberal and judicious policy of the Spanish Governors, and it will be sufficient to note only the more important events.

EARLY NAVIGATION OF THE MISSISSIPPI.

It is difficult to realize in these days the perils and delays incident to the early navigation of the Mississippi. It is to us now the unobstructed and natural highway of commerce and travel, connecting the West and far North with the warm and fruitful South, and bearing to the ocean the various products of rich and populous regions. A hundred years ago it was no less majestic in its strength and beauty, but its ministrations to the needs of civilized humanity had hardly begun; it rolled its splendid flood through a wild and solitary wilderness, and the sound of the winds in the forest mingled with the monotone of flowing waters in a murmurous rythm that sunk or swelled only with the fluctuations of nature. There were no towns along its banks, no rushing steamboats on its surface; and rarely only Indian canoes formed a transitory feature in its landscapes and the shouts of savage voices were heard. With the birth of white settlements in the great Valley the solitude of the Father of Waters was gradually invaded. In their rude craft the early voyageurs had to struggle hard against the swift current, and a voyage from New Orleans to St. Louis was then a thing of months, not of days, and required nearly as much preparation as a one across the Atlantic. During Cruzat's second administration navigation was much impeded and disturbed by piratical bands which harbored at certain points on the woody shores and instituted a system of depredations on settlers or others passing up and down the river. These bands were principally controlled by two men named Culbert and Magilbray, who had a permanent rendezvous at a place called Cotton Wood Creek. The usual programme of the pirates was to attack the vessels of voyageurs at some place where a surprise could be readily effected, and having compelled the affrighted crews to seek safety on shore or by surrender, they would plunder the boats and the persons of prisoners of all valuables. The vicinity of Grand Tower, a lofty rock situated about half way between St. Louis and the mouth of the Ohio, became a dreaded spot also through the deeds of these river marauders, and many tales exist in the memories of old citizens of acts of violence perpetrated near these places. Early in the year 1787 an event occurred which inaugurated severe measures by the government against the pirates, resulting in their dispersion. M. Beausoliel, a New Orleans merchant, started from New Orleans for St. Louis with a barge richly freighted with merchandise. A strong breeze prevailed as this vessel was approaching Cotton Wood Creek. The pirates were in waiting to make an attack, but were frustrated by the swift progress of the vessel, and they dispatched a body of men up the river for the purpose of heading off the expected prize. The point chosen for the attack was an island, since called Beausoliel's Island, and was reached in about two days. The barge had put ashore and was easily captured and the crew disarmed, when the captors turned her course down the river. On the way down an unexpected deliverance was effected through the daring of a negro named Casotte, who, by pretending joy at the capture of the vessel, was left free and employed as a cook. He maintained a secret understanding with Beausoliel and some of his men, and at a given signal the party effected a sudden rising. They defeated the pirates after a brief struggle, who were all either killed or captured. Beausoliel deemed it prudent after this alarming experience to return to New Orleans, and in passing Cotton Wood Creek kept as near the opposite shore as possible. On reaching New Orleans a full report of the doings of the pirates and the capture and deliverance of the barge was made public, and convinced the authorities and the people that strong measures were absolutely necessary to terminate these perils to life and property on the river. The Governor issued an order that all boats bound for St. Louis the following spring should make the voyage together, thus insuring mutual protection. This was carried out and a little fleet of ten boats started up the river. On approaching Cotton Wood Creek, some of the men in the foremost boat perceived some persons on shore near the mouth of the creek. A consultation was held with the crews and passengers of the other boats, and it was determined that while a sufficient number of men should remain to protect the boats the remainder would form a party to attack the robbers in their haunt.

On reaching the place the courageous voyageurs found that their enemies had disappeared, but four boats were discovered in a bend of the creek, laden with a miscellaneous assortment of valuable plunder, and in a low hut, situated among the trees at a little distance from the bank, a large quantity of provisions and ammunition was found, with cases of guns and various other weapons, indicating the numerous captures which had been made by these outlaws. All of this property was removed, together with the boats and contents, and carried to St. Louis, where a large number of the articles were identified by the owners.

The arrival of the fleet of barges created quite a commotion in the settlement, and was considered so memorable that the year 1788 received the name of "*L'annee des Dix Bateaux*," or the year of the ten boats. A most fortunate result of this descent was that although no blood was shed it practically led to the dispersion of the bands, and but few subsequent depredations are reported to have occurred.

Prior to the event just narrated and in the year 1785, the people of St. Louis experienced a serious alarm and loss of property, owing to a sudden and extraordinary rise in the Mississippi river. The American Bottom was covered with water, and Cahokia and Kaskaskia were threatened with being swept out of existence. Most of the buildings in St. Louis were situated on Main street, and the rise of the waters above the steep banks spread general dismay. The flood subsided, however, nearly as rapidly as it had risen, averting the necessity of abandoning the houses, which had been commenced. The year received the name of "*L'annee des Grandes Eaux*," or the year of the great waters. No rise in the river equal to this has occurred since excepting in 1844 and 1851, which floods are remembered by most of our citizens.

CONCLUDING EVENTS UNDER THE SPANISH DOMINATION.

In the year 1788 the administration of Don Francisco Cruzat terminated, and Manual Perez became Commandant-General of the West Illinois country at the post of St. Louis. At this time the population of this and the neighboring settlements numbered nearly 1200 persons, while that of Ste. Genevieve was about 800. The administration of Perez was prosperous, and like his predecessor he was generally esteemed by the inhabitants. He brought about a settlement of friendly Indians in the vicinity of Cape Girardeau, where he gave them a large grant of land. They consisted of Shawnees and Delawares, two of the most powerful tribes east of the Mississippi river, and the object was to oppose through them the Osage Indians, a strong Missouri tribe who were constantly making incursions on the young settlements. This scheme is said to have operated satisfactorily.

In 1793 Perez was succeeded by Zenon Trudeau, who also became popular, and instituted various measures for the encouragement of immigration. In the year 1792 the honey-bee is chronicled to have first appeared, following as it were civilization from the East, and its coming was hailed with delight. The grave difficulties which had sprung up between the American Colonies and Spain, respecting territorial boundaries and the navigation of the Mississippi, were adjusted by treaty in October, 1795, but more serious trouble subsequently arose from the same cause.

During the administration of Trudeau St. Louis and the other settlements in that portion of the country expanded rapidly. Under the influence of the exceedingly favorable terms offered to settlers, and the fact that the fear of Indian attacks was greatly diminished, quite a number of citizens of the United States left the country east of the Mississippi, over which English control was now practically broken up, and took up their residence in the Spanish dominions. St. Louis improved in appearance, and new and neat buildings began to supplant, in many places, the rude log huts of earlier years. Trade received a new impetus, but the clearing of the country in its vicinity and the development of agriculture still made but slow progress. The dealing in peltries was the principal business, and in their effort to expand their exchanges with Indian tribes, traders became more energetic and daring in their excursions and traveled long distances into the interior westward, and forced their rude boats up the swift Missouri to many points never before visited.

Trudeau closed his official career in 1798 and was succeeded by Charles Dehault Delassus de Delusiere, a Frenchman by birth, but who had been many years in the service of Spain. The winter of the succeeding year was one of extraordinary severity and received the title of "*L'annee du Grande-hiver,*" or year of the hard winter. The same year that Delassus commenced his administration was signalized by the arrival of some galleys with Spanish troops under Don Carlos Howard, and was called "*L'annee des galeres,*" or year of the galleys. This Governor caused a census to be taken of Upper Louisiana settlements, from which we extract the following, showing the population of the places named in the year 1799: St. Louis, 925; Carondelet, 184; St. Charles, 875; St. Ferdinand, 276; Marius des Liard, 376; Meramec, 115; St. Andrew, 393; Ste. Genevieve, 949; New Bourbon, 560; Cape Girardeau, 521; New Madrid, 782; Little Meadows, 72. Total, 6,028. Total number of whites, 4,948; free colored, 197; slaves, 883.

It will be seen from these figures that St. Charles then nearly equaled St. Louis in population, while Ste. Genevieve exceeded it; and if any then living ever dreamed of one of these settlements becoming the center and seat of Western empire, the prophecy would probably have been in favor of the brisk town at the mouth of the Missouri.

On the 15th of May, 1801, the small pox broke out in St. Louis and vicinity with fearful severity. It was a new malady among the healthy settlers, and, as was usual when particularly impressed by an event, they commemorated the year by a peculiar title, calling it "*L'annee de la Picotte,*" the year of the small-pox. About this time the increase in immigration created a furore for speculation in land, and some immense grants were obtained.

THE RETROCESSION OF LOUISIANA TO FRANCE AND ITS PURCHASE BY THE UNITED STATES.

On the 1st of October, 1800, the treaty of Ildefonso was consummated, by which Spain, under certain conditions, retroceded to France the territory of Louisiana; and in July, 1802, the Spanish authorities were directed to deliver possession to the French commissioners. This event, however, did not take place until the month of December, 1803, when M. Laussat on behalf of France was placed in control. The supremacy of England on the high seas at this period practically prevented France from instituting any possessory acts by transferring troops to the newly-acquired territory, and she wisely resolved to accept the offer of the United States and sell the vast territory to that government. This famous purchase, accomplished during the administration of President Jefferson, was formally concluded on the 30th of April, 1803; and in December following, M. Laussat, who had just received control of the Province from the Spanish authorities, transferred it to the United States, represented at New Orleans for that purpose by Governor Claiborne and General Wilkinson, the commissioners appointed. The sum of money paid by the United States for the territory acquired was about $15,000,000. The agent of France for receiving possession of Upper Louisiana from the Spanish authorities was Amos Stoddard, a captain of artillery in the service of the United States. He arrived in St. Louis in March, 1804, and on the 9th of that month Charles Dehault Delassus, the Spanish Commandant, placed him in possession of the territory, and on the following day he transferred it to the United States. This memorable event created a wide-spread sensation in St. Louis and the other young towns in the vicinity. Most of the people were deeply attached to the old government, and although they were in sympathy with the vigorous Republic which had sprung into existence in the East, and dimly appreciated the promise of its future, yet it was with feelings of regret and apprehension that they saw the banner of the new government unfurled in place of the well-known flag of Spain. There were, however, many among St. Louis citizens who rejoiced at the transfer, and their anticipations of its prosperous influence on their town were speedily realized, for business generally became more animated, while the population rapidly increased by an energetic and ingenious class of settlers from the East and other points, mostly representatives of the Anglo-Saxon race, always the most successful in urging forward the prosperity and development of a country.

The date of this transfer marks an interesting epoch in the growth of St. Louis and the Western country. If, as we believe, before the year 1900 St. Louis will be the leading city of the North American Continent, her history will form a marvelous chapter in the chronicles of the life and development of modern nations. Nearly within the bounds of a century a rude settlement in a far inland wilderness will have expanded into a mighty metropolis, the rich capital and throbbing heart of the greatest nation in the world, the center of modern civilization, knowledge and arts; a city of vast manufacturing and commercial interests, in which every branch of human industry is represented; a second Babylon, on the banks of a river beside which the Euphrates was a streamlet; with iron roadways for the cars of steam branching out in all directions, and whose empire extends from the wild billows of the Atlantic to the calmer waters of the Pacific, from the cold lakes of the North to the warm waters of the Mexican Gulf. Here indeed is a historical picture which words can scarcely depict, which illustrates the power of human activities far more wondrously than the colossal but isolated structures of the people of the olden time.

ST. LOUIS UNDER THE RULE OF THE UNITED STATES.

A temporary government for St. Louis and Upper Louisiana was promptly provided for by Congress, Captain Stoddard being appointed to exercise the functions and prerogatives formerly vested in the Spanish Lieutenant-Governor. In the excellent historical sketch of Louisiana written by that officer, some interesting particulars are given of St. Louis at the time of the transfer to the United States. The town consisted of about 180 houses, and the population in the district numbered about 2,280 whites and about 500 blacks. The total population of Upper Louisiana is stated at 9,020 whites and 1,320 blacks. Three-fifths of the population of Upper Louisiana were Anglo-Americans. According to the same authority, St. Louis then consisted of two long streets running parallel to the river, with a number of others intersecting them at right angles. There were some houses, however, on the line of the present Third street, which was known as "*La rue des Granges*," or the street of barns, as before mentioned. The church building, from which Second street then derived its name, was a structure of hewn logs somewhat rude and primitive in appearance. West of Fourth street there was little else but woods and commons, and the Planters' House now stands upon a portion of the space then used for pasturage purposes. There was no post-office, nor indeed any need for one, as there were no official mails. Government boats ran occasionally between New Orleans and St. Louis, but there was no regular communication. The principal buildings were the Government house on Main street near Walnut street, the Chouteau mansion on the block between Main and Second and Market and Walnut streets, the residence of Madame Chouteau on the next block north, and the fort, St. Charles, near the present intersection of Fifth and Walnut streets. The means of education were of course limited in character, and as peltries and lead continued to be the chief articles of export, the cultivation of the land in the vicinity of the town progressed but slowly. There is a tradition that St. Louis received the *sobriquet* of *Pain Court* (short bread), owing to the scarcity of the staff of life in the town. Indeed there appears reason to believe that, in a commercial point of view, Ste. Genevieve at this time was a much more important place than St. Louis.

Captain Stoddard, on assuming control, published a circular address to the inhabitants, in which he formally announced that Louisiana had been transferred to the possession of the United States, and that the plan of a permanent territorial government was under the consideration of Congress. He briefly alluded to preceding events as follows: "It will not be necessary to advert to the various preliminary arrangements which have conspired to place you in your present political situation. With these it is presumed you are already acquainted. Suffice it to observe that Spain, in 1800 and 1801, retroceded the colony and province of Louisiana to France, and that France, in 1803, conveyed the same territory to the United States, who are now in the legal and peaceful possession of it. These transfers were made with honorable views and under such forms and sanctions as are usually practiced among civilized nations." The remainder of the address is devoted to an eloquent exposition of the new political condition of the people and of the privileges and benefits of a liberal republican government.

The fur trade, which had led to the founding of St. Louis, continued for many years to be the principal business of the people. Here, as elsewhere, the Indian tribes forged the weapons for their own destruction. They eagerly sought the opportunity to exchange with the white men the fruits of the chase for the articles and commodities of a higher civilization. They were the principal agents in developing the fur trade of the North and West, and by so doing hastened the incoming of that indomitable race destined to build, over their slaughter and decay, the glorious structure of American liberty. These primitive races wasted and faded with the birth of a nation, whose evangel was to bless and metamorphose the New World; and even had there been no Revolutionary war to usher in the American Union, there is enough in the fate of the aborigines of the country to authenticate the remark of Theodore Parker that "all the great charters of humanity have been written in blood."

During the fifteen years ending in 1804 the average annual value of the furs collected at St. Louis is stated to have been $203,750. The number of buffalo skins was only 850; deer, 158,000; beaver, 36,900 pounds; otter, 8,000; bear, 5,100. A very different state of things existed twenty or thirty years later, when beaver were nearly exhausted and buffalo skins formed the most important article of trade. The commerce consisted principally of that portion of furs that did not find its way directly to Montreal and Quebec through the lakes.

The supplies of the town, especially of groceries, were brought from New Orleans, and the time necessary for a trip was from four to six months. The departure of a boat was an important event, and generally many of the inhabitants collected together on the shore to see it off and bid good-by to the friends who might be among the passengers. Wm. C. Carr, who arrived about the 1st of April, 1804, states that it took him *twenty-five days* to make the trip from Louisville, Ky., by river. On the same authority it is stated that there were then only two American families in the place—those of Calvin Adams and William Sullivan. Mr. Carr remained in St. Louis about a month, and then, attracted by the greater lead trade of Ste. Genevieve, went to that place to reside, but returned in about a year, convinced that St. Louis was a better location. In the same year Col. Rufus Easton, John Scott, and Edward

Hempstead came to reside in the country. Mr. Scott settled at Ste. Genevieve; Mr. Hempstead went to St. Charles, then called Petite Cote, where he remained for several years, and then came to St. Louis; Mr. Easton remained in St. Louis.

In 1802 James Pursley, an American, with two companions, started on a hunting expedition from St. Louis to the source of the Osage, but extended his course westward. After various dangers and adventures he reached the vicinity of Santa Fe, and is said to have been the first American who traversed the great plains between the United States and New Mexico.

In 1804 the United States dispatched Lewis and Clark and Major Pike to explore the sources of the Mississippi, the Arkansas, the Kansas, and the Platte rivers. Hunters from St. Louis and vicinity formed their companions, or preceded them, and were to be found on nearly all the rivers east of the Rocky Mountains. Mr. Auguste Chouteau, about the same-time, had outfitted Loisel, who established a considerable fort and trading post on Cedar Island, a little above the Big Bend of the Missouri; so that about the time that St. Louis became a town of the United States, the great regions west and north of her were being gradually opened to settlement. Forty years had elapsed since Laclede had founded the settlement, and yet, compared with the development of subsequent times, its growth had not been very rapid. It was but a straggling river village with few buildings of any consequence, and was cut off from the world of trade and civilization by its great distance from the seaboard and the vast unpeopled country surrounding it. The inhabitants were mostly French, and the social intercourse was simple and friendly, with but faint traces of class distinctions. There was only one resident physician, Dr. Saugrain, who lived on Second street, and one baker, Le Clerc, who baked for the garrison and lived on Main street near Elm. The only American tavern was kept by a man named Adams, and this, with two others kept by Frenchmen named Yostic and Laudreville, both on Main street near Locust, were, we believe, the only establishments of the kind in the town. The names of the more prominent merchants and citizens at this time are familiar at present to nearly all of our citizens, owing to many of the families still being represented, and the fact that their names, most appropriately, have been wrought in with the nomenclature of our streets. Among them we may mention Auguste and Pierre Chouteau, Labadie, Sarpy, Gratiot, Pratte, Tayon, Lecompt, Papin, Cabanne, Lebaume, Soulard, Hortez, Alvarez, Clamorgan, Debreuil and Manuel Lisa. The Chouteaus lived on Main street, and Pierre, whose place was near the present intersection of that street with Washington avenue, had nearly a whole square encircled by a stone wall, and in which he had a fine orchard. Manuel Lisa lived on Second street; the establishment of Labadie & Sarpy was on Main near Chesnut, and the Debreuils had a fine place on Second between Pine and Chesnut streets.

On the 26th of March, 1804, by an act of Congress the Province of Louisiana was divided into two parts, the Territory of Orleans and the District of Louisiana, the latter including all north of the 33d parallel of latitude. The executive power of the Government in the Territory of Indiana was extended over that of Louisiana, the Governors and Judges of the former being authorized to enact laws for the new District. Gen. William Henry Harrison, then Governor of Indiana, instituted the American authorities here under the provisions of this act, his associates being, we believe, Judges Griffin, Vanderberg, and Davis. The first courts of justice were held during the ensuing winter in the old fort near Fifth and Walnut streets, and were called Courts of Common Pleas. On the 3d of March, 1805, by another act of Congress the District was changed to the Territory of Louisiana, and James Wilkinson was appointed Governor, and with Judges R. J. Meigs and John B. C. Lucas, of the Superior Court, formed the Legislature of the Territory. The executive offices were in the old Government building on Main street, near Walnut, just south of the Public Square, called *La Place d'Armes*. Here Gen. Wilkinson was visited by Aaron Burr when the latter was planning his daring and ambitious conspiracy. When Wilkinson was appointed there were in each of the Districts of St. Charles, St. Louis, Ste. Genevieve, and Cape Girardeau a civil and military Commandant, as follows: Col Meigs for the first, Col. Hammond for St. Louis, Maj. Seth Hunt for Ste. Genevieve, and Col. T. B. Scott for the last-named place. These officers were superseded by the organization of courts, and the names of the districts subsequently became those of counties. This system of legislation was maintained for several years, with occasional changes in officers.

In 1806 Gen. Wilkinson established the fort of Belle Fontaine, on the south side of the Missouri, a few miles above its mouth; but it was practically abandoned early the following year, when he was ordered South to assist in arresting the Burr conspiracy. During part of 1806 Joseph Browne was Secretary of the Territory and Acting Governor, and J. B. C. Lucas and Otho Shrader were Judges. The following year Frederic Bates was Governor, with the same Judges in office. Next year Merriweather Lewis, with the same Judges, formed the Legislature, and continued to do so until 1811.

On the 9th of November, 1809, the town of St. Louis was first incorporated, upon the petition of two-thirds of the taxable inhabitants and under the authority of an act of the Territory of Louisiana, passed the previous year.

On the 4th of June, 1812, the country received the name of the Territory of Missouri, and the government was modified and made to consist of a Governor and Legislative Assembly, the upper branch of which, numbering nine councilors, were selected out of twice that number, nominated to the Governor by the lower branch. At this time the Territory had first conceded to it the right of representation in Congress by one delegate. Anterior to this change in the government there are some events which deserve particular notice. Shortly after the country became part of the United States a post-office was permanently created in the town, the first postmaster being Rufus Easton. The first newspaper was established July, 1808, by Joseph Charless, and received the name of the *Missouri Gazette*. It was first printed on a sheet of writing-paper not much larger than a royal-octavo page. This journal was the germ of the present *Missouri Republican*, one of the largest in circulation and most influential journals of the country. The necessity of some means of transportation to and fro across the river had led to the establishment of a small ferry, which was first kept by Calvin Adams and proved a paying enterprise. His ferry consisted of two pirogues tied together with planks laid across the top, and his charge for bringing over man and horse was $2. In the August of this year two Iowa Indians were tried for murder before the Court of Oyer and Terminer, Judges Lucas and Shrader presiding. It created a good deal of excitement, but owing to some want of jurisdiction in the case the prisoners escaped the sentence of death which was passed upon them. On the 16th of September the first execution for murder in the Territory took place, the criminal being a young man who had shot his step-father. In the autumn of the next year Governor Lewis, while on a journey to Louisville, committed suicide by shooting himself while under the influence of aberration of mind.

The Municipal Government, at this time, consisted of a Board of Trustees, elected under the provisions of the charter mentioned above. The Missouri Fur Company was formed in St. Louis in 1808, consisting principally of Pierre Chouteau, Manuel Lisa, William Clark, Sylvester Labadie, Pierre Menard, and Auguste Pierre Chouteau, the capital being $40,000. An expedition was dispatched under the auspices of this company, in charge of Major A. Henry, and succeeded in establishing trading posts upon the Upper Missouri—one on Lewis river, beyond the Rocky Mountains, and one on the southern branch of the Columbia, the latter being the first post established on the great river of the Oregon Territory. In 1812 this company was dissolved, most of the members establishing independent houses in the trade and for furnishing outfits to private adventurers. Among these may be mentioned the houses of Berthold & Chouteau, B. Pratte, J. P. Cabanne, and M. Lisa. The hunters and trappers at this time formed a considerable part of the population of St. Louis, and were principally half-breed Indians and white men so long accustomed to such pursuits that they were nearly similar in habits to the natives. Notwithstanding the preponderance of this reckless element, it does not appear that the town was disorderly, and crime and scenes of violence were of rare occurrence.

The first members of the Territorial Legislature, elected in 1812, sat during the ensuing winter in the old house of Joseph Robidoux, on Main, between Walnut and Elm streets. It was in this year that the terrible earthquake occurred at New Madrid and vicinity, and created wide-spread dismay. The waters of the Mississippi were greatly agitated by the subterranean convulsion, and several boats with their crews were engulfed. New Madrid, which stood upon a bluff fifteen or twenty feet above the summer floods, sank so low that the next rise covered the ground to the depth of four or five feet. The channel of the river was affected materially, and the bottoms of some small lakes in the vicinity were so elevated that they became dry land.

The first English school was opened in St. Louis in 1808, by Geo. Tompkins, a young Virginian, who, when he started in the enterprise, was nearly without funds and with but few acquaintances. He rented a room on the north side of

Market street, between Second and Third, for his school, and during his leisure hours pursued the study of law. The first debating society known west of the Mississippi was connected with this school, and the debates were generally open to the public and afforded interesting and instructive entertainment. This energetic young school-teacher studied law to some purpose, for he ultimately became Chief Justice of the Supreme Court of Missouri. Among the members of the society he organized were Dr. Farrar, Dr. Lowry, Major O'Fallon, Edward Bates, and Joshua Barton — names afterward rendered eminent by ability and public service. The population of the town in 1810 was about 1400. In May, 1812, the chiefs of the Osage, the Shawnees, Delawares, and other tribes, came here to accompany Gen. Wm. Clark to Washington, the purpose being to consummate some negotiations then pending and to impress the savages with some true idea of the greatness and power of the Government. This Gen. Clark was the brother of Gen. George Rogers Clark, so distinguished in the West during the Revolutionary war, and was the companion of Lewis in the famous expedition to the Upper Missouri, and had remarkable experience and judgment in dealing with the Indians. The war of 1812 between the United States and England produced but little effect upon our city, so far removed inland, but the people took a lively interest in the progress of the conflict, and participated in the general rejoicing over its honorable close.

In August, 1816, the Bank of St. Louis was incorporated, being the first institution of the kind in the town. The following gentlemen composed the commissioners: Auguste Chouteau, J. B. C. Lucas, Clement B. Penrose, Moses Austin, Bernard Pratte, Manuel Lisa, Thos. Brady, Bartholomew Berthold, Samuel Hammond, Rufus Easton, Robert Simpson, Christian Wilt, and Risdon H. Price. At an election, held on the 20th of the following month, Samuel Hammond was elected President, and John B. N. Smith Cashier. The career of this bank was not successful, and continued for something over two years, when it came to a disastrous close. On the 1st of February, 1817, the Missouri Bank was incorporated, the commissioners appointed by the stockholders to receive subscriptions being Charles Gratiot, Wm. Smith, John McKnight, J. B. Cabanne, and Mathew Kerr. The first President was Auguste Chouteau, and the Cashier Lilburn W. Boggs.

A census published in the *Missouri Gazette*, December 9, 1815, and taken by John W. Thompson, states that the number of souls in the town was 2,000, and the total population of county and town 7,395.

On the 2d of August an event occurred which marked the commencement of a new epoch in the history of St. Louis. Heretofore its growth had been dependent upon human energies alone, but now a new agency was to enter into its commercial life, and which was to enable her to reap the full benefit accruing from the noble river that rolled past her to the sea. The first steamboat arrived on the day named. It was called the "Pike," and was commanded by Capt. Jacob Reed. The inhabitants were, as might be expected, greatly interested and delighted as the novel craft touched the foot of Market street, many of them having never seen a vessel of the kind before. Some Indians who were in town were so alarmed at the unusual spectacle that they receded from the shore as the boat neared, and could not be persuaded to come in the vicinity of the monster, for such it seemed to them, although in reality but a tiny little vessel. She was propelled by a low-pressure engine, and had been built at Louisville. The second boat which arrived here was the "Constitution," commanded by Capt. R. P. Guyard, and the 2d of October, 1817, was the date of her arrival. In May, 1819, the first steamboat stemmed the tide of the Missouri; it was the "Independence," Capt. Nelson commanding, and went up as far as "Old Franklin," after a passage of seven running days. The first steamboat from New Orleans, the "Harriet," commanded by Capt. Armitage, reached here on the 2d of June, 1819, making the voyage in twenty-seven days.

In 1817 the first board of school trustees was formed, which may be regarded as the commencement of the present unsurpassed school system. They were: Wm. Clark, Wm. C. Carr, Thos. H. Benton, Bernard Pratte, Auguste Chouteau, Alexander McNair, and John P. Cabanne. During the following year the application of Missouri for admission into the Union gave rise to a most exciting political agitation, in which the whole nation participated. The Southern members of Congress insisted that the new State should be admitted without restriction as to slavery, while the members from the North as bitterly opposed any extension of the slave system. It is not our province to more than mention the interesting and important aspect of the discussion that ensued, as it is a subject fully treated in the political history of the country. The result was the celebrated "Missouri Compromise," which in effect allowed the formation of the Missouri constitution without restriction, but declared that slavery should not extend in any new-formed State north of 36 degrees 40 minutes north latitude. The convention which framed the first Constitution of the State of Missouri assembled in 1820 in this city. The place of meeting was the Mansion House, then a building of considerable importance on the corner of Third and Vine streets, now known as the City Hotel.

Mr. John Jacob Astor established a branch of his house in this city in 1819, under the charge of Mr. Samuel Abbott, and it was called the Western Department of the American Fur Company. This company entered upon a most successful career, embracing in its trade the northern and western parts of the United States, east of the Rocky Mountains. About this time the old Missouri Fur Company was revived, with new partners, among whom were Maj. John Pilcher, M. Lisa, Thomas Hempstead, and Capt. Perkins. We may incidentally mention that in 1823 a hunting and trapping party of this company, under Messrs. Jones and Immel, while on the Yellow Stone, were attacked by Black Feet Indians. The leaders and several of the party were killed, and those who escaped were robbed of whatever property they had with them. This company only continued a few years, and was not successful. The important expedition of Gen. Wm. H. Ashley took place also in this year, and resulted in the discovery of the Southern pass of the Rocky Mountains, and the opening of commercial intercourse with the countries west of the same. The

General encountered fierce opposition from the Indians, and lost fourteen men, and had ten wounded in a fight at the outset of the expedition.

A city directory was published in 1821, which furnishes some interesting information respecting the condition of the town at the time, and from which we make the following extracts:

"It is but about forty years since the now flourishing but yet more promising State of Missouri was but a vast wilderness, many of the inhabitants of this country yet remembering the time when they met together to kill the buffalo at the same place where Mr. Philipson's ox saw and flour mill is now erected, and on Mill creek, near to where Mr. Chouteau's mill now stands. What a prodigious change has been operated! St. Louis is now ornamented with a great number of brick buildings, and both the scholar and the courtier could move in a circle suiting their choice and taste.

"By the exertions of the Right Rev. Bishop Louis Wm. Du Bourg, the inhabitants have seen a fine cathedral rise at the same spot where stood an old log church. * * * This elegant building was commenced in 1818, under the superintendence of Mr. Gabriel Paul, the architect, and is only in part completed. As it now stands it is 40 feet by 135 in depth and 40 feet in height. When completed it will have a wing on each side running its whole length 22½ feet wide and 25 in height, giving it a front of 85 feet. It will have a steeple the same height as the depth of the building, which will be provided with several large bells expected from France. The lot on which the church college and other buildings are erected embraces a complete square, a part of which is used as a burial ground.

* * * * * * * *

"It is a truly delightful sight, to an American of taste, to find in one of the remotest towns in the Union, a church decorated with *original* paintings of Rubens, Raphael, Guido, Paul Verouese, and a number of others by the first modern masters of the Italian, French and Flemish schools. The ancient and precious gold embroideries which the St. Louis Cathedral possesses would certainly decorate any museum in the world. All this is due to the liberality of the Catholics of Europe, who presented these rich articles to Bishop Du Bourg, on his last tour through France, Italy, Sicily, and the Netherlands. Among the liberal benefactors could be named many princes and princesses, but we will only insert the names of Louis XVIII., the present King of France, and that of the Baroness Le Candele de Ghyseghern, a Flemish lady, to whose munificence the Cathedral is particularly indebted, and who, even lately, has sent a fine, large and elegant organ, fit to correspond with the rest of the decorations. The Bishop possesses beside, a very elegant and valuable library containing about 8,000 volumes, and which is without doubt, the most complete scientific and literary repertory of the Western country, if not of the Western world. Though it is not public, there is no doubt but the man of science, the antiquary and the linguist, will obtain a ready access to it, and find the Bishop a man at once endowed with the elegance and politeness of the courtier, the piety and zeal of the apostle, and the learning of a father of the church. Connected with this establishment is the St. Louis College, under the direction of Bishop Du Bourg. It is a two-story brick building and has about sixty-five students, who are taught the Greek, Latin, French, English, Spanish, and Italian languages, mathematics, elementary and transcendent, drawing, &c. There are several teachers. Connected with the college is an ecclesiastical seminary, at the Barrens, in Ste. Genevieve county, where divinity, the oriental languages and philosophy are taught.

"St. Louis likewise contains ten common schools; a brick Baptist church, 40 feet by 60, built in 1819, and an Episcopal church of wood. The Methodist congregation hold their meetings in the old Court House, and the Presbyterians in the Circuit Court room." We gather the following additional facts from the same work: There were three newspapers then in the city, the *St. Louis Enquirer*, *Missouri Gazette*, and *St. Louis Register*.

* * * * * * * *

"Eight streets run parallel with the river, and are intersected by twenty-three others at right angles; three of the preceding are in the *lower* part of the town, and the five others in the *upper* part. The streets in the lower part of the town are narrow, being from thirty-two to thirty-eight and a half feet in width; those on 'the Hill' or upper part are much wider. 'The Hill' is much the most pleasant and salubrious, and will no doubt become the most improved. The lower end of Market street is well paved, and the trustees of the town have passed an ordinance for paving the sidewalks of Main street, being the second from and parallel to the river, and principal one for business. This is a very wholesome regulation of the trustees, and is the more necessary, as this and many other streets are sometimes so extremely muddy as to be rendered almost impassable. It is hoped that the trustees will next pave the middle of Main street, and that they will proceed gradually to improve the other streets, which will contribute to make the town more healthy, add to the value of property, and make it a desirable place of residence. On the Hill, in the center of the town, is a public square, two hundred and forty by three hundred feet, on which it is intended to build an elegant court-house. The various courts are held at present in buildings adjacent to the public square. A new stone jail of two stories, seventy feet front by thirty deep, stands west of the site of the court-house. Market street is in the middle of the town, and is the line dividing the north part from the south. Those streets running north from Market street have the addition of *North* to their names, and those running in the opposite direction, *South*. For example: North Main street, South Main street, North A, &c. street, South A street. The houses were first numbered by the publisher of this Directory, in May, 1821. The fortifications erected in early times for the defense of the place stand principally on the Hill. They consist of several circular stone towers, about fifteen feet in height and twenty in diameter, a wooden block-house and a large stone bastion, the interior of which is used as a garden by Captain A. Wetmore of the United States army.

"Just above the town are several Indian mounds and remains of antiquity, which afford an extensive and most charming view of the town and beautiful surrounding country, situated in the two States of Missouri and Illinois, which are separated by the majestic Mississippi, and which is likewise observed in the scene, as he glides along in all his greatness. Adjacent to the large mound, nearest the town, is the Mound Garden, belonging to Colonel Elias Rector, and kept by Mr. James Gray as a place of entertainment and recreation. The proprietor has displayed considerable taste in laying it out in beds and walks, and in ornamenting it with flowers and shrubbery. In short, it affords a delightful and pleasant retreat from the noise, heat and dust of a busy town.

"There is a Masonic hall in which the Grand Lodge of the State of Missouri, the Royal Arch, and the Master Masons' Lodges are held. Connected with this excellent institution is a burying-ground, where poor Masons are interred at the expense of the fraternity. The council chamber of Governor Wm. Clark, where he gives audience to the chiefs of the various tribes of Indians who visit St. Louis, contains probably the most complete museum of Indian curiosities to be met with anywhere in the United States, and the Governor is so polite as to permit its being visited by any person of respectability at any time.

* * * * * * * *

"Population in 1810, 1,000; in 1818, 3,500, and at this time (1821), about 5,500. The town and county contain 9,732. The population is much mixed, consisting principally of Americans from every part of the Union, the original and other French, of whom there are one hundred and fifty-five families, and foreigners of various nations; consequently the society is much diversified and has no fixed character. This, the reader will perceive, arises from the situation of the country, in itself new, flourishing and changing; still, that class who compose the respectable part of the community are hospitable, polite and well informed. And here I must take occasion, in justice to the town and country, to protest against the many calumnies circulated abroad, to the prejudice of St. Louis, respecting the manners and dispositions of the inhabitants. Persons meet here with dissimilar habits produced by a different education, and possessing various peculiarities. It is not therefore surprising that, in a place composed of such discordant materials, there should be occasional differences and difficulties. But the reader may be assured that old-established inhabitants have little participation in transactions which have, so far, so much injured the town.

"St. Louis has grown very rapidly. There is not, however, so much improvement going on at this time, owing to the check caused by general and universal pressure that pervades the country. This state of things can only be temporary here, for it possesses such permanent advantages from its local and geographical situation that it must, ere some distant day, become a place of great importance, being more central with regard to the whole territory belonging to the United States than any other considerable town, and uniting the advantages of the three great rivers, Mississippi, Missouri and Illinois, of the trade of which it is the emporium.

"The Missouri Fur Company was formed by several gentlemen of St. Louis in 1819, for the purpose of trading on the Missouri river and its waters. The principal establishment of the company is at Council Bluffs, yet they have several others of minor consequence several hundred miles above, and it is expected that the establishment will be extended shortly up as high as the Mandan villages. The actual capital invested in the trade is supposed to amount at this time to about $70,000. They have in their employ, exclusive of their partners on the river, twenty-five clerks and interpreters and seventy laboring men.

"It is estimated that the annual value of the Indian trade of the Mississippi and Missouri rivers is $600,000. The annual amount of imports to this town is stated at upwards of $2,000,000. The commerce by water is carried on by a great number of steamboats, barges and keel-boats. These center here, after performing the greatest inland voyages known in the world. The principal articles of trade are fur, peltry and lead. The agricultural productions are Indian corn, wheat, rye, barley, oats, buckwheat, tobacco and other articles common to the Western country. Excellent mill-stones are found and made in this county. Stone coal is abundant, and saltpetre and common salt have been made within a few miles. Within three or four miles are several springs of good water, and seven miles southwest is a sulphur spring. In the vicinity are two natural caverns in limestone rocks. Two miles above town, at North St. Louis, is a steam saw-mill, and several common mills are on the neighboring streams. The roads leading from St. Louis are very good, and it is expected that the great national turnpike from Washington will strike this place, as the commissioners for the United States have reported in favor of it.

"There were two fire engines with organized companies, one of which was stationed in the northern, the other in the southern part of the town. Two steam ferry-boats, the property of Mr. Samuel Wiggins, were in regular operation between the city and the opposite shore, and the river at the ferry was one mile and one-eighth in width. "Opposite the upper part of the town and above the ferry is an island about one mile and one-half in length and containing upwards of 1,000 acres, the property also of Mr. Wiggins. A considerable sand-bar has been formed in the river adjoining the lower part of the town, which extends far out and has thrown the main channel over on the Illinois side; when the water is low it is entirely dry and covered with an immense quantity of drift-wood nearly sufficient to supply the town with fuel, costing only the trouble of cutting and hauling. This is of great consequence to the inhabitants, particularly as the growth of wood is small in the immediate neighborhood on this side of the river. Wood is likewise brought down the river in large quantities for disposal."

Only about four years had elapsed from the arrival of the first steamboat at St. Louis to the time this directory was published, yet it is evident that municipal growth had been exceedingly rapid; business of all kinds, particularly in furs, peltries, lead, and agricultural productions, had expanded greatly, while numbers of steamboats, barges, and other craft were constantly engaged in the river commerce. In fact, even at this early period the inhabitants appear to have had some idea of the great future before their city. The career of St. Louis as an incorporated city may be dated from December 9, 1822, when an act was passed by the State Legislature entitled "An act to incorporate the inhabitants of the town of St. Louis;" and in

April following, an election took place for Mayor and nine Aldermen, in accordance with the provisions of the act. William Carr Lane was elected Mayor, with the following Aldermen: Thomas McKnight, James Kennerley, Philip Rocheblane, Archibald Gamble, Wm. H. Savage, Robert Nash, James Loper, Henry Von Phul, and James Lackman. The new city government proved a most effective one, and immediately set about the improvement of the city. An ordinance was passed for the grading of Main street and compelling citizens to improve streets in front of their lots. The salary of the Mayor was only $300 per annum, but he applied himself with as much earnestness and assiduity to the public service as if he were receiving the present salary of $4,000. Before proceeding to sketch the progress of St. Louis as an incorporated city, the following items may be mentioned as illustrating the progress of building up to that time: Chouteau's row in block No. 7 was begun in 1818 and finished in 1819. During the same years three other buildings of an important character were erected; the first by Gen. Clark, the second by Bernard Pratte, at the corner of Market and Water streets, and the third, a large warehouse, by A. Chouteau, in block No. 6. The Catholic Church, a large brick building on Second street, long since demolished, was constructed in 1818, and on Christmas day, 1819, divine service was performed there for the first time. The first paving which was laid in St. Louis was executed by Wm. Deckers, with stone on edge, on Market street, between Main and Water. In 1821 the first brick pavement was laid on Second street, and finally it may be mentioned that the first *brick* dwelling was built in 1813 by William C. Carr. There was, at the time we now speak of, but little indications of settlement on the eastern bank of the river opposite St. Louis, but the long strip of land near the Illinois shore had already earned the right to the title of Bloody Island, as more than one fatal duel had taken place there. The first was that between Thos. H. Benton, subsequently so distinguished a citizen, and Charles Lucas. The difficulty between the parties originated during a trial in which both were engaged as counsel. Col. Benton, believing himself insulted, challenged Mr. Lucas, who declined on the ground that statements made to a jury could not properly be considered a cause for such a meeting. The ill feeling thus created was aggravated by a subsequent political controversy, and Mr. Lucas challenged Mr. Benton, who accepted. The meeting took place on Bloody Island on the morning of August 12, 1817, pistols being the weapons used. Mr. Lucas was severely wounded in the neck, and owing to the effusion of blood, was withdrawn from the field. A temporary reconciliation followed this duel, but the feud between the parties broke out afresh shortly afterwards, and another duel took place on Bloody Island, resulting in the killing of young Lucas at the age of twenty-five. This deplorable rencounter occurred on the 27th of September, 1817. During the following year another duel occurred on Bloody Island, which also resulted fatally, the combatants being Captains Martin and Ramsey, of the U. S. army, who were stationed at the Fort Belle Fountaine, on the Missouri river. Ramsey was wounded and died a few days afterwards, and was buried with Masonic and military honors. On the 30th of June, 1823, a hostile meeting took place at the same locality between

Joshua Barton, District Attorney of the United States, resident at St. Louis, and Thos. C. Rector. The parties met in the evening, and Mr. Barton fell mortally wounded. An article which appeared in the *Missouri Republican*, charging Gen. Wm. Rector, then United States Surveyor, with corruption in office, was the cause of the duel. The General was in Washington at the time, and his brother, Thos. C. Rector, warmly espoused his cause, and learning that Mr. Barton was the author of the charge, sent him the challenge which resulted so fatally. Various other rencounters between the adherents to the "code of honor" took place at later dates on Bloody Island, so that the reader will see that its sanguinary appellation had a reasonable and appropriate origin. The more prominent of the other duels which occurred there will be mentioned when we reach their appropriate dates.

Notwithstanding the disastrous conflicts between the Indians and the followers of the Rocky Mountain and Missouri Fur Companies, which occurred in 1823, the progress of trade and exploration, under the daring leadership of Gen. Wm. H. Ashley and others, was not seriously retarded. Benj. O'Fallon, U. S. agent for Indian affairs, writes to Gen. Wm. Clark, superintendent of Indian affairs, giving an account of the misfortunes to Gen. Ashley's command, and adds: "Many circumstances have transpired to induce the belief that the British traders (Hudson's Bay Company) are exciting the Indians against us, either to drive us from that quarter, or reap with the Indians the fruits of our labors." It is evident from all the records of that time, that trade and exploration in the Upper Missouri and Rocky Mountain region were environed with extraordinary hardships and perils, and nothing but the greatest courage, energy, and endurance could have accomplished their advancement. In 1824 Gen. Ashley made another expedition, penetrating as far as the great Utah Lake, near which he discovered another and a smaller, to which he gave his own name. In this vicinity he established a fort, and two years afterwards a six-pound cannon was drawn from Missouri to this fort, 1200 miles, and in 1828 many loaded wagons performed the same journey. Between the years 1824 and 1827 Gen. Ashley's men sent furs to this city to the value of over $200,000. The General, having achieved a handsome competence during his perilous career, sold out all his interests and establishments to the Rocky Mountain Fur Company, in which Messrs. J. S. Smith, David E. Jackson, and Wm. L. Sublette were principals, Mr. Robert Campbell then holding the position of clerk. The followers of this company penetrated the far West in every direction and had many conflicts with the Indians, and "traversed every part of the country about the southern branches of the Columbia, and ransacked nearly the whole of California." It is stated on good authority that during the five years from 1825 to 1830, of the number of our men engaged in the fur trade two-fifths were killed by the Indians or died victims to the dangers of exploring a wilderness.

In 1824 Frederic Bates was elected Governor, defeating Gen. Wm. Ashley after an exciting political contest; but he did not long enjoy the honors of the position, for he was attacked by pleurisy and died in August of the following year.

We now reach the date of an interesting event in the history of St. Louis, namely, the visit of Lafayette, who reached Carondelet on the 28th of April, 1825, and the next morning came up to the city. He was tendered a most enthusiastic reception, as many of the citizens were not only of the same nationality but all were familiar with his name and fame. He landed opposite the old Market House, where half the town were assembled awaiting his arrival and received him with cheers, took his seat in a carriage, accompanied by Wm. Carr Lane, Mayor, Stephen Hempstead, an officer of the Revolution, and Col. Auguste Chouteau, one of the companions of Laclede. Apart from private hospitalities, a splendid banquet and ball were given the distinguished visitor at the Mansion House, then the prominent hotel and situated on the northeast corner of Third and Market streets. Lafayette was at this time sixty-eight years of age but still active and strong; he was accompanied by his son, George Washington Lafayette, and some distinguished gentlemen from the South. The next morning he left for Kaskaskia, being escorted to the boat by crowds of citizens who in every way manifested their esteem and respect, and his visit has always been regarded as a memorable local incident.

During this year measures were taken to locate a permanent route across the plains. Major Sibley, one of the commissioners appointed by government, set out from St. Louis in June, accompanied by Joseph C. Brown and Captain Gamble, with seven wagons containing various goods for trading with the Indians on the road. The party selected a route to Sante Fe, which afterwards was adopted as the general highway for intercourse and trade.

The first Episcopal church of any architectural importance was erected in this year at the corner of Third and Chestnut streets. It afterwards passed into the hands of the Baptists, and finally disappeared as business houses multiplied in the vicinity. The first Presbyterian church was erected in 1825, near the corner of Fourth and St. Charles streets, and was consecrated by the Rev. Samuel Giddings, but also disappeared as business limits expanded. The first steps towards building a Court House were taken in 1826, and the building, a large one of brick, was erected in the following year, and which was destined to be succeeded by the present superb structure of stone. Antoine Chenie built the first three-story house on Main street in 1825, and it was occupied by Tracy & Wahrendoff and James Clemens, Jr.; Jefferson Barracks was commenced in July, 1826, and Center Market in 1827. The U. S. Arsenal was authorized by Congress in 1826, and was commenced during the next year on the block where it is now situated, but it was many years before it was completed. An ordinance was passed in 1826 changing the names of the streets with the exception of Market street. From 1809 those running west from the river, excepting Market, had been designated by letters, and they now received in most instances the names by which they are at present known. From the last date to 1830 no events of prominent interest mark the history of St. Louis. Different ordinances were passed for the grading, paving and general improvement of streets; and the growth of the city, if not rapid, was steady and satisfactory. Daniel D. Page was elected Mayor in 1829 and proved an energetic and valuable executive. Dr. Robert Simpson was elected Sheriff by a large majority over Frederic Hyat, his opponent. The branch Bank of the United States was established here during this year. Col. John O'Fallon was appointed president, and Henry S. Coxe cashier, and during the years it continued in existence possessed the public confidence and closed its career without disaster.

In 1830 the number of brick buildings in the city increased considerably, as the multiplication of brick-yards brought that material more into general use; a bridge was erected across Mill creek on lower Fourth street; and, architecturally and commercially, there were evidences of solid advancement. The large yards and gardens, which surrounded so many of the dwellings and stores of earlier times, gradually disappeared with the growth of improvements. Some excitement was caused this year by the decisions rendered by Judge James H. Peck, of the United States District Court, in regard to land claims, which were of a stringent character. Judge Lawless, who was interested as counsel in some cases in which Auguste Chouteau and others, and the heirs of Mackey Wherry, were plaintiffs *vs.* the United States, having avowed the authorship of a rather severe criticism which appeared in one of the newspapers on some decisions of Judge Peck, was committed to prison for contempt of court. He was released after a few hours, on a writ of *habeas corpus*, and subsequently preferred charges against Judge Peck before the House of Representatives, which, however, were dismissed after some examination. On the first day of August in this year the corner-stone of the Cathedral on Walnut street, between Second and Third, was laid with religious ceremonies, and this building is now the oldest place of worship in the city, as all those erected previously have given place to other edifices.

The population of the city in 1831 was 5,963. Various measures were adopted this year for public improvement, and an ordinance was passed for building the Broadway market. The Missouri Insurance Company was incorporated with a capital of $100,000, and George Collier was elected president. In August a most shocking and fatal duel occurred on Bloody Island. Spencer Pettis, a young lawyer of promise, was a candidate for Congress, his opponent being David Barton. Major Biddle made some severe criticisms on Mr. Pettis through the newspapers, and a challenge passed and was accepted. They fought at five paces distant, and at the first fire both fell mortally wounded. Mr. Pettis died in about twenty-four hours, while Major Biddle survived only a few days. The former had just gained his election, and Gen. Wm. H. Ashley was elected to fill the vacancy caused by his death.

In 1832 the famous expedition of Capt. Bonneville took place, and important steps were made in the opening of the great country to the West. Fort William was established on the Arkansas by the Messrs. Bent of this city. Messrs. Sublette and Campbell went to the mountains. Mr. Wyeth established Fort Hall on the Lewis river, and the American Fur Company sent the first steamboat to the Yellow Stone. The Asiatic cholera visited the city this summer, having first invaded Eastern and Southern cities. It first broke out at Jefferson Barracks, and, notwithstanding the most energetic sanitary measures, soon spread through the town with alarming severity. The population was then 6,918, and the deaths averaged, for some time, more than thirty a day. The disease prevailed for little over a month, then abated and disappeared. In this fall Daniel Dunklin, the Jackson candidate, was elected Governor, and L. A. Boggs Lieutenant-Governor. During the next year an effort was made to impeach Wm. C. Carr, one of the Circuit Judges, and one of the oldest citizens, the charge being that he was wholly unqualified for judicial station. On examination of the case before both Houses of the Legislature he was acquitted. Dr. Samuel Merry was elected Mayor, but was declared ineligible on the ground of being a receiver of public moneys, which office he held under the appointment of the President, and the next autumn Col. John W. Johnson was elected in his place. The taxable property was valued, in 1833, at only $2,000,000, and the whole tax of the year on real and personal property amounted only to $2,745.84. The tonnage of boats belonging to the port was hardly 2,000, and the fees for wharfage not more than $600.

In 1834 Mr. Astor retired from business and sold his Western department to Messrs. B. Pratte, P. Chouteau, Jr., and Mr. Cabanne, who conducted the business until 1839. A few years after this latter date nearly the entire fur trade of the West was controlled by the house of Pierre Chouteau, Jr., & Co. and the firm of Messrs. Bent & St. Vrain.

The business of the city was now developing rapidly, although the lack of proper banking facilities made itself felt somewhat injuriously; and while the unfortunate careers of the Bank of St. Louis and the Bank of Missouri had tended to make the people distrustful of such institutions, the want of them was generally recognized. During 1835–6 applications were made to the Legislature to supply this deficiency, but without success, and finally the banks of the other States were invited to establish branches in this city. Immigration at this period was unusually large, and a vigorous activity pervaded every department of business. As an illustration of this we quote from one of the newspapers: "The prosperity of our city is laid deep and broad. * * * * * Whether we turn to the right or to the left, we see workmen busy in laying the foundation or finishing some costly edifice. The dilapidated and antique structure of the original settler is fast giving way to the spacious and lofty blocks of brick and stone. But comparatively a few years ago, even within the remembrance of our young men, our town was confined to one or two streets running parallel with the river. The 'half-moon' fortifications, the 'bastion,' the tower, the rampart, were then known as the utmost limits. What was then termed 'The Hill,' now forming the most beautiful part of the town, covered with elegant mansions, but a few years ago was covered with shrubbery. A tract of land was purchased by a gentleman now living, as we have understood, for two barrels of whisky, which is now worth half a million of dollars. * * * * * * Intimately connected with the prosperity of the city is the fate of the petition pending in Congress for the removal of the sandbar now forming in front of our steamboat landing."

The number of boats in 1835, exclusive of barges was, 121; aggregate tonnage 15,470 tons, and total wharfage collected $4,573. In March of this year the sale of the town commons was ordered by the City Council, and in accordance with the act of the Legislature nine-tenths of the proceeds was appropriated to the improvement of streets and one-tenth to the support of public schools. The sum realized for the latter was small, but it assisted materially in laying the foundation of the present system, so extensive and beneficent in its operation. John F. Darby was elected Mayor in 1835, and during that year a meeting of citizens was called for the purpose of memorializing Congress to direct the great national road, then building, to cross the Mississippi at St. Louis, in its extension to Jefferson City. Mr. Darby presided at the meeting and George K. McGunnegle acted as secretary. The popular interest in railroad enterprises which at this time prevailed in the East soon reached as far as St. Louis, and on the 20th of April, 1835, an Internal Improvement Convention was held in this city. Delegations from the counties in the State interested in the movement were invited to attend. Dr. Samuel Merry acted as chairman and Mr. McGunnegle as secretary. The two railroad lines particularly advocated were from St. Louis to Fayette, and from the same point to the iron and lead mines in the southern portion of the State. A banquet at the National Hotel followed the convention, and the event had doubtless an important influence in fostering railroad interests, always so important in the life of a community.

A most exciting local incident occurred shortly after the sitting of the convention. A negro named Francis L. McIntosh had been arrested for assisting a steamboat hand to escape who was in custody for some offense. He was taken to a justice's office, where the case was examined, and the prisoner, unable to furnish the requisite bail, was delivered to Mr. Wm. Mull, deputy constable, to be taken to jail. While on the way there, Mr. George Hammond, the Sheriff's deputy, met Mr. Mull and volunteered to assist him in conducting his charge to the jail. The three men walked on together, and when near the northeast corner of the Court House block the negro asked Mr. Hammond what would be done to him for the offense committed. He replied in jest, "perhaps you will be hanged." The prisoner in a moment jerked himself free from the grasp of Mull and struck at him with a boatman's knife; the first stroke missed, but another followed inflicting a severe wound in the left side of the constable. Mr. Hammond then siezed the negro by the collar and pulled him back, when the latter struck him in the neck with the knife, severing the important arteries. The wounded man ran some steps towards his own home, when he fell from loss of blood and expired in a few moments. The negro fled after this bloody work, pursued by Mull, who raised the alarm by shouting until he fainted from loss of blood. A number of citizens joined in the pursuit, and the murderer was finally captured and lodged in jail. An intense public excitement was created and an angry multitude of people gathered round the jail. The prisoner was given up to them when demanded, by the affrighted jailor, and he was seized and dragged to a point near the corner of Seventh and Chestnut streets, where the cries of the mob—"burn him! burn him!"—were literally carried into effect. The wretched culprit was bound to a small locust tree, some brush and other dry wood piled around him and set on fire. Mr. Joseph Charles, son of the founder of the *Republican*, made an ineffectual effort to dissuade the crowd from their awful purpose, but he was not listened to, and in sullen and unpitying silence they stood round the fire and watched the agonies of their victim. In 1836 the corner-stone of the St. Louis Theater was laid at the corner of Third and Olive streets, on the site now occupied by the Custom House and Post Office, the parties principally interested in the enterprise being N. M. Ludlow, E. H. Bebee, H. S. Coxe, J. C. Lavielle, L. M. Clark and C. Keemle. The building erected was quite a handsome one, and the theater was carried on for a number of years until the property was purchased by the United States and the present government buildings erected. The Central Fire Company of the city of St. Louis was also incorporated this year. The first steam flour mill erected in St. Louis by Captain Martin Thomas was burned down on the night of the 10th of July this year. On the 20th of September the daily issue of the *Missouri Republican* commenced.

On the 1st of February, 1837, the Bank of the State of Missouri was incorporated by the Legislature with a capital of $5,000,000. The first officers elected were John Smith, president of the parent bank, with the following directors: Hugh O'Neal, Samuel S. Rayburn, Edward Walsh, Edward Dobyns, Wm. L. Sublette and John O'Fallon, all of St. Louis. A branch was also established at Lafayette, and J. J. Lowry was appointed president. Not long after the passage of the act incorporating the State Bank, another was passed excluding all other banking agencies from the State. The new bank with its great privileges and brilliant prospects opened business in a house owned by Pierre Chouteau on Main street near Vine. The total tonnage of the port in 1836 was 19,447 tons, and the amount of wharfage collected between $7,000 and $8,000. In 1837 the Planters' House was commenced, but owing to the financial embarrassments of the year the progress of the building was slow. Early this summer Daniel Webster visited the city and was received with the utmost cordiality and enthusiasm. It was expected that Henry Clay would accompany him, but he was prevented by business engagements. The distinguished guest and his family stopped at the National Hotel and remained for several days. A public festival or barbecue was given them in a grove on the land of Judge Lucas, west of Ninth street, and the occasion became peculiarly memorable from the fact that Mr. Webster delivered an eloquent speech.

The general financial disasters of 1837 were felt to a serious extent in St. Louis, and the Bank of the State of Missouri suspended temporarily. On September 26th David Barton, a colleague of Col. Thos. H. Benton in the U. S. Senate, and one of the most distinguished citizens of the State, died in Cooper county, at the residence of Mr. Gibson. In the summer of the next year Thos. M. Doherty, one of the Judges of St. Louis county, was mysteriously murdered on the road between this city and Carondelet, and the murderers were never discovered. In the fall Gen. Wm. Clark died. He was the oldest American resident in St. Louis, was the first Governor of the Territory of Missouri, and as superintendent of Indian affairs rendered important public services. During this year Kemper College, which was built principally through the exertions of Bishop Kemper, was opened. The medical department was formed shortly after, and owed its origin to Drs. Joseph N. McDowell and J. W. Hall. On the 20th of November the Legislature met at Jefferson

City, and during its session, which lasted until February, 1839, some important acts were passed in connection with St. Louis. The Criminal Court was established, over which the Hon. James B. Bowlin presided as Judge for several years. A bill was passed to incorporate the St. Louis Hotel Company, under the auspices of which the Planters' House was completed. A Mayor's Court was also established for the purpose of disposing of trials for breach of city ordinances. A charter was granted to the St. Louis Gaslight Company, but the streets were not lighted with gas by this corporation for many years afterwards. The present gas company holds its exclusive privileges under this charter; and although the original intention of the Legislature was that the city should have the authority to purchase the works at a certain specified period, this has not been done and probably never will be. The charter expires by limitation in 1889. Christ Church was erected during this year, on the southwest corner of Chestnut and Fifth streets, but after a few years yielded up its site to business edifices. Considerable agitation was current about this time, owing to the action of the officers of the Bank of the State of Missouri in refusing to receive the notes of any suspended banks on deposit or in payment at their counter. This resolution was caused by the financial disturbance that pervaded the country and the fact that a number of banks in different States of the Union had again suspended specie payments. A strong effort was made by the merchants of the city to procure a rescinding of the resolution, and ten gentlemen, among the most prominent and wealthy in the city, offered to legally bind themselves to indemnify the bank against any loss that might be sustained by the depreciation of the notes of any of the suspended banks. The directors, however, after a consultation, refused the proposition and adhered to their cautious policy, notwithstanding that some of their best patrons withdrew their deposits in irritation at this course. The result, however, showed that the bank acted wisely, and the public confidence in it was rather increased than impaired. The County Court ordered the commencement of an important addition to the Court House, commenced in 1825–6, and the corner-stone was laid with the usual ceremonies in the presence of a large concourse of citizens

The total arrivals of steamboats at this port during the year 1839 was 2,095; departures 1,645. In the spring of 1840 the corner-stone of the Catholic church attached to the St. Louis University was laid and a number of other buildings erected. During this year the unfortunate affray between Mr. Andrew J. Davis, proprietor of the *Argus*, and Mr. Wm. P. Darnes occurred, arising from some severe remarks published in the journal named reflecting on the latter. The parties chanced to meet on Third street near the National Hotel, and Mr. Davis received several blows on the head from an iron cane in the hands of Mr. Darnes, and subsequently died from the effects. The trial of Darnes took place in November, and he was found guilty of manslaughter in the fourth degree and fined $500. The steamer Meteor made the trip from New Orleans to this city in five days and five hours during the early part of this season, being the quickest trip ever made up to that time. The Hon. John F. Darby, the Whig candidate, was elected Mayor in April, and at the election for county officers in

August the same party was successful. There were ten insurance companies in existence in St. Louis in the year 1841, many of which carried on a semi-banking business.

In April, two young men, Jacob Weaver and Jesse Baker, met a shocking and violent death. They slept in a room in a large stone building on the corner of Pine and Water streets, occupied in front by Messrs. Simonds & Morrison, and in the rear by Mr. Wm. G. Pettus, banker and broker. An alarm of fire came from this building early on Sunday morning, April 18th, and one of the firemen in forcing open the rear door discovered the body of Jacob Weaver lying in a pool of blood and evidently the victim of a cruel murder. The remains of Jesse Baker were discovered the next day in the ruins of the building, which was nearly destroyed, and hardly a doubt remained that he had also been murdered. It may be mentioned that A. S. Kemball, first engineer of the Union Fire Company, was killed during the progress of the fire by a portion of the wall falling on him. Subsequent investigations into the crime led to the arrest of four negroes named Madison, Brown, Seward and Warrick, who it was shown had been influenced to enter the building by the hope of robbery. They were all convicted of murder in the first degree, and were executed upon the island opposite the lower part of the city, and the four-fold execution became so memorable an event that the time was often alluded to as that "when the negroes were hung."

The Legislature extended the city limits considerably this year, and the Mayor and Aldermen were authorized to divide the city into five wards. At the municipal election in April John D. Daggett was elected Mayor, and in the same month the Planters' House was opened by Messrs. Stickney & Knight as proprietors.

There were now in the city two colleges, the St. Louis University and Kemper College, with a medical school attached to each. The churches were as follows: two Catholic; two Presbyterian; two Episcopal; two Methodist; one Baptist; one Associate Reform Presbyterian; one Unitarian; one German Lutheran, and two for colored congregations. There were two Orphan Asylums, one under the charge of the Sisters of Charity, and one under the control of Protestant ladies. The Sisters' Hospital was in operation, and there were several hotels, the principal of which was the Planters' House; six grist-mills, six breweries, two foundries, and a number of other manufactories of different characters. Steamboat building had also been established as a permanent business, the originators being, it is stated, Messrs. Case & Nelson, and on all sides there were indications that the city was fairly launched on a prosperous career.

Among the prominent events of 1842 were the election of Hon. Geo. Maguire as Mayor, in April, and the laying the corner-stone of the Centenary Church, at the corner of Fifth and Pine streets, on the 10th of May. This edifice long remained a prominent place of worship, but finally, in 1870, was changed into a business establishment. In the autumn of the year the Hon. John B. C. Lucas died, one of the earliest citizens of St. Louis, and who had received from President Jefferson the appointment of Judge of the highest court in Missouri when it was the District of Louisiana. He was a man generally esteemed and respected, and his name is prominently and forever identified with the earlier years of our city. In the spring of the year, the "St. Louis Oak" was turned out from the boat-yard of Captain Irwine, ready to enter into the Galena trade, for which she had been built, and is stated to have been the first steamboat entirely built here, including machinery, engines, etc. In the May term of the St. Louis Criminal Court, the Hon. Bryan Mullanphy, Judge of the Circuit Court, was arraigned for alleged oppression in the discharge of his judicial duties. The matter originated from the Judge having imposed three fines of $50 each on Ferdinand W. Risque, a lawyer. Mr. R., feeling some indignation while in the court room at a certain ruling which was contrary to that he had expected, made some contemptuous gesture or expression of countenance, and the Judge ordered him to be seated, and for each refusal imposed a fine, and finally ordered him to be removed from the court room by the sheriff. Judge Mullanphy was acquitted.

There were now two public schools in St. Louis, one on Fourth, the other on Sixth street, and they were numerously attended, indicating that the people fully appreciated a general system of public instruction. On the third of July the steamer Edna, a Missouri river boat, which had left St. Louis the night before with a large number of emigrants on board, exploded her boiler with terrible results. Fifty-five persons lost their lives by this catastrophe, and there was a large list of injured. Gen. Henry Atkinson died this year at Jefferson Barracks, where his remains were interred. The only other incident we will mention was the murder of Major Floyd, at his residence near the Fair Grounds, on the night of the 10th of August. The crime was perpetrated by a party of five men, who robbed the house and escaped. A young man named Henry Johnson was convicted and executed for the crime, although he solemnly protested his innocence to the last moment.

In March, 1843, Audubon, the French naturalist, visited the city on his way to the Yellow Stone, in the interest of his favorite science. The business of the city improved generally this year, and there was no small activity in commerce and in building. The State Tobacco Warehouse was in course of erection, as well as some sixty stores on Front, Main and Second streets, and some three to four hundred other buildings.

In June, 1844, Macready visited the place, and being then at the highest point of his fame and abilities, he created quite a general local sensation. He was succeeded by Forrest, who divided with him popular admiration. Judge P. Hill Engle died in the early part of the year. A Catholic church of some importance was commenced in Soulard's addition. A most memorable and disastrous rise in the Mississippi took place this year. About the 8th or 10th of June the river commenced to rise rapidly, while intelligence was received of the rising of the Illinois and Missouri rivers. The levee was soon covered, and by the 16th the curb-stones of Front street were under water, and the danger to property and business became quite alarming. At first it was regarded as merely the usual "June rise," but the continued expansion of the flood soon convinced the inhabitants of its unprecedented and alarming character. Illinoistown and Brooklyn were nearly submerged, the occupants of the houses being driven to the upper stories. The American Bottom was a turbid sea. The town of Naples was inundated, boats plying in the streets; and from all places on the rivers came intelligence of heavy losses to stock and property, and the surface of the Mississippi was nearly covered with immense masses of drift trees and other substances torn from the shores. As the reports reached St. Louis that the inhabitants of the towns and villages on the Illinois shore, and other places on the river, were in danger, active measures were taken for their relief. Captain Saltmarsh, of the steamer Monona, particularly distinguished himself by offering the use of his boat gratis. Between four and five hundred persons in St. Louis and vicinity were driven from their homes, and great distress prevailed. To procure means to alleviate this, a meeting of citizens was held in front of the Court House, and a list of committees appointed to obtain subscriptions, and quite a large amount was collected. The river reached its greatest height here on the 24th of June, when it was seven feet seven inches above the city directrix. A few days before this, the glad intelligence was received that the Upper Missouri and Illinois were falling, but the effect was not immediately evident here, and the water did not reach the city directrix in its abatement until the 14th of July. The rise of 1844 obtained a greater elevation than any previous similar event. The great flood of 1785, known as *L'annee des Grandes Eaux,* was surpassed, as were also the floods of 1811 and 1826. The number of buildings erected in 1844 was 1,146, and notwithstanding the misfortune of the great flood, the year was one of general prosperity.

St. George's Episcopal Church was organized in 1845, the Rev. E. C. Hutchinson being pastor. During the summer of this year Col. Wm. Sublette died in Pittsburgh, on his way East for the benefit of his health. He belonged to one of the old families of St. Louis, and his name has been alluded to more than once before in this sketch. In August an election was held for members to the Convention to revise the Constitution, and was attended with much public interest. The City Hospital was commenced, but was not finished in its present form for several years afterward. The erection of Lucas Market was also commenced.

The Mercantile Library Association was formed in 1846, and ultimately led to the erection of the fine building now occupied by them on Fifth street. The originators of the library were John C. Tevis and Robert K. Woods, and the first meeting of citizens in connection with the project was held at the counting room of Mr. Tevis on the evening of December 30, 1846. There were eight gentlemen present, namely: Col. A. B. Chambers, Peter Powell, Robert K. Woods, John F. Franklin, R. P. Perry, Wm. P. Scott, John Halsall and John C. Tevis, all merchants except Col. Chambers. On the 13th of January following, a meeting was held in accordance with a public call, at Concert Hall, and the Association was organized by the adoption of a constitution. On the 16th of February rooms were rented at the corner of Pine and Main streets, and in April it was open to the members. At the end of the first year the cash receipts amounted to $2,689, the members numbering 283, with 1,680 volumes in the library. The association prospered rapidly and finally a joint stock company, designated the Mercantile Library Hall Association, was formed, the main object being the erection of a suitable building for the library. The first president was Alfred Vinton. On the 10th of June, 1851, it was determined to purchase a lot on the corner of Fifth and Locust streets at a cost of $25,500. A design for the building by Robert S. Mitchell was adopted and the present edifice erected. The estimated cost was $70,000, which, with the price of the lot, made the total expenditure $95,500. To illustrate the growth of this noble institution we may add that the present building is now insufficient for its accommodation, and the question of erecting another, fire-proof in character, at a cost of $350,000 is being seriously considered.

On the 10th of January of this year Mrs. Ann Biddle died. She was the daughter of John Mullanphy, who was the possessor of great wealth and had established the male department of the Mullanphy Orphan Asylum, besides being identified with other enterprises of a noble and charitable character. Mrs. Biddle was the widow of Major Biddle, who was killed in the duel with Mr. Pettus on Bloody Island, and shortly after her husband's death established a Female Orphan Asylum, and even surrendered her fine residence on Broadway for religious and charitable purposes. In her will she left an appropriation for a Widows' and Infants' Asylum, whilst her private charities, of which there is no earthly record, are believed to have been very large. The inclosed monument near Tenth and Biddle streets, with its inscription, "Pray for the souls of Thomas and Ann Biddle," is familiar to many of our readers. The spot for the monument was designated by Mrs. Biddle, who bequeathed a sum of money for the purpose of its erection. It is appropriately placed in close contiguity with the noble institutions with which the names of the deceased are identified. The harbor of St. Louis again attracted public attention this year, owing to a sand-bar forming in the river nearly in front of the landing, extending from Duncan's Island nearly to Cherry street, and interruption of commerce became so evident that the municipal and general governments were compelled to take some active measures, which resulted in the removal of the obstructions. An idea of the proportions now assumed by the commerce of the city may be gathered from the fact that in 1845 there were nearly 2,100 steamboats connected with the port, the aggregate tonnage being 358,045, and the number of keel and flat boats was 346.

The war declared between the United States and Mexico created this year an unusual excitement in St. Louis. Numerous volunteers came forward, and the St. Louis Legion, a military organization, prepared for the field. A meeting of citizens was held with the view of raising supplies for the volunteers, and Col. J. B. Brant started a subscription with $1,000, and Lucas Mullanphy, Robert Campbell, Alfred Vinton, Benjamin Stickney and others subscribed liberally, and a few days afterwards the Legion departed for the South, under command of Col. Easton, with a grand public farewell demonstration in their honor. The corner-stone of the Odd Fellows' Hall had been laid April 26th, 1845, and on the 26th of October of this year the building was dedicated.

In the early part of 1847 the Boatmen's Savings Institution was incorporated, and it commenced a career which has proven not only successful, but most beneficial to the public. The most prominent event of this year was the public anniversary celebration, on the 15th of February, of the founding of St. Louis. The grand features of the day were an imposing public pageant and a banquet. At an early hour the various societies and other bodies participating marched to the place of rendezvous, and at ten o'clock the procession moved in the following order: Chief Marshal Col. Thornton Grimsley and his aids, followed by the military companies, and the Apprentices' Library Association bearing banners. Then came the Committee of Arrangements, and next the invited guests, the latter being the most interesting portion of the procession. In an open carriage was seated Mr. Pierre Chouteau, president of the day, and the only survivor of those who accompanied Laclede when he founded the city on the 15th day of February, 1764. The other occupants of this carriage were Pierre Chouteau, Jr., and P. Ligueste Chouteau, his sons, and Gabriel S. Chouteau. In the next carriage were the Hon. Wm. C. Carr, Col. John O'Fallon and Gen. Wm. Milburn, and in other carriages were many others of the old inhabitants of the city. Without further specifying the features of this procession, some of which were highly interesting and unique, illustrating all the industries and trades, we will state that after carrying out the line of march the pageant ceased, and the Hon. Wilson Primm, orator of the day, addressed the multitude from a stand on the east side of Fourth street, fronting the Court House, eloquently reviewing the history of St. Louis from its founding to the date of the celebration. The address was carefully prepared and contained a quantity of valuable historical data not previously, we believe, presented in literary form. The banquet took place in the State Tobacco Warehouse and proved an exceedingly brilliant affair. Among the speakers we may mention Col. L. V. Bogy, Col. Campbell, Hon. Wm. C. Carr, Mr. Thos. Allen, Mr. Crockett, Col. Kennett, Dr. Linton, Mr. Darby, Mr. Treat, George R. Taylor and others. A ball at the Planters' House closed the proceedings of the memorable day. On December 20th of this year the telegraph lines connecting with the East reached East St. Louis, and our city was placed in telegraphic communication with the leading cities of the country. On the 28th of the same month an important meeting of citizens took place, to consider the advisability of the city subscribing $500,000 towards the construction of the Ohio and Mississippi Railroad, the route of which from Cincinnati through Vincennes had been established. A committee of seven, comprising Messrs. Hudson, Gamble, Kennett, Darby, Kayser, Yeatman and Collier, were appointed for the purpose of petitioning the Legislature to authorize the subscription. The measure being supported by a general vote of the people, the subscription was finally made. The two most important agents in the development of commerce—the telegraph and the railroad—were now identified with the growth of St. Louis, and her advancement became accelerated greatly through their influence.

No public events of a very important character mark the year of 1848, but the career of the city, commercially and in reference to general improvements, was satisfactory. On the 22d day of June Edward Charless died in his fiftieth year. His death excited no small amount of public attention and regret, as he was very generally known, having come to this country at a very early period, with his father Joseph Charless. Several public meetings were held in connection with the intelligence of the victorious operations of our arms in Mexico and the exciting reports of the revolutions in France and Germany. Towards the close of the year rumors prevailed of the approach of the cholera, which for more than a year previous had appeared in Europe and subsequently at different points in the United States. A few cases occurred here, and the authorities were stirred up to active sanitary precautions, but the dreaded disease did not develop itself until the ensuing spring. In April, 1849, the Bellefontaine Cemetery was established, the ground being previously known as the "Hempstead Farm," and was purchased from Luther M. Kennett. The names of the trustees mentioned in the act of incorporation are: John F. Darby, Henry Kayser, Wayman Crow, James E. Yeatman, James Harrison, Charles S. Rannells, Gerard B. Allen, Philander Salisbury, Wm. Bennett, Augustus Brewster and Wm. M. McPherson. The cemetery is now one of the most beautiful in the country. This year was one of the most disastrous in the history of St. Louis, owing to the outbreak of the cholera and the occurrence of a terrible conflagration. About ten o'clock on Thursday night, May 19, a fire broke out on the steamer White Cloud, lying at the wharf between Vine and Cherry streets, and the steamboat and fire bells soon spread the alarm throughout the city. The flames rapidly enveloped the steamer, and, notwithstanding vigorous efforts to check their course, communicated to three or four other boats in the vicinity. The White Cloud became loosened from the wharf and drifted down the river with the current, the blazing wreck came in collision with a number of other steamers, and in a short time twenty-three or four boats were in flames. The dreadful disaster did not, however, stop here. A stiff breeze prevailed from the northeast, and an avalanche of fiery embers was whirled over the buildings on the levee, and soon a number of them were in flames. The first which caught fire were near the corner of Locust street, and the conflagration rapidly extending south and westward, assumed the most stupendous proportions, and the utmost excitement and dismay prevailed over the city. Without sketching in detail the devastation of the terrible calamity, we may say that it was by far the most serious of the kind that has ever visited St. Louis. All the buildings, with only a few exceptions, from Locust to Market, and between Second and the river, were destroyed or badly injured, and the progress of the fire was only arrested by blowing up buildings with gunpowder. In one of these explosions Mr. T. B. Targee, the well-known auctioneer, was killed, and several others injured. Twenty-three steamboats, three barges and one canal boat were destroyed, the total value being estimated at about $440,000. The whole value of property destroyed reached over $3,000,000. The occurrence of the fire was a serious blow to our city, but the energy of its citizens was displayed in the manner with which they labored to repair its ravages, and the evidences of desolation and ruin soon disappeared, and new buildings were erected of a more substantial character than the old, and Main street was considerably widened.

We turn from the fire to the second great calamity of the year. As before stated, the coming of the cholera was heralded during the fall of '48, and early in the ensuing spring it reappeared, the number of deaths increasing daily as the summer approached, and in June it assumed a virulent epidemic form and spread dismay throughout the community. At the time of the outbreak of the disease the sanitary condition of the city was exceedingly bad, the present sewer system having hardly been commenced, and most of the alleys were unpaved and in a shockingly dirty condition. When the cholera declared itself the authorities adopted energetic sanitary measures, but without avail, and the mortality increased steadily. As is generally the case, there was a conflict of opinion respecting the disease among the physicians, and at first the medical board pronounced the use of vegetables injurious, and the City Council passed an ordinance prohibiting their sale within the city limits, but this was shortly afterwards revoked. The Council finally, on recommendation of the Committee of Public Health, adopted quarantine regulations, and a site for quarantine was adopted on Arsenal Island. Notwithstanding all the efforts made, the number of deaths increased to over 160 *per diem*, which in a city with a population of less than 64,000 indicates the truly alarming extent of the epidemic. The second day of July was observed as a day of humiliation and prayer, but it was not until late in the month that there was any sensible abatement in the epidemic, and about the middle of August it had nearly disappeared. Between June 25th and July 16th the greatest mortality occurred, and from April 30th to August 6th the total number of deaths from all causes was 5,989, of which 4,060 were from cholera, and among the host of victims were many well-known citizens and several prominent physicians. The disasters of this year seriously interrupted the progress of our city, but their effects were soon repaired, a bountiful harvest was gathered, and with the general improvement of the locality devastated by the fire, business revived and commercial facilities were extended. During the year the immense emigration to California, owing to the discovery of the gold fields and the general impression of the vast wealth and resources of the Far West, brought the project of a great railroad route across the continent prominently before the minds of our people. It was determined to call together a Mass Convention in St. Louis, for the purpose of considering the enterprise, and invitations were sent to the prominent citizens of nearly every State in the Union. The convention assembled on the 15th of October, in the Court House, and was called to order by Judge A. T. Ellis of Indiana. The result of the deliberations was a general conviction of the necessity of the road, and an influential committee was appointed to prepare an address to the people of the Union, soliciting their co-operation in inducing Congress to take the requisite action towards the end desired. It is thus evident that St. Louis citizens were the first to move in the great enterprise of a continental railroad, and there are many living to-day who participated in these preliminary measures, who now witness the practical fulfillment of the stupendous achievement which they inaugurated. The fine building on the corner of Seventh and Myrtle streets, then connected with the medical department of the St. Louis University, was built during this year, and owes its origin to the munificence of

Col. John O'Fallon. Louis A. Labeaume was this year elected Assistant Treasurer of the United States, and his bondsmen were all St. Louis citizens, representing an aggregate wealth of over $6,000,000.

An exciting and bloody affair occurred at the City Hotel on the night of the 29th of October. A day or so before, two unknown gentlemen arrived at the hotel on the corner of Third and Vine streets, then kept by Theron Barnum, and some trouble in reference to accommodations arose between them and Mr. Kirby Barnum, nephew of the proprietor, but it was settled without anything serious having occurred. On the night mentioned, Mr. Kirby Barnum retired to his room, and shortly after a shot was fired through the window, which fatally wounded him, and in attempting to leave the room he fell in the hall. Wm. Albert Jones, who occupied a room on the same floor, on opening his door to ascertain the cause of the firing, was shot dead, and H. M. Henderson and Captain W. D. Hubbell, who were rooming with him, were both wounded. The affair produced intense excitement, and the two strangers, who were Frenchmen named Gonsalve and Raymond Montesque, were accused of the crime. On the first trial the jury did not agree, and at the second, Gonsalve, who had confessed his guilt and alleged "God made him do it," was acquitted on the ground of insanity, and Raymond was shown to be innocent. The only other incident we will mention in connection with the year is the extraordinary robbery at the bank of the State of Missouri, the sum of $120,000 having disappeared from the vaults, but the perpetrators were never discovered.

ST. LOUIS FROM 1850 TO 1870.

The twenty years embraced between 1850 and 1870 were those of the greatest development of the city as well as of the commercial energies of the entire nation. Before that period the growth of St. Louis had been comparatively slow, and although within less than a century an astonishing superstructure had been reared upon the rude foundation laid by Laclede, the real wonders of our city's history were things yet to be achieved. In 1850 the population of the city was about 74,000, less than one-fourth of that of the present. Our railroad system, our iron manufactures, our public institutions in a great measure, our hotels and business palaces, our parks, sewerage system, broad avenues, beautiful private residences, and the other innumerable features and elements which go to make up a great city, were either not in existence or barely commenced. Within two decades, what a magnificent expansion has been wrought! and yet there is no question but it will be greatly exceeded by that of the next twenty years.

In the preceding sketch we have glanced somewhat in detail at the rise and progress of our city from its foundation up to a time within the memory of most of our citizens, but its character will not permit us to continue further the narration of events in chronological order. Our object has been to connect with this book, devoted mainly to the delineation of the destiny of St. Louis, some faint portraiture of her historic past, and it is not our province to pursue the work over later years, with the events of which nearly all are familiar. It is a curious fact that from the year 1849, during which occurred such terrible disasters, may be dated the more rapid development of our city. Forth from the ruins of conflagration and the gloom of the shadow of death, she emerged on a bright and broad career with pulses bounding in exuberant life. It is indeed astonishing to review the mighty steps in civic progress which mark every year in the decades above mentioned. The Railroad Convention held in 1849 was followed quickly by substantial fruits, and on the 4th of July, 1851, ground was broken in the practical commencement of the Pacific Railroad, the company having been organized some time previously through the exertions of such citizens as Thos. Allen, James H. Lucas, Daniel D. Page, John O'Fallon and other public-spirited gentlemen. The following year witnessed the commencement of the Ohio and Mississippi Railroad, also the Terre Haute and Alton; and in 1852 the Chicago and St. Louis Railroad, then called the Alton and Sangamon line, was opened to Carlinville by a public excursion. On the 30th of June, 1855, the Ohio and Mississippi was opened to Vincennes, and on the 4th of July of that year an excursion of citizens took place to the last-named place. Thus our now spendid railroad system was inaugurated, and the rapidity of its development is significantly illustrated when we refer to the list given in another part of this work, by which it is seen we have twenty-four trunk lines converging at St. Louis, nearly all in practical operation, connecting our city with every portion of the country, and sending out daily trains to the Atlantic and Pacific, the great Lakes of the North and the waters of tropical seas. In every other department of business enterprise our progress was equally rapid and steady. Massive business structures sprung up as if by magic along the lines of our leading streets, and with the multiplication of residences the territory of the city increased every day. The splendid Lindell Hotel, commenced in 1857, gave us one of the most important structures of the kind to be found in the country, and until its lamentable destruction by fire in 1867 it formed one of the grand adornments of our city. The beautiful garden at Tower Grove, commenced in 1850, assisted materially the growth of the western part of the city. Other parks and public squares were speedily formed, and the work of street opening and other public improvements were carried on uninterruptedly by the city authorities. Our sewer system was energetically elaborated, and the old method of supplying our citizens with water was supplanted by well-constructed waterworks, which have now again given place to a new system, with settling reservoirs at Bissell's Point and storage reservoir at Compton Hill, constructed at a cost of nearly $4,000,000. The other improvements effected during the period indicated are too numerous to be specifically mentioned. Manufactories of all kinds came into existence in different portions of the city, and the wharf north and south was improved and the elevator was constructed, together with a number of storehouses and warehouses. The public school system, from its small beginnings before mentioned, has expanded to unequaled proportions, and now the enrollment of scholars is nearly 32,000, total number of district schools 41, number of colored schools 6; and besides there are the Normal and High Schools and the departments in connection with the Polytechnic. All of our public school buildings, with perhaps a few exceptions, which will soon be abolished, are handsome, substantial structures, and form a prominent architectural feature in our city. In order, however, to fully appreciate the educational system of St. Louis, we must include also the universities and private schools and public libraries, which perform so important a work for the public. The aggregate, we think, fairly establishes the statement that our facilities for public instruction and the distribution of knowledge are unequaled in proportion by any city of the world.

In December, 1855, a charter was obtained for the St. Louis Agricultural and Mechanical Association, and officers were appointed May 5th, 1856, as follows: J. Richard Barret, President; T. Grimsley, A. Harper and H. C. Hart, Vice Presidents; H. S. Turner, Treasurer; G. O. Kalb, Agent and Recording Secretary, and Oscar W. Collett, Corresponding Secretary. The present site of the Fair Grounds was purchased from Col. John O'Fallon, suitable buildings were erected, and in the fall of 1856 the first fair was held. It proved a most satisfactory success, and so the career of the association was fully inaugurated, and it has resulted in substantial and important benefits to St. Louis. The fairs were interrupted during the exciting and troublous years of the war, but recommenced in 1866, and each year since have increased in interest and attendance, and now transcend any event of the kind in the country. In fact they have ceased to be representative merely of the arts and industries, stock and agricultural products of one State: they are *National* exhibitions, with a premium list of great liberality; and if their future growth correspond with their past, their fame will extend beyond the boundaries of our country, and they will become international in character.

The formation of our system of street railroads corresponds in vigor and rapidity with the general growth of the city during this period. It was not until 1859 that the old omnibus lines began to give place to this improved method of local transportation, and we have now nine or ten separate and distinct lines in full operation, running between 160 and 170 cars and carrying a total of between seven and eight thousand passengers each day.

Among the important public structures erected we may mention the Custom House and Post Office in 1859, John Hogan being the first Postmaster. This building is now inadequate to the wants of the city, and will soon doubtless be replaced by a magnificent structure in a different locality at a probable cost of between two and three millions of dollars.

In 1857 the site was purchased for the Southern Hotel, and the work of excavating was commenced in the following spring. The laying of masonry progressed steadily until December 4th, 1858, when it ceased temporarily, and having been covered to protect it from frost and rain it remained in this condition until April 14th, 1860, when work was resumed and continued until August 15th, 1861, when it was again suspended until June 17th, 1862. The splendid hotel was finally opened to the public September 6th, 1865, the lessees being Messrs. Laveille, Warner & Co., and the establishment representing in federal currency nearly one million and a half of dollars. The scale of the house is indicated by the following items: 17,000 yards of carpeting were required to carpet it, and 1,400 gas-burners to give it light; it has about 350 rooms with over 3,000 feet of corridor; the main one on each story is 257 feet long, with three others crossing it at right angles in length from about 80 to 200 feet. Other fine hotels came into being during the period of which we are speaking, and notwithstanding the destruction of the Lindell the hotel facilities of St. Louis correspond with the wants of the city, and already measures are being discussed for largely increasing them. The Exchange, finished in 1859, is a handsome and imposing building, but will soon be supplanted by one more commensurate with our expanding commerce. The Polytechnic, finished in 1867, is now the stately headquarters of the public school department, while the handsome building of the Masonic Temple, of more recent construction, adds materially to the adornment of the same locality. The County Insane Asylum was commenced in 1865 and finished in April, 1869. It is situated about two miles west of Tower Grove, the justly celebrated place of Mr. Shaw, and the total cost was about $900,000, including the furniture and the expense of boring the artesian well. The capacity of the institution is about 300 patients. The beautiful building of the new jail, now nearly completed, was commenced in 1869, and forms architecturally one of the most attractive public buildings in the city, and reflects great credit on the architect, Mr. Thomas Walsh. The total cost will be about $550,000. The Court House was completed in 1862, and some particulars of its history and cost will be found elsewhere. In mentioning these buildings we have only selected a few instances illustrating the development of the city. Had we space to present a full statement of the various important edifices erected during the last twenty years the list would be lengthened almost indefinitely. Ranges of magnificent stores have been built along our principal streets, almost innumerable church edifices and hospitals, asylums, and other eleemosynary institutions, have arisen in various directions, and there are very few cities on the continent with a greater number of elegant private residences.

In this brief summary of the progress of St. Louis during the last two decades our object has been merely to indicate rather than describe, and we have passed over in silence the scenes and events of the war. From a thriving inland city she has advanced to the proud position of the metropolis of the West, whose architectural and commercial standing is a visible prophecy of her destiny as the future Babylon of the Old and New Worlds. Her past may well be a matter of pride to the people identified with her career, and whose intellectual and nervine force has made her what she is; but more so should be the glorious aggregate that now foreshadows the grander developments to come. Everything speaks of greatness. The mighty arches of steel soon to span our glorious river will form the greatest bridge ever built by man, and over which will pass the trade of more than half the world; our population steadily expands, and the human tide that flows in upon us under the magnetic influence of increasing prosperity seems to know no ebb, the mineral resources of our State have only inaugurated their development, and the smoke of the Carondelet iron furnaces by day and their lurid illumination by night, like the symbol of Divine protection in the olden time to the chosen people, guarantee blessings different but not less real in character, while the vast country westward is filling yearly with busy millions and all tributary to our city. Thus on all hands are promises for the future, and the energies of our people grow more active and concentrated. Is it strange, therefore, that with this unequaled spectacle of human growth before us, these thundering prophetic voices sounding round us, we should believe devoutly that our city is destined to be the Capital of this Nation and the Future Great City of the Globe? It is not an ardent enthusiast that conceives the idea, but a phalanx of solid realities that enunciate it as the sure consummation of their combined power.

ST. LOUIS AND ITS CHARTERS.

The town of St. Louis was first incorporated on the 9th day of November, 1809, by the Court of Common Pleas for the District of St. Louis, upon the petition of two-thirds of the taxable inhabitants, under authority of an act of the Legislature of the Territory of Louisiana, passed June 18th, 1808, entitled "An act concerning towns in this Territory." The Judges constituting the Court were Silas Bent, President, and Bernard Pratte and Louis Labeaume, Associates. The charter granted by the Court was the only one under which the town existed until 1822, when it was incorporated as a city. It is to be found in the records of the Court in Book A, page 334, in the following words:

"On petition of sundry inhabitants of the town of St. Louis, praying so much of said town as is included in the following limits to be incorporated, to-wit: Beginning at Antoine Roy's mill on the banks of the Mississippi river, thence running sixty arpents west, thence south on said line of sixty arpents in the rear until the same comes to the Barriere Denoyer, thence due south until it comes to the Sugar Loaf, thence due east to the Mississippi, from thence by the Mississippi to the place first mentioned. The Court having examined the said petition and finding that the same is signed by two-thirds of the taxable inhabitants residing in said town, order the same to be incorporated and the metes and bounds to be surveyed and marked and a plat thereof filed of record in the Clerk's office." David Delawnay and Wm. C. Carr were appointed Commissioners to superintend the first election of five trustees in accordance with the law.

The next act in reference to incorporation is entitled "An act to incorporate the inhabitants of the town of St. Louis, approved December 9th, 1822." The limits stated in this act are as follows: Beginning at a point in the middle of the main channel of the Mississippi river, due east of the southern end of a bridge across Mill creek, at the lower end of the town of St. Louis; thence due west to a point at which the line of Seventh street extending southwardly will intersect the same; thence northwardly along the western side of Seventh street, and continuing in that course to a point due west of the northern side of Roy's tower; thence due east to the middle of the main channel of the river Mississippi; thence with the middle of the main channel of the said river to the beginning. By this act the town, bounded as above given, was "erected into a city" by the name of the city of St. Louis, and the inhabitants constituted a body politic and corporate under the name and style of the Mayor, Aldermen and Citizens of the City of St. Louis.

An act supplementary to that last mentioned was passed January 15, 1831, but without any alteration of the boundaries. On the 16th of January, 1833, an additional act was passed dividing the city into four wards. On the 26th of February a new charter was passed by the Legislature, which reiterated the boundaries of the act of 1822, but contained new and more specific provisions for municipal government. On February 8, 1839, a new charter was again promulgated by the Legislature, which was much more elaborate than any of the preceding, being divided into articles, a formality not previously observed. This established the boundaries as follows: Beginning at a point in the middle of the main channel of the Mississippi river due east of the mouth of Mill creek (so called); thence due west to the mouth of said creek; thence up the center of the main channel of said creek to a point where the southern side of Rutgers street, produced, shall intersect the same; thence westwardly along the southern side of said street to the intersection of the same with the western line of Seventh street, produced; thence northwardly along the western line of Seventh street to the northern line of Biddle street; thence eastwardly with the northern line of Biddle street to the western line of Broadway, to a point where the southern boundary of survey number six hundred and seventy-one, produced, shall intersect the same; thence eastwardly along the southern boundary of said survey to the Mississippi river; thence due east to the middle of the main channel of the Mississippi river; thence down with the middle of the main channel of said river to the place of beginning.

On the 15th of February, 1841, an act amendatory to the foregoing again changed the boundaries as follows: Beginning at a point in the middle of the main channel of the river due east of the southeast corner of St. George, in St. Louis county; thence due west to the west line of Second Carondelet avenue; thence north with the west line of said avenue to the north line of Chouteau avenue; thence northwardly in a direct line to the mouth of Stony creek, above the then existing north line of the city; thence due east to the middle of the main channel of the Mississippi river, and thence south to the place of beginning.

On February 8, 1843, an act was approved entitled "An act to reduce the law incorporating the city of St. Louis and the several acts amendatory thereof, into one act, and to amend the same." This act did not change the city limits. Another act similar in title to that just mentioned was approved March 3, 1851, but it left the limits as last quoted.

Various supplementary and amendatory acts besides these mentioned were passed in reference to the city, but the next extension of the limits was made by an act specifically for that purpose, which was approved December 5, 1855. This act made the line of Keokuk street the southern boundary of the city, to a point six hundred and sixty feet west of Grand avenue; thence northwardly and parallel to the line of Grand or Lindell avenue at a distance of six hundred and sixty feet therefrom, until the line intersects the Bellefontaine road; thence northeast to the line dividing townships 45 and 46 north, range seven east; thence eastwardly with said line and in the same direction to the middle of the main channel of the Mississippi river; thence southwardly with the meanderings of said channel to place of beginning.

In 1866 the Legislature granted another charter for the city of St. Louis, which divided the city into ten wards but left the boundaries unchanged. The act was approved March 19, 1866.

In 1867 another charter was obtained which added Carondelet to the city by extending the southern limits, but this extension did not go into effect until the first Tuesday in April, 1870. The city proper remained unchanged as to boundaries, and the extension authorized received the designation of the "New Limits." This charter divided the city into twelve wards. It remained unchanged until 1870, when an act was passed by the Legislature entitled "An act to revise the charter of the city of St. Louis and to extend the limits thereof." There was no actual extension of the limits made by this act, but the provisions of the previous charter in reference to the incorporation of Carondelet as part of the city were again enacted, it being provided that for the first five years not more than one-half of the rates of taxes authorized for the old limits should be levied on the property in the "new limits."

This is the existing charter of the city, but whether it will be so or not after the next session of the Legislature is quite problematical. Last winter an important bill was introduced in the House by Mr. W. H. Stone, of the St. Louis delegation, consolidating the governments of St. Louis city and county and extending the limits of the city to include the entire territory of St. Louis county. This bill elicited much attention and comment, but was not acted upon by the Legislature, and will probably come up again for consideration at the session next winter. In some of its details it may be imperfect, but the general extension of limits proposed is advisable and necessary in anticipation of the destined development of the city. Municipal growth is not circumscribed by the invisible lines of corporate authority, but it should not be even slightly retarded by the want of appropriate legislation.

HISTORY OF THE COURT HOUSE.

The Court House building which towers above our city, and gives to it, when viewed from a little distance, an aspect like London with its St. Paul's, is one of the most massive and imposing architectural structures of the kind in the country, and the following historical particulars respecting it will be interesting to our readers:

On the 14th of December, 1822, an act was approved entitled "An act concerning a Court House and Jail in the county of St. Louis," and, in accordance with its provisions, Thomas Sappington of Gravois, Ludwell Bacon of Bonhomme, Robt. Quarles of St. Ferdinand, and Pierre Chouteau, Jr., and Wm. Carr Lane, of the town of St. Louis, were appointed Commissioners to select a proper site within the town of St. Louis, whereon to erect a Court House for said county. The Commissioners were also authorized to receive proposals from all persons willing to make donations of lands for the purpose named, and to accept any donation that might seem to them most beneficial to the county; and to cause a deed of conveyance to be executed, whereby the land so donated should be conveyed to the Justices of the County Court and their successors in office. Under the authority conveyed in this act, the Commissioners named selected the site now occupied by the Court House, which was donated for the purpose by the proprietors, John B. C. Lucas and Auguste Chouteau; the date of the report of the Commissioners being August 25, 1823. It is stated that under the old *regime*, the whipping-post was placed at a point on the site now occupied by the Court House. The first step towards the erection of the building was taken by the County Court on the 9th of November, 1825, the Justices then being Joseph V. Garnier, Peter Ferguson, and Francis Nash; when the sum of $7,000 was appropriated for the purpose, and Alexander Stuart was appointed Commissioner to superintend the work. On the 7th of February, 1826, an additional appropriation in the sum of $5,000 was made, and on the 9th of the same month Mr. Stuart submitted plans for the building, which were approved, the estimate of the cost being $12,000. Some difficulty appears to have occurred relative to the plans adopted, for on May 1, 1826, a plan prepared by Messrs. Morton & Laveille was approved, and $2,000 additional was appropriated. Stuart's plan was apparently thrown overboard, and the contract for the erection was awarded to Joseph C. Laveille and George Morton, for $14,000, and bears date May 26, 1826. At a meeting of the Court, held on July 26th of the same year, Henry S. Geyer was appointed Commissioner to superintend the building of the Court House, vice Alexander Stuart, resigned. This building was completed on the 10th of August, 1833, the entire cost being $14,416.16.

In June, 1838, the public business had so increased, and the necessity for greater accommodations was so evident, that the court asked for proposals for clerks' offices on the southwest corner of the square (Fifth and Market streets), to be 132 feet long by 36 feet in width. In September, 1838, another public notice was given, and an offer of $100 for the best plan for a building on the Public Square, either adjoining the Court House or adjacent thereto. A plan submitted by Henry Singleton on July 8th, 1839, was adopted, and the designer was appointed architect and superintendent. This was really the commencement of the present imposing structure, and the first contract for work was made by Mr. Singleton with Joseph Foster, for the carpenter work, on August 12, 1839, and in April, 1842, a contract for the cut-stone work of the rotunda was awarded to J. H. Hall. The work progressed slowly until 1851, when Robert S. Mitchell was appointed architect and superintendent, and he immediately proceeded to tear down the old building, which stood where the east wing was to be erected, and in October, 1852, contracted with Mr. Bernard Crickard for the cut-stone work for the wing. It was subsequently decided by the Court to have the north and south wings, and on the 28th of May, 1853, Mr. Mitchell contracted with Mr. Crickard for the cut-stone work of the south wing, and in July, 1853, for the six stone columns in the portico of the east wing. In May, 1857, the court superseded Mr. Mitchell and appointed Thomas D. P. Lanham to the office at a remuneration of four per cent. on the amount of work done under his supervision. The County Court was abolished by the Legislature, and on the first Monday in August, 1859, the Board of County Commissioners were elected, and on the 21st of September following the Board declared the office of architect and superintendent vacant, and the day after appointed William Rumbold to the office at a salary of $125 per month. The work from this period progressed with steadiness. The design for the dome prepared by Mr. Lanham was rejected, and the wrought-iron dome devised by Mr. Rumbold was adopted, having been carefully tested, and the contract for the erection awarded to Mr. James McPheeters. Without further pursuing the different steps in the progress of the work, we will state that the splendid building, after the lapse of a quarter of a century from the time of its commencement, was pronounced completed at the beginning of July, 1862.

The cost of the work was as follows:

Cut-stone work	$383,647 05
Other stone work	48,455 91
Iron work	151,342 22
Brick and material	71,115 23
Plastering	21,054 65
Carpentry	146,607 19
Painting and glazing	21,650 13
Roofing	23,825 49
Sundries, labor, material, etc	288,329 71
Architect and superintendent	43,844 33
Total cost	$1,199,871 91

EXECUTIVE OFFICERS OF ST. LOUIS SINCE 1810.

1810	Auguste Chouteau	Chairman.	1841	John D. Daggett	Mayor.
1811	Charles Gratiot	"	1842	George Maguire	"
1812	Charles Gratiot	"	1843	John M. Wimer	"
1813	Charles Gratiot	"	1844	Bernard Pratte	"
1814	Clement B. Penrose	"	1845	Bernard Pratte	"
1815	Elijah Beebe	"	1846	Peter G. Camden	"
1816	Elijah Beebe	"	1847	Bryan Mullanphy	"
1817	Elijah Beebe	"	1848	John M. Krum	"
1818	Thomas F. Riddick	"	1849	James B. Barry	"
1819	Peter Ferguson	"	1850	Luther M. Kennett	"
1820	Pierre Chouteau, Sen	"	1851	Luther M. Kennett	"
1821	Pierre Chouteau, Sen	"	1852	Luther M. Kennett	"
1822	Thomas McKnight	"	1853	John How	"
1823	William Carr Lane	Mayor.	1854	John How	"
1824	William Carr Lane	"	1855	Washington King	"
1825	William Carr Lane	"	1856	John How	"
1826	William Carr Lane	"	1857	John M. Wimer	"
1827	William Carr Lane	"	1858	Oliver D. Filley	"
1828	William Carr Lane	"	1859	Oliver D. Filley	"
1829	Daniel D. Page	"	1860	Oliver D. Filley	"
1830	Daniel D. Page	"	1861	Daniel G. Taylor	"
1831	Daniel D. Page	"	1862	Daniel G. Taylor	"
1832	Daniel D. Page	"	1863	Chauncey I. Filley	"
1833	*Samuel Merry	"	1864	James S. Thomas	"
1834	John W. Johnston	"	1865	James S. Thomas	"
1835	John F. Darby	"	1866	James S. Thomas	"
1836	John F. Darby	"	1867	James S. Thomas	"
1837	John F. Darby	"	1868	James S. Thomas	"
1838	William Carr Lane	"	1869	Nathan Cole	"
1839	William Carr Lane	"	1870	Nathan Cole	"
1840	John F. Darby	"	1871	Joseph Brown	"

* Disqualified in consequence of holding office under the general government. John W. Johnston elected Mayor in his stead.

THE CITY PARKS.

There is no more striking evidence of high civilization than the reproduction in the heart of a great city of the sweet and serene beauties of nature, for it is only true culture that appreciates the fact that the useful and beautiful are combined in a higher sense. How delightful is it to slip from the busy, dusty life of business thoroughfares, into the fragrant, sylvan quietude of a beautiful park! how refreshing to mind and body, reassuring us that no mere mechanical, irrational force has created the maze of buildings we have left behind, but the toiling hands and the practical yet tender and compassionate spirit of enlightened mankind, which, while urging the development of the useful-remembers to foster the beautiful, and the means of pure and health-giving recreation. In St. Louis, while there is no park at present on a scale corresponding with the needs of the community in this respect, this feature of adornment, and we might say necessity, is not lacking. We have a number of parks and some very beautiful ones, and so situated that nearly every section of the city has one contiguous. Lafayette Park is one of the most beautiful places of the kind in the country, and grows more attractive each year. The following table furnishes a glance at the area, situation, etc., of our parks as they exist at present:

NAME OF PARK.	DIMENSIONS.	AREA.	DISTANCE AND DIRECTION FROM COURT HOUSE.
Carondelet Park	600x230 feet.	3 17-100 acres.	4 1-3 miles S. S. West.
Laclede Park	600x230 "	3 17-100 "	3 3-5 miles S. S. West.
Gravois Park	600x600 "	8 252-1000 "	3 1-2 miles Southwest.
Lafayette Park	1142x1142 "	29 956-1000 "	1 1-2 miles Southwest.
Washington Square	792x330 "	6 "	3-8 of a mile W. (7 blocks).
Missouri Park	508x336 "	3 346-1000 "	3-5 of a mile W. N. W.
Carr Square	372x305 "	2 607-1000 "	9-10 of a mile Northwest.
Jackson Place	300 feet diameter.	1 622-1000 "	1 2-3 miles Northwest.
Clinton Place	300 " "	1 622-1000 "	1 2-3 miles Northwest.
Marion Place	300 " "	1 622-1000 "	1 2-3 miles Northwest.
St. Louis Place	2320x300 feet.	15 303-1000 "	2 miles Northwest.
Hyde Park	789x690 "	11 833-1000 "	2 1-2 miles N. N. West.
Exchange Square	1180x560 6-12 "	15 18-100 "	1 3-4 miles North.
Tower Grove Park	1180x7458 "	276 76-100 "	3 1-2 miles Southwest.
Benton Park	605x1060 "	15 50-100 "	1 1-2 miles S. S. West.
		395 94-100 acres.	

Tower Grove Park will be opened to the public during the present year.

THE ST. LOUIS PARK OF FRUITS.

With other works of magnitude, begun and in progress by the business men of St. Louis, is a great Park of Fruits, destined to extend over one thousand acres. From the annual address of its able originator and superintendent, Mr. C. H. Haven, to the members of the Association, we take pleasure in extracting the following remarks, showing it to be in truth "the creation of the first park of the kind in the United States, of such an extent and usefulness, when completed, as will make it a matter of pride as well as profit to all concerned in its formation. The originality of, as well as benefit derived from this work, consist in possessing, as we now do, in the cultivated grounds of our first or Missouri River division, and in determining to have, on the beautiful site of our second or Pacific Railroad division, all the accessories of a park of flowers, such as avenues, drives, seats, etc., but distributed *among fruits of every description, instead of flowers,* while such a park, through the invitations given by our members, will be visited by and attract men of capital, and valuable emigration from all countries desirous of ascertaining, from actual observation, the worth and productiveness of the upland counties of our State, which form the nearest back-country to St. Louis for one hundred and fifty miles south and west of her; which counties should be the first to be settled, on account of the home trade it will give rise to, amounting to several millions of dollars annually, and which can never be diverted to any other point.

"Such a park, we submit, will be of lasting benefit to St. Louis, while it will become the favorite resort of our members and their families forever when seeking health and recreation, or when desirous of obtaining, fresh from our vines and fruit trees, their valuable products, or from our cellars the pure wines stored therein. There are now 437 members of the Association."

STREET RAILWAYS IN ST. LOUIS.

In 1843 Erastus Wells, now our respected and valuable Representative in Congress from the First District, and Calvin Case, established the first omnibus in St. Louis, the rolling stock consisting of one omnibus. It differed considerably from the kind now in use, having no glass windows but curtains instead, and elliptic springs in place of the present low flat ones, and was built in this city at a cost of $200. The route was from Third and Market, along Third and Broadway to North Market street; and the receipts for the first six months did not exceed $2.50 per day. In 1844 the enterprising proprietors put on another coach, and within five years increased their business considerably, and had from twelve to fifteen busses running, and for the first two years Mr. Wells drove one of them himself. In 1844 Michael Sutter started a line on Second street and Carondelet avenue, running from Market street to the Arsenal. During the ensuing year Mr. M. Kounts established a line on Market street, running between Main street and Camp Spring; the same year T. O. Duncan and John C. Vogel started a line on Franklin avenue, between Broadway and Twenty-fifth street, having purchased for the purpose from Case & Wells their pioneer omnibus for $100. In 1846 Luther Case commenced a line on Fourth and Seventh streets, between Green street and Flora Garden. In 1850, Calvin Case, Erastus Wells, Robert McO'Blenis, and Lawrence Mathews, forming the firm of Case & Co., purchased all the lines in the city, and established a coach line between here and Belleville, Ill., and subsequently one on Olive street between Fourth and Seventeenth streets. In January, 1856, the copartnership was dissolved by the death of the senior member, who was killed in the memorable accident on the Pacific Railroad, at the Gasconade bridge. The different lines were owned and operated by the surviving partners, but separately, until 1859, when the street railway mania reached St. Louis, and the omnibuses were speedily superseded.

The St. Louis, Missouri, Citizens' and People's Railway Companies were formed in the spring of 1859, and the first company that started their cars was the Missouri, on their Olive street line, on July 4, 1859. The first President was Erastus Wells, who has filled that position up to the present time. They have now nine miles of track. The St. Louis commenced operations during the same summer, and has now fifteen miles of track; D. H. Armstrong was the first President. The People's Line commenced running in the autumn of the same year; Col. R. M. Renick, President, and has now six miles of track. The Citizens' got under way in August, 1859; B. Gratz Brown, President, with six miles of track. In 1862 the Union Railway started; B. Gratz Brown, President, and with six miles of track. In 1864 the Tower Grove & Lafayette Company commenced running; R. M. Renick, President, and seven miles of track. The Lindell Railway Company got under way in 1866; Dwight Durkee, President, with nine miles of track. The same year the Bellefontaine Railway Company went into operation; Mr. Krum, President, and six miles of track. The Suburban Railway Company was started in 1860; A. R. Easton, President, and four miles of track. The total length of street railway in St. Louis is about 70 miles, and from 160 to 170 cars are employed each day, carrying from six to seven thousand passengers. Not less than 1,400 horses are required in the business of these lines, and over 500 men are constantly employed. It is thus seen that the increase in this line of business has fully corresponded with the general growth of the city. Twenty-eight years ago there was one omnibus running, carrying not more than fifty passengers per diem; now we have nine distinct lines, each doing a prosperous business and representing a large amount of invested capital. There is something appropriate and fitting in the fact that the man who was mainly instrumental in laying the foundation of this extensive business is now one of the representatives of St. Louis in Congress. Mr. Wells is a prominent representative of the self-made men of the West. His career has been valuable in many ways to St. Louis, and his political elevation is an evidence that his fellow-citizens appreciated his worth, and his earnest labors in behalf of the city.

STREET IMPROVEMENTS, ETC., IN ST. LOUIS.

The following particulars have been obtained from the office of the City Engineer: Total length of street pavement in St. Louis, 174 miles; total length of sidewalk pavement in St. Louis, (about) 300 miles; total length of wharf pavement (11½ miles river front), 2½ miles; total length of water-pipe laid in St. Louis, 102 miles; total length of sewers in St. Louis, 117 miles; total number of streets, 600. The total length of public sewers in the city is 24½ miles; total cost, $1,730,389.08. Total length of district sewers, 92½ miles; total cost, $1,948,000.

PUBLIC SCHOOL SYSTEM.

The vast importance of our system of public instruction renders the following *resume* of general interest in addition to what has already been said:

In 1812 Congress passed an act setting apart certain vacant lands in the Territory of Missouri, situated in or adjoining to St. Louis, St. Charles and other settlements, for the support of schools in those "towns and villages." Other acts amendatory and supplementary to this were passed in 1824 and 1831. Out of these grants a large school fund for St. Louis, amounting to upwards of $2,000,000, has accumulated. Adding to this the value of property in use for school purposes, we have a total of $3,500,000 permanent investment for the city schools, and under the management of the corporate body known as the Board of President and Directors of Public Schools in St. Louis. The Board has not only the sole and exclusive control of the public schools and the school funds, but it possesses also the power of levying and collecting a city tax not exceeding one-half of one per cent. With these ample means at its disposal it has built up a magnificent system of schools, furnishing free education to the youth of the city in all the branches required, from the lowest primary grades up to the finished education for the man of business.

In 1860, when the population of St. Louis was 160,773, the number of pupils in the public schools was 11,563; in 1870, with a population of 310,864, the number had increased to 24,347. This increase took place during a decade in which war nearly broke up the schools for a considerable period. It will be noted that the per cent of the entire population in the public schools had increased during the decade from seven per cent. in 1860, to eight per cent. in 1870, notwithstanding the immense increase of the city.

The rate of increase for the present year (1870–1871) is still greater, and testifies to the efficient management and growing popularity of the system of public schools as well as to the growth of the city.

For the year ending June 1871, the number of pupils enrolled in the day schools	28,283
Pupils enrolled in evening schools	3,609
Total	31,892

Total number of teachers	548
Total number of separate schools, including one Normal School, one High School, six colored schools, forty-one district schools	49

About 1,600 of the pupils were enrolled in colored schools (held in separate buildings).

Most of the schools have German taught in them by competent teachers, so that pupils of German parentage may attend the public schools without the danger of losing the knowledge of their native tongue while they acquire the English.

A flourishing Public School Library, containing upwards of twenty-five thousand well-selected books, is a novel feature in the system, but is a great practical success. Children learn how to read and what to read, and continue the habits learned in school through life.

MISSOURI SCHOOL STATISTICS.

TABLE *showing the Number of Schools, Universities, &c., Teachers and Pupils in the State, also the Income Supporting Public Instruction.*

	No. of Schools.	TEACHERS.		PUPILS.		Endowment.	Taxation.	Public Funds.	Other sources and tuition.
		Male.	Female.	Male.	Female.				
CLASSICAL	78	260	309	4,891	5,281	$27,821	$957	$2,160	$404,595
Universities	2	39	13	589	170	10,000	......	......	75,000
Colleges	32	130	56	2,618	2,039	17,300	957	160	153,825
Academies	44	82	240	1,684	3,072	521	......	2,000	175,770
PROFESSIONAL	26	102	8	1,200	297	10,800	......	......	126,400
Law	1	6	......	30	1	......	......	......	3,000
Medicine	7	67	......	286	......	......	......	......	24,800
Theology	2	6	......	68	......	10,800	......	......	......
Technological.									
Schools of Mining*	1	......	......	......	......	......	......	......	......
Schools of Art	1	......	2	1	15	......	......	......	800
Other Schools of art and music	8	4	6	75	126	......	......	......	57,000
Commercial	6	19	......	740	155	......	......	......	40,800
Military.									
PUBLIC SCHOOLS	5,867	4,349	2,860	159,279	152,017	2,300	2,231,303	560,839	63,070
Normal	3	7	10	75	172	300	2,435	194	1,700
High	45	63	54	2,570	2,864	......	38,817	7,608	23,418
Grammar	42	35	42	1,461	1,638	1,000	35,318	4,830	11,078
Graded, Common	337	218	717	23,782	26,865	1,000	693,405	121,970	8,410
Ungraded, Common	5,440	4,026	2,037	131,391	120,478	......	1,461,328	426,237	18,464
PRIVATE SCHOOLS	567	277	478	11,440	14,506	......	20,000	......	484,576
Day	531	238	401	10,827	13,003	......	......	......	379,211
Boarding	33	34	72	467	1,414	......	......	......	102,865
Parochial	1	2	......	100	......	......	......	......	2,000
Charity	1	......	1	......	50	......	......	......	500
School of Instruction for Blind	1	3	4	46	39	......	20,000	......	......
Total	6,460	4,728	3,316	171,919	166,820	13,100	2,251,303	560,839	674,046

* Not yet organized.

The rapid growth of Missouri and St. Louis is not confined alone to the developments of their material interests, but extends with equal encouragement to every department of activity and improvement. Considering the great embarrassments imposed by four years of blighting war, education has in spite of an impoverished treasury made rapid advances.

In 1860 there were in the State 4,120 public schools which were attended by 175,855 pupils. By the census returns for 1870, as seen above, there are now 5,867 public schools in the State, which are attended by 311,296 pupils.

POPULATION.

TABLE *showing the Census of the City of St. Louis according to Nationalities and Color.*

BORN IN UNITED STATES.

STATES.	White.	Colored.	Indians.
Alabama	426	559	
Arkansas	246	274	
California	123	1	1
Connecticut	628	6	
Delaware	231	11	
Florida	56	28	
Georgia	340	205	
Illinois	6,720	174	7
Indiana	2,439	32	
Iowa	1,424	26	
Kansas	278	9	
Kentucky	3,706	2,010	
Louisiana	1,882	611	
Maine	712		
Maryland	1,502	174	
Massachusetts	2,542	27	
Michigan	746	66	
Minnesota	145	8	1
Mississippi	554	911	2
Missouri	121,931	12,281	9
Nebraska	58	1	
Nevada	1	1	
New Hampshire	343	3	
New Jersey	955	8	
New York	9,250	38	
North Carolina	190	243	
Ohio	6,880	362	
Oregon	2		
Pennsylvania	5,878	210	2
Rhode Island	150	3	
South Carolina	150	148	
Tennessee	1,439	1,764	
Texas	129	89	
Vermont	578	4	
Virginia	2,235	1,647	1
West Virginia	45	9	
Wisconsin	660	8	
District of Columbia	251	30	
TERRITORIES.			
Alaska			
Arizona			
Colorado	20	1	
Dakota	5	1	
Idaho			1
Indian	5		
Montana	9		4
New Mexico	27	9	
Utah	18		
Washington	4		
Wyoming	1		

BORN IN FOREIGN COUNTRIES.

COUNTRIES.	White.	Colored.	Indians.	Chinese.
Africa	7	8		
Asia	27	1		
Atlantic Islands	3			
Australia	27			
Austria	751			
Belgium	254			
Bohemia	2,652			
British America:				
Canada	1,841	16	6	
N. Brunswick	58			
Newfoundland	4			
Nova Scotia	74			
Brit'h America, not specified	9			
Total Brit. America				
Central America	4	1		
China				
Cuba	17	1		
Denmark	178			
England	5,366			
Europe, not specified	94	8		
France	2,788			
Germany:				
Baden	5,881			
Bavaria	6,430			
Brunswick	269			
Hamburg	310			
Hanover	8,858			
Hessen	4,849			
Lubec	9			
Mecklenburg	186			
Nassau	482			
Oldenburg	220			
Prussia	24,269			
Saxony	1,775			
Weimar	3			
Wurtemburg	2,566			
Germany, not specified	2,933			
Total Germany	59,040			
Great Britain, not specified	5			
Greece	2			
Holland	643			
Hungary	126			
Ireland	32,239			
Italy	785			
Mexico	25	5	2	
Norway	67			
Pacific Islands	1			

POPULATION—*Continued.*

BORN IN UNITED STATES.

STATES.	White.	Colored.	Indians.
At sea under United States flag	1	....	......
Not stated	625	53	2
Total U. S.	176,540	22,045	30

RECAPITULATION.

Total Whites	288,737	
" Colored	22,088	
" Indians	38	
" Chinese	1	
" Natives		198,615
" Foreign		112,249
Grand total	310,864	310,864

BORN IN FOREIGN COUNTRIES.

COUNTRIES.	White.	Colored.	Indians.	Chinese.
Poland	292	......	......	......
Portugal	14	......	......	......
Russia	86	......	......	......
Sandwich Islands	1	......	......	......
Sardinia	1	......	......	......
Scotland	1,202	......	......	......
South America	15	2	......	......
Spain	45	......	......	......
Sweden	237	......	......	......
Switzerland	2,949	......	......	......
Turkey	2	......	......	......
Wales	147	......	......	......
West Indies	74	1	......	......
At sea	45	......	......	......
Not stated	....	......	......	......
Total foreign	112,197	43	8	1

By the census of 1860 the total foreign-born population of the county was 96,086. The colored population then consisted of 1,865 free and 4,346 slave, the total population of the county being 190,524.

TABLE *showing the White and Colored Population of St. Louis County.*

ST. LOUIS COUNTY.	White.	Colored.	Indian.	Chinese.	Native.	Foreign.	Total.
Bonhomme	5,304	858	...	...	4,704	1,458	6,162
Central	8,120	803	...	...	6,017	2,906	8,923
Carondelet	5,000	297	...	...	3,609	1,778	5,387
Meramec	2,853	583	...	...	2,705	731	3,436
St. Ferdinand	6,262	952	...	...	5,346	1,868	7,214
St. Louis	8,395	805	3	...	5,817	3,386	9,203
ST. LOUIS	288,705	22,117	38	...	188,608	112,256	310,864
First Ward	32,099	1,607	2	...	23,389	10,319	33,708
Second Ward	21,295	580	...	...	12,166	9,689	21,855
Third Ward	23,109	754	15	...	13,341	10,537	23,878
Fourth Ward	36,633	2,538	2	...	26,363	12,810	30,173
Fifth Ward	26,257	3,510	7	...	19,624	10,150	29,774
Sixth Ward	20,408	1,104	...	...	15,116	6,396	21,512
Seventh Ward	16,875	1,630	3	...	12,603	5,105	18,508
Eighth Ward	19,659	7,051	...	...	18,600	8,110	26,710
Ninth Ward	22,268	649	1	4	13,368	9,574	22,922
Tenth Ward	19,430	1,173	...	...	12,298	8,325	20,623
Eleventh Ward	31,885	687	8	...	19,018	13,562	32,580
Twelfth Ward	18,787	834	...	...	12,722	6,899	19,621
	324.729	26,415	41	4	226,806	124,383	351,189

LATITUDE AND LONGITUDE OF THE CITY OF ST. LOUIS.

The following is the report of Prof. Hilgard, of the Coast Survey, on the observations made to determine the exact geographical position of St. Louis, and which demonstrates the same to be sufficiently central for the National Capital or the emporium of all nations :

LATITUDE AND LONGITUDE OF THE OBSERVATORY AT WASHINGTON UNIVERSITY, ST. LOUIS, MISSOURI.

The observations of the southern limit of totality of the solar eclipse which occurred on August 7, 1869, having been made at a point near St. Louis, by a party under the direction of Major J. Pitzman, County Surveyor of St. Louis county, it became important to ascertain with precision the geographical position of that point, in order that by comparison with a corresponding point of observation on the northern limit, the position of the central line of eclipse and the apparent diameter of the moon might be inferred.

It was judged advisable to make the requisite observations of latitude and longitude at some point within the city and refer the eclipse station to the same by triangulation, both on account of the convenience of observers and because the geographical position of St. Louis had never been before ascertained with precision. Arrangements were therefore made with the officers of the Washington University, in pursuance of which piers for the instruments of the Coast Survey were erected by them on the grounds of the university, and a temporary building was put up over them at the expense of the Coast Survey.

The observations for latitude were made in December, 1869, by Mr. O. H. Tittmann, of St. Louis, aid in the Coast Survey, with a 28-inch zenith telescope by twenty-six observations upon nine pairs of stars. The resulting latitude is 38 deg. 38 min. 3.2 sec.

The following are the individual results, arranged in the order of magnitude, and the successive means of the greatest and least, and so on :

38 deg. 38 min.	0.3 sec.	5.9 sec.	3.10 sec.	38 deg. 38 min.	2.1 sec.	4.4 sec.	3.25 sec.
	1.0	5.3	3.15		2.2	4.2	3.20
	1.1	5.0	3.05		2.3	4.1	3.20
	1.3	4.7	3.00		2.7	4.0	3.25
	1.5	4.7	3.10		2.9	3.7	3.30
	1.7	4.7	3.20		3.1	3.6	3.35
	2.1	4.5	3.30				

From the accordance of which we infer by the calculus of probabilities that the resulting mean value has no greater uncertainty than two-tenths of a second of arc.

The observations for longitude were deferred until the following April on account of the unfavorable season. They were made by Prof. Wm. Eimbeck, of St. Louis, in conjunction with the United States Observatory at Washington.

At St. Louis the instruments used were a 26-inch transit and sidereal chronometer, the correction of which was determined by the observation of not less than 17 stars on each night.

After star observations, the chronometer was compared by coincidences of beat with another chronometer going to mean time, which was then carried to the telegraph office, whence signals, coincident with its beats, were sent to Washington, and recorded on the chronograph at the United States Observatory, on which the beats of the sidereal clock were at the same time registered. Next, the Washington clock was put into the circuit, and its beats, repeated at St. Louis, noted by coincidences with those of the mean time chronometer, which was finally carried back to the observatory, and again compared with the siderial chronometer, in order to make certain that no derangement had taken place during transportation.

The observations at Washington were made by Professor Wm. Harkness, U. S. N., with the 12-feet telescope of the transit circle.

The following are the results of four different nights on which observations were obtained at both places, and signals successfully exchanged:

St. Louis.	West of Washington.
April 12	52m 36.92
" 23	36.89
" 26	36.95
" 30	36.97
Mean	52m 36.93

The greatest difference from the mean is 0.04 or one twenty-fifth part of a second.

The difference in time or longitude between the two places derived from the signals sent *eastward* will appear too *small* by the length of time required for the transmission of signals along the telegraph wire and through the repeating and recording instruments, and too *large* by the same amount from the signals sent *westward*. The effect disappears in the mean of the two comparisons, and half their difference measures the time of transmission, which, in the present case, was 0.16, or about one-seventh of a second of time.

In order to ascertain the personal equation between the two observers, Professor Eimbeck subsequently proceeded to Washington, and observed the time at a point in the meridian of the transit circle, with the transit and chronometer used at St. Louis, and compared his time so obtained with that observed by Professor Harkness, with the transit circle and chronograph in the same manner in which the comparison had previously been made when observing at St. Louis. It was thus ascertained that Eimbeck was on the average later than Harkness by 0.08 sec., by which amount the longitude above given must be diminished. At the same time, the transit circle being 0.07 sec. west of the center of the observatory to which the longitudes are referred, we must add that quantity and obtain finally for the longitude of the station in St. Louis west of Washington 52 min. 36.92 sec., which value is not uncertain more than two-hundredths of a second. The Washington Observatory being 5 hours 8 minutes 12.0 seconds west of Greenwich, we obtain for the station in St. Louis 6 hours 00 minutes 48.92 seconds.

In order to reduce the observed values to the center of Court House, we must deduct from the latitude 25.7 seconds, and from the longitude 3.63 seconds, so that we have finally for the Court House of St. Louis:

	Deg.	Min.	Sec.
Latitude	38	37	37.5
	H.	M.	S.
Longitude	6	0	45.29
	Deg.	Min.	Sec.
Or in arc.	90	11	19.35

The public are indebted to the Western Union Telegraph Company for the free use of their lines, kindly granted through General Anson Stager, Superintendent of the Western Division, for the purpose of the foregoing determinations. Special acknowledgment is due to Mr. M. D. Crain, of the Western Union telegraph office in St. Louis, for his assistance in the transmission of signals and messages, which was rendered gratuitously, as was all the arduous and long-continued work of Professor Eimbeck.

J. E. HILGARD,
In charge of Coast Survey office.

THE WATER SUPPLY.

In a different portion of this work we have spoken of the water supply of St. Louis, and described the new and extensive system of waterworks now in successful operation, and we have to add only some statements respecting the quality of the water used by our people. The Mississippi river is not only the source of the prosperity of our city, more than any other agency, but as it supplies the water necessary for the inhabitants, and consumed in the various industrial processes, it is the perennial and essential fountain of individual and commercial life. The discolored appearance of the water as ordinarily taken from the river, very naturally creates the impression that its use must be prejudicial to health, although even a stranger must admit its peculiar sweetness and purity of taste. The fact, however, is now fully demonstrated, alike by practical experience and scientific analysis, that this water is excellently adapted for human use, and that in mingling its yellow flood with the Mississippi, the Missouri river has in nowise deteriorated, but rather improved, the quality and wholesomeness of the original stream. Contrary to the popular idea upon the subject, clearness in river water forms rather an objection than a recommendation for its general use. The Wabash and Illinois rivers are clear, but the water is inferior in quality to that of the Missouri, and the people living on the Meramec bottom do not use the water of that river, although clear, but supply their wants from other sources. Among sailors, the water obtained from the river at New Orleans is in high repute, and they say that it and the water of the Nile are the best in the world for long sea voyages, keeping fresh and sweet during periods when that obtained from other sources is almost unfit for use. One reason assigned for the preservative qualities is, that the Missouri river water, flowing down from the snow mountains, is too cold for animalcula to live in it, and being free from vegetable matter, and with a current so swift that stagnation is impossible, and rarely overflowing the banks except in high floods, there is nothing mingling in it that can contaminate, while the confluence of the various tributaries only increases the admixture of sand and alluvial without adding any elements calculated to deteriorate. The Missouri or Mississippi water is, consequently, excellently adapted for human use, while the attractiveness of perfect clarity can be secured by the cheap and simple process of letting the sediment settle before use, so that this one objection is easily removed. Nearly every person who has once become accustomed to the use of our river water prefers it to any other on account of its constant sweetness and freshness of taste, and even in the country, the people living on the Missouri river prefer the river water for drinking to that which they can obtain elsewhere. It is said of Col. Benton, when in Congress, that he had his drinking water at one time shipped from St. Louis to Washington. The superior quality of this water has been frequently tested, and our fellow-citizen, Mr. Easterly, daguerrean artist, whose business demands the purest water, has bestowed some careful labor on the subject with very satisfactory results. We present the following interesting statements prepared by that gentleman for publication more than two years ago:

"Allow me, as a party interested, to call attention to a few facts that have come under my own observation in relation to the much abused water of the Mississippi. In the winter of 1844, I made the trip by sea from New York to New Orleans, on the packet ship Mississippi. Our commander was Capt. Hillard, who was saved from the burning steamer Lexington, on Long Island Sound, by lashing himself to a bale of cotton. He was a man noted for coolness in danger, and strictly truthful on all subjects. The captain assured me that the water we were drinking was taken on board the ship at New Orleans, had made the trip from there to Liverpool with a cargo of cotton, from Liverpool to New York, and was then on its way back to New Orleans. He said that they had taken water on board at Brooklyn, New York, but that it was not so good. He also told me that the Mississippi water would keep longer at sea than any water known to sea-faring men, and next in quality was the water obtained at Brooklyn. In a later conversation with the mate, he confirmed all that the captain had said on the subject. We used ice in the water most of the time, and I confess that to my taste it was as pure as the water from my native hills in Vermont.

"Capt. Hillard's statement induced me to further investigate the subject, and in the summer of 1847, by way of experiment, I filled a five-gallon stone jar from the hydrant, and placed it in a small hall-room in the fourth story of Glasgow's row, then over the Mercantile Library Hall. The room was closed for two and a half months from the first of June, and the hot sun poured in at the east window at will. At the end of this period the water was found on examination to be perfectly clear and pure to the taste, except that it was warm. I drank of it freely and frequently, and no bad result followed.

"On the 20th of June, 1850, I started on a pleasure trip to the falls of St. Anthony, on the steamer Anthony Wayne, the first steamer that ever made a landing at the Falls. Between St. Louis and the mouth of the Missouri river I filled a five-gallon demijohn with water from the current of the river, placed it on the upper deck of the steamer, where it would be most exposed to the weather and hot sun, in which condition it remained until we again reached St. Louis, which was fifteen days from the time of starting. I then subjected it to the weather and sun as much as possible until the middle of November. I then bottled a portion of it, and have it now, subject to the inspection of the scientific and curious. It is now nearly seventeen years old, clear, pure and sweet to the taste, and has never undergone the process of fermentation which some believe necessary to the purification of water. I will here state that the sand was allowed to settle of itself without the aid of any of the articles sometimes used for clearing the water, all of which will cause it to taint, except alum.

"In 1866 I used a saturated solution of alum in the proportion of one fluid ounce to eight gallons of water, and, on applying our test for daguerreotype uses, found the water sufficiently pure for all practical purposes; and to finish a daguerreotype on silver plate, we must have pure water, especially for removing the gilding solution, which is the last washing. The test (well known to every chemist and druggist in the country) is a few grains of nitrate of silver in a small quantity of water, and if pure no change is perceptible, but if impure the water will change color or turn milky. Let the water settle without the aid of alum, and the nitrate of silver will change the color to a milky appearance on account of the lime in the water, but with the alum in proper quantity, no perceptible change takes place—a proof that the water is pure, or as nearly so as water can be when exposed to the atmosphere. We now use it for chemical purposes where we once thought distilled water indispensable.

"It is a well-known fact that all or nearly all of the spring and well water in the West will taint by standing twenty-four hour in a bucket or pitcher, while the Mississippi water will get warm, but remain sweet to the taste for days and months, in a clean vessel."

The most recent analysis of our river water is that made by Dr. Theodore Fay, chemist of the Board of Water Commissioners, which is given in the following form, exhibiting the comparative quality of the water obtained from the old and new reservoirs:

Water drawn from Hydrant (Old Supply).

Solid matter separated by filter	232	grains per gallon.
Hardness	7.05	
Oxydizable organic matter	.504	grains per gallon.
Carbonate of lime	5.60	" " "

Settled Water drawn from Hydrant (New Supply).

Hardness	8.75	
Oxydizable organic matter	.784	grains per gallon.
Carbonate of lime	7.17	" " "

Animalcula in considerable number.

Dr. Fay, in connection with the above, makes the following explanation:

"The above statement in regard to the difference in organic matter and hardness is hardly a fair test, on account of the excess of time that the water remained exposed to the sun, and solution of a portion of the lime used in the construction of the reservoirs and culverts, in which many thousands of bushels have been used. It is my opinion that we will have as good water from the Mississippi as any in the United States when the clay and sand are removed."

In view of these considerations, and others which they suggest, the question of the water supply for St. Louis is finally and satisfactorily settled. In this, as in other essential elements, Nature has prophetically provided for the great destiny of our city.

HEALTHFULNESS OF ST. LOUIS.

The statistics recently presented in the able report of Dr. Wm. L. Barrett, Health Officer, fully demonstrate the healthfulness of St. Louis as a place of residence. The following official table shows conclusively that the death-rate here is below that of any of the important cities of the country.

PRINCIPAL CITIES.	Population, United States Census, 1870.	Deaths in 1870	Ratio of Deaths per 1000 of Population.
New York	927,436	27,175	29.3
Philadelphia	657,179	16,750	25.5
St. Louis	312,963	6,670	21.3
Chicago	299,370	7,342	24.5
Baltimore	267,599	7,262	27.1
Boston	253,984	6,096	24.0
New Orleans	184,688	6,942	37.6
San Francisco	150,361	3,351	22.3

The following official tables also contain some interesting statistics respecting population and mortality, &c.

TABLE *showing the Population, Mortality and per centage of same by Wards; the Area, Sewerage and Population according to the number of Acres in each Ward.*

	NUMBER OF DEATHS DURING												Total.	Population.	Per cent. of Mortality.	Area in Acres.	Average Population per Acre.	NO. OF ACRES.	
	January.	February.	March.	April.	May.	June.	July.	August.	September.	October.	November.	December.						Drained.	Not Drained.
First Ward	39	44	44	40	34	49	86	61	60	48	37	35	540	34,008	1.58	4,884	1.58	67	4,817
Second "	48	52	50	43	31	46	67	51	58	51	40	41	578	12,155	2 60	950	23.32	133	817
Third "	50	37	44	39	40	50	86	46	50	51	42	43	577	24,178	2.38	580	41.68	179	401
Fourth "	43	36	39	34	29	48	60	45	48	54	34	47	517	38,873	1.32	850	45.73	238	612
Fifth "	46	34	38	35	29	39	67	48	50	57	44	41	528	30,074	1.75	550	54.68	196	354
Sixth "	43	31	36	31	31	45	61	46	45	53	33	39	494	20,013	2.46	650	32.31	410	240
Seventh "	47	41	42	36	38	48	60	53	51	51	38	47	562	18,601	3.	480	38 85	313	167
Eighth "	48	42	35	36	42	54	61	67	53	52	40	41	581	26,910	2.16	210	132.90	200	10
Ninth "	53	46	53	48	46	64	67	75	55	53	39	39	648	22,322	2.41	420	53.14	165	255
Tenth "	49	49	42	47	48	63	82	64	58	45	48	35	641	20,923	3.06	270	77.49	153	117
Eleventh "	41	36	35	38	34	49	65	47	44	48	32	41	531	32,786	1.61	1,000	32.78	159	841
Twelfth "	40	29	30	29	27	41	63	43	38	51	37	43	473	20,021	2.36	1,460	13.80	54	1,396
Total	547	477	488	456	429	591	848	646	610	615	464	494	6,670	312,963	2.12	12,294	48 27	2,267	10,027

TABLE *of Population, Increase, Mortality, &c., in the City of St. Louis, from 1847 to 1870 inclusive.*

YEAR.	Population.	Increase of Population.	Mortality.	Per cent. of Mortality	REMARKS.
1847...	47,974	....	....	......	
1849..	63,471	15,494	8,423	13.27	Year of the cholera.
1851...	74,438	10,967	4,361	5.99	
1853...	84,116	9,678	3,766	4.38	
1855...	95,542	13,426	5,122	5.25	
1856...	121,813	24,271	3,602	2.14	City limits extended.
1857...	126,266	4,453	3,103	2.46	
1858...	135,355	9,089	4,104	3.03	
1859...	143,800	8,445	4,521	2.13	
1860...	153,800	10,000	5,945	3.86	
1861...	153,800	....	5,035	3.30	1861 and 1862 were years of the war, in which there was no increase.
1862...	153,800	....	5,866	3.16	
1863...	157,182	3,382	5,744	3.63	
1864...	164,456	7,274	6,720	4.08	
1865...	178,690	14,234	5,501	3.08	
1866...	204,327	25,637	9,465	4.63	Year of cholera.
1867...	216,477	12,150	6,538	3.02	" "
1868...	250,000	33,523	5,193	2.07	
1869...	284,967	34,967	5,884	2.06	
1870...	312,963	27,996	6,670	2.12	

It will be readily observed from the above that there is no uniformity in the ratios of increase of population and mortality. In fact, as the city has expanded in its material development its healthfulness has improved, of course largely arising from the elaboration of the sewerage system and the general improvement of the sanitary condition. This fact suggests another more significant and of wider application to the family of man. The growth of great cities does not deteriorate the health of a country, and the multiplication of population does not raise, but actually diminishes, the death-rate. A vast metropolis, with its countless houses and myriad people, is after all not a stronghold of death; and although its inevitable visitations are more appalling because presented in aggregate form, they are really numerically less than if the same diseases were working their way through the same number of people living in a ruder and more dispersed fashion. The ratio of mortality among the primitive Indian tribes was considerably greater than that which we find in later periods when the increasing population began to eddy into towns and cities. In numbers there is strength and also better food, better shelter, and other elements of health.

MERCHANTS AND COMMERCE OF ST. LOUIS.

THE MERCHANTS.

If the boy is father to the man, with equal propriety may the village be said to be the progenitor of the metropolitan city. The same energy of character in both, the same elements of organization, are developed as prophecies of future eminence. These may not be apparent at the beginning, because the grand characteristics which are to distinguish either may not have found their appropriate field of appreciation and action in the mind of the people; the embryo, however, existed, and when greatness was achieved its parentage is traceable with all possible certainty. When Laclede selected the site now occupied by the Future Great City of the continent, it was because the locality was conducive to the leading design—the successful operations of the business of the early founders, the fur trade. Above and below it the rivers of the North, West and East, debouched into the main stream of the Mississippi, on all of which was found the wealth they sought, and opened a field of hardy and remunerative enterprise sufficiently broad to attract the attention of the boldest spirits. The idea was not conceived at that day that the rich soil penetrated by these rivers would teem, in half a century, with the richest products of agriculture, and that these inland waters would eventually bear upon their bosom a commerce of greater value and of more beneficial influences to humanity than the world had hitherto known; yet that pre-eminent object was then inaugurated by a determinate power which shapes destinies and appropriates resources. The pirogue of the trapper was the pioneer of the steamer, and his indomitable will and courage the intuitive forces destined to subdue the wilderness and open up this magnificent domain to civilization and the beauties and comforts of progressive art. Looking forward at that time, not one of those early voyageurs or projectors, however intuitive, could discover the first intimation of the ultimate result of his labors; looking back, there is not an individual but can read plainly and legibly the connection existing between the design and the consummation, the commencement and the realization. The village founded by trappers has grown into a city erected by merchants and artisans; the broad expanse of plain, varied by valley and hill, has yielded to the plowshare and exchanged its savage aspect for the economic glories of harvest fields and happy homes.

At the time, however, when the Mississippi Valley attracted the attention of Spanish and French adventurers, and subsequently of American citizens—for three nationalities have claimed the magnificent country—the growth of cities was the work of centuries, emigration was on a small scale, transportation was of the most primitive order, science had developed little of mechanical skill and power to overcome distances and impediments. The ocean had not been crossed by steamships, while river navigation depended entirely on simple muscle. In the energy and brightness of the boy the future man might be discerned, because individual achievements had their precedents thickly scattered throughout the history of the race, while the formation of communities had resulted from the aggregations of ages rather than from the advantages of location or the wealth of soil and mineral resources. In a thousand years, therefore, the daring flight of a poetic fancy might reckon on the march of Empire towards the West and class it as the last act in the world's drama; but that in a century such a scene should be presented was beyond the human intellect to conjecture or entertain. It may be doubted if Laclede ever dreamed of a commerce beyond the commodities of furs and skins, of a settlement greater than that which offers protection by rude stockades against a savage enemy, and comforts superior to the most limited demands of humanity. The elements on every hand of progress and greatness, as we see and appropriate them, were so many obstacles to the development of such a result—a seal on the future of a more opaque and impenetrable character to hide the supposition from the reason or imagination. Rapid streams, dense forests, extended prairies, and the isolation of a vast interior forbade the idea of civilized industries and the concentrated influences of settlements to resist the treachery and combined power of the murderous Indian. His policy was to preserve the hunting-grounds in their primeval wildness, for which these grand provisions of nature seemed peculiarly adapted. Indeed, we need not go back to that time and to the trappers' village to gather up the notions of the geologists, the statesmen and the merchants of that period, as they cogitated along the banks of the Mississippi or polled and cordelled upon the Missouri and Illinois; for not longer ago than yesterday the enlightened men of the present supposed the broad belt of land between our State line and the Rocky Mountains to be a desert, incapable of cultivation, and closed out by drought and inhospitable barrenness from the inroads of civilization. On our western border, however, the work of settlement goes on with continuous improvement from year to year, until for a thousand miles beyond the Missouri line the Great American Desert is dotted with thriving villages, and even cities, and begins to blossom like the rose. The remotest rainl-ine is already passed, and the successful experiment of cultivation even without irrigation has already been made and found to be practicable. It is in these constant developments of new resources that we find the strength which steadily builds up, and must continue to enlarge, this metropolitan city.

There were in the nature of the service to be performed by the early pioneers characteristics of moral power which have had much to do in shaping and directing the destiny of St. Louis. The men who sought this wide and wild theater for their exploits were of no ordinary mould. They were self-reliant and determined. Danger was their constant companion and steadiness of purpose their cardinal virtue. Of all who turned their backs on the safety and comforts of home, of whatever nationality, and set their faces hitherward to brave the perils and share the labors of a constantly exposed frontier life, each was a well-defined individuality. None other crossed the Mississippi at that day and ventured into the *terra incognita* which lay beyond, guarded as it was by real dangers and by the more terrible apprehensions which spring from exaggerated legends and imaginary horrors. Their dependence was upon themselves; their safety rested alone within the citadel of their own indomitable will and determined action. Individuality of character begets responsibilities in almost all cases of intrinsic worth. A prominent man cannot afford to be indifferent to his obligations, public or private. His promises and pledges must be met promptly, else his standing becomes a mark for peculiar derision and defamation. This ingredient in the character of the early settlers of the Great Valley has exercised ever since a high-toned influence not only in administrative duties which belong to all departments of duty, but in the trade relations which have been established throughout the country. The subject of the boyhood of this community was introduced for the purpose of adverting to these moral agencies, showing that the implantations of independent thought and action, of energy and integrity early made, have taken deep root and have distinguished and continue to distinguish our commercial men to the present time. They began with no fanciful schemes of suddenly acquired fortunes, but adopted the plain and solid basis of hard work and fair equivalents. Wild speculations were not indulged, and it may be doubted if such vagaries found a lodgment in their brain. Buy and pay promptly was the secret of success, the motto of business. This slow and sure policy seems to have been adopted—too slow, it may be said, and probably was; for even now, with all the evidences of a brilliant future, the brakes are applied to the wheels of progress with singular and provoking obstinacy. Never was development allowed a safer process. No scheme of early aggrandizement was adopted, but the pioneers simply depended upon natural means to acquire competence without resorting to any of those excitements in which speculation finds its main agencies.

Capital was considered the basis of success, and a character was established by our traders which has clung to their successors with remarkably good effects. The boy was father to the man in his patient industry, his indomitable independence, his self-reliance and individuality, and his freedom from experiments of doubtful propriety, in which recklessness forms generally a too large ingredient. Then the material of the community was composed of men of enterprise, who were able to brave dangers, were fond of adventure, and not easily deterred by arduous labors and personal sacrifices. Each prominent individual had the reputation of the settlement to bear, and each was willing to take the responsibility of that reputation, though it involved his pecuniary means or his life. How well these characteristics were exemplified in subsequent times, when St. Louis began to assume the position of a commercial point, is one of the proudest portions of its history. The financial convulsions of the country were felt here with the same violence with which they shook the established centers of business in the East, but they were met by resistances of personal effort and forbearance, of local pride and magnanimity, of determined purpose and self-sacrifice—the offspring of those qualities which had triumphed over physical dangers and overcome the discomforts of the wilderness, which were not found elsewhere. Men stood in the doors of our banking institutions, and by a pledge of their private fortunes subdued the evil spirits of alarm and doubt. They threw themselves in the breach and re-established confidence. The honor of the city rested upon their prompt, decided action, and they were quick to respond. A remarkable instance of this kind occurred in the financial disturbance of 1855, when the entire country was shaken by a crisis that involved both the pecuniary and political interests of the nation. It was a pressure upon our civic institutions which tried beyond precedent at that day the principles of self-government, and tested the powers of popular domination. When other communities went under, hopelessly wrecked by the storm of disaffection and partisan fury, the people of Missouri, directed by calm, decisive leaders, who had won their positions through the practical school of imminent danger and personal adaptations, re-established order and preserved the honor of the commonwealth. Credit and patriotism were boldly asserted, and the victory honorably achieved. Capital began to look to the west bank of the Mississippi for the citadel of integrity, and here that proud distinction has been found, in a score of conflicts that have imperiled commercial credit since, as it had on less memorable occasions imperiled it before. The honors won by the metropolis of the Adriatic were repeated here—the one the refined center of Eastern commerce, the other the rude beginnings of a capital destined to be erected in the wilds of the Western Empire. St. Louis was unknown when

"Venice sate in state throned on her hundred isles,"

but the same inviolate honor in trade relations which embellishes the history of the old *regime* of business obligations and extended transactions, still works its influence in the successful achievement of metropolitan greatness. Looking back through those periods of financial struggles, there are comparatively few of our merchants who took advantage of the stress of circumstances to avoid calamity, benefit their position, or yield to inglorious imbecility or defeat. They met the liabilities of the day with open frankness, and, generally free from the encumbrances of unreasonable liabilities and speculative investments, were able with renewed industry to start afresh in the race of enterprise.

Large business centers have been started since the early trappers settled this site as the rendezvous of their operations, and every inch of ground has been contested for commercial supremacy by them. For a while, aided by outside capital and the appliances of modern influences, the contest has seemed doubtful, and artificial stimulants have threatened to triumph over natural advantages. The very strength of this locality has seemed but to assist in its prostration. Situated between the agricultural interests of the North and South, its trade was the exchange of the commodities of both, and it soon became the battle-field for the extension or contraction of an institution which finally shook the very foundations of the Republic. Its grand position invited the contest, and all the forces of anti-slavery influences were pointed in this direction. National means were employed, corporate powers invoked, individual and combined efforts brought into requisition to crush or render nugatory the inherent strength of this business emporium. Our rivers were to be superseded by railroads, and our plain old style of honest dealing laughed out of countenance by a mode of glittering operations which had no basis but that of fancy, and no powers but those of excitement. The conflict broke at last in actual war, and during its prolonged existence, with the guns of both parties directed against us, our trade languished, and those points which presented no strategic advantages and were really without the circle of business and political consideration, were vastly benefited. St. Louis must lose the supremacy of her position, even though it requires millions to overcome her natural advantages, was the language and determination of the party who looked upon slavery as a morally abhorred system and political monstrosity. Self-reliant, the descendants of the fur traders had sought no outside influences, and, secure in their position, they awaited the results with calm indifference; still developing her energies by those slow processes which wait upon positive demands her citizens followed the plain requirements of the day. When the army of occupation began to penetrate the far West, and improvements became necessary to retain the business relations established in the East, and South, and North, our people were ready for action and entered upon the duty with proper zeal and activity.

It is one of the characteristics of true merit that it is reliable and distinguished under all circumstances. If slavery was supposed to be peculiarly adapted to the staple articles of agriculture and the mining wealth of the State, it has been found since its abrogation that universal emancipation has far stronger ingredients in its nature to enrich materially her condition, and draw hither the wealth of population, of labor and of capital. From that gigantic civil revolution which tore asunder the bands which supported our industries—the foundations on which was erected the superstructure of our local forces—the State has become doubly powerful and prosperous; she has thrown herself at one bound within the influences of a sympathy which pervades an advanced civilization the world over, and gives to this internal region those moral correspondent qualities so necessary to the true development of physical resources. Our population, therefore, mingles in its veins the blood of all nations—blood which possesses the fire of adventure, the stamina of enterprise, the daring necessary to achieve personal independence.

An allusion to an incident in the history of the city may be permitted which illustrates the texture of those moral elements of character derived from the crude looms of the early settlers of the trappers' village. In 1849 St. Louis was visited with the triple furies of fire, blood and pestilence. The best portion of her business locations were reduced to ashes; five thousand of her people died with a disease that bid defiance to medical skill; her rivers rose and flooded her productive bottom-lands Ruin stalked through her streets and pervaded the country tributary to her commercial support. At this trying moment, with that self-reliant and indomitable will which carried her founders safely through the ordeals to which they were exposed, she met the responsibilities of the trial with an independent spirit, a prowess of resistances and recuperative energies of the highest type. Honorable as it is to our nature that sympathy finds a lodgment not alone in individual bosoms, but in communities and nations, our citizens asked no aid from this benevolent feeling to meet the exigencies of the hour. Not a dollar was asked or received from contiguous or distant cities. The bravery and self-reliant characteristics of the trapper shone out in the artisan, merchant and professional man of the present, and an immediate effort was put in requisition to redeem losses and repair devastations. Such an exhibition of unconquerable will, of inherent strength, is surely a forcible prognostic, a grand prophecy of the ultimate destiny of our beloved metropolis.

THE COMMERCE.

We have glanced in the aggregate at the characteristics of the merchants of St. Louis which have so constantly imparted a vigorous vitality and rapidity to her commercial growth, and it will be appropriate to turn from such a subject to the existing commerce of the city. In the historical review, to be found in preceding pages, a general idea has been given of the rise and progress of the trade of St. Louis during the earlier years, when a thriving river town but faintly foreshadowed the magnificent metropolis of the future. We have looked upon it in its infancy, and now present some facts and figures which illustrate its extent and character in the present and indicate the vaster proportions to be attained in the future. In presenting facts and figures respecting the trade, manufactures, etc., of St. Louis, we are necessarily compelled to do so in the most compact form, and to leave to the reader the thoughts and comparisons naturally suggested by the statistical statements made. It is not our purpose to review in detail each branch of business, but to group only the more important, from which the aggregate may be fairly inferred.

MANUFACTURES OF ST. LOUIS.

The industrial interests of St. Louis have received a grand impulse during the past year, and the general result shows a large increase over any preceding year. The following statement will show the advancement of St. Louis as a manufacturing city during the last ten years:

Capital invested in manufactures in 1860	$12,733,948
" " " in 1870	48,387,150
Making a clear gain of 284 per cent. in ten years, or 24 4-10 per cent. per annum.	
The value of raw material used in 1860 was	$16,212,699
" " " in 1870 was	63,427,509
Making a gain of 269 per cent. in ten years, or 26 9-10 per cent. per annum.	
The value of products in 1860 was	27,610,070
" " in 1870 was	109,513,950
A gain of 296 per cent. in ten years, or 29 6-10 per cent. per annum.	

The following shows the extent of investments and operations in reference to some of the more important articles:

Capital invested in manufacture of pig-iron	$4,398,165
Value of material used	2,266,815
Value of product	3,180,815
Capital invested in foundries	2,593,850
Value of material	2,676,991
Value of product	4,605,887
Capital invested in manufacture of agricultural implements	660,000
Value of materials used	295,000
Value of product	745,000
Capital invested in flour mills	6,408,600
Value of material used	8,230,660
Value of product	11,224,441
Capital invested in planing mills, and sash and door factories	2,454,750
Value of material used	2,854,158
Value of product	4,759,790
Capital invested in breweries	2,198,708
Value of material	1,750,931
Value of product	3,557,583
Capital invested in pork and beef packing	$3,032,800
Value of material	5,419,432
Value of product	7,929,700
Capital invested in manufacture of tobacco	1,520,900
Value of material	1,674,068
Value of product	8,094,083
Capital invested in manufacture of steam machinery	1,871,400
Value of material	596,070
Value of product	1,509,112
Capital invested in manufacture of white lead, oils and paints	975,000
Value of material	961,662
Value of product	1,633,500
Capital invested in manufacture of sugar	1,000,000
Value of material	3,430,000
Value of product	3,678,250

BANKS AND BANKING.

There are forty-eight incorporated banks and private banking houses in St. Louis, with an aggregate working capital of about eighteen millions. On the 15th of October last each of the forty-eight made a statement to the managers of the Clearing House, which showed the following aggregates:

Paid-up capital stock	$12,307,147 00
Surplus and undivided profits	5,490,585 00
	$17,797,732 00

It is fair to presume that since that date the amount has increased to eighteen millions. The aggregate of deposits at same date was thirty-two millions, and loans and discounts thirty-nine millions.

Two had capital and surplus exceeding	$3,000,000
Five " "	1,000,000
Five " "	500,000
Eight " "	250,000
Twelve " "	100,000
Sixteen " less than	100,000

The operations of the banks through the Clearing House are given below, and indicate not only the increase in the banking business of the city, but also all other kinds of business, as the banks are only a part of the means by which other kinds of business are done. This statement shows the monthly clearings, comparatively, for the years 1869, 1870, 1871:

MONTHS.	1869.	1870.	1871.
January	$57,688,226 36	$59,233,322 62	$75,610,677 56
February	46,064,787 12	53,281,286 50	59,424,324 18
March	52,407,642 54	62,040,575 18	71,264,501 96
April	51,373,701 20	65,716,992 00	69,938,400 72
May	53,787,979 92	73,618,227 16	73,427,624 74
June	53,353,781 62	68,248,274 80	71,791,607 72
July	50,935,806 04	69,083,282 28	....
August	50,540,733 14	64,381,275 20	....
September	50,608,439 94	59,975,993 84	....
October	56,447,015 18	65,766,001 62	....
November	61,415,146 20	64,504,192 86	....
December	68,966,034 26	75,105,121 08	....
Totals	$653,589,293 52	$780,954,545 14	....
Monthly average	$54,465,774 46	$65,079,545 43	$69,933,105 83

FLOUR AND GRAIN.

One of the natural results of the situation of our city as the center of a fertile and extensive wheat region has been the rapid development of the flour trade, and in this branch of domestic manufacture she is already famous, we might say, on both sides of the Atlantic, while the receipts of grain are also steadily on the increase. During the past year the manufacture of flour has increased from 1,068,592 barrels in 1869 to 1,251,773 barrels in 1870. The following exhibit furnishes a condensed view of the operations of our millers during the past four years:

	1870.	1869.	1868.	1867.
Received	1,491,626 bbls.	1,310,555 bbls.	805,836 bbls.	944,075 bbls.
Manufactured	1,351,773 "	1,068,592 "	859,154 "	765,298 "
Sold and shipped direct from country mills	407,561 "	297,860 "	245,822 "	180,370 "
Total	3,250,960 bbls.	2,677,007 bbls.	1,910,812 bbls.	1,889,743 bbls.

The total receipts and exports for six years ending 1870 were as follows:

TOTAL RECEIPTS FOR SIX YEARS.

ARTICLES.	1870.	1869.	1868.	1867.	1866.	1865.
Flour (reduced to wheat)	7,458,130	6,552,775	4,029,180	4,720,375	6,043,630	5,805,190
Wheat	6,638,253	6,736,454	4,353,591	3,571,593	4,410,305	2,452,722
Corn	4,708,838	2,395,713	2,800,277	5,155,480	7,233,671	3,162,313
Oats	4,519,510	3,461,844	3,259,132	3,455,388	3,467,253	4,173,229
Rye	210,542	266,056	367,961	250,704	375,417	217,568
Barley	778,518	757,600	634,590	705,215	548,796	846,230
Total bushels	24,313,791	20,170,442	15,444,731	17,848,755	22,079,072	17,657,252

TOTAL EXPORTS FOR SIX YEARS.

ARTICLES.	1870.	1869.	1868.	1867.	1866.	1865.
Flour (reduced to wheat)	13,453,695	10,863,805	7,496,685	7,252,375	8,503,700	7,607,325
Wheat	634,562	1,715,005	543,234	321,888	635,817	62,860
Corn	3,636,060	1,298,863	1,611,618	4,318,937	6,757,199	2,591,558
Oats	3,144,744	2,103,002	1,952,579	2,244,756	2,624,044	3,083,864
Rye	100,254	110,447	192,555	56,076	225,458	31,445
Barley	70,451	57,134	64,426	55,720	89,751	50,000
Total bushels	21,039,766¾	16,148,756	11,860,097	14,249,752	18,835,969	13,427,052

The direction of the trade is thus indicated: Total shipments southward during the year 1870, 1,713,913 barrels. Total shipments eastward, 933,591 barrels. Total shipments to other points, 43,235. Total shipments during the year, 2,690,730 barrels.

There is every reason to be satisfied with the condition of the grain trade of St. Louis, while there are the most encouraging prospects for the future.

PROVISIONS.

The following figures show the growth as well as indicate the present *status* of the packing business in this city:

HOGS PACKED AT ST. LOUIS FOR NINE SEASONS.

	1869-70.	1868-69.	1867-68.	1866-67.	1865-66.	1864-65.	1863-64.	1862-63.	1861-62.
No. Hogs	241,316	231,937	237,160	183,543	123,335	191,890	244,600	178,750	84,093
Average net w't	190 50-100	189 27-100	193 91-100	222 34-100	208 91-100	178 50-100	179	207	224 50-100

This department of business is one very much dependent on facilities for handling and the means of easy communication with the States and sections of country producing the stock. A few years must necessarily make St. Louis the first packing point in the West, as she possesses all the material advantages requisite to secure that position.

PACKING AT THE FIVE PRINCIPAL WESTERN CITIES.

	Jan. 21, 1871	Jan. 21, 1870	Whole Season, 1869-70
St. Louis	264,699	221,222	241,326
Chicago	649,036	454,637	685,959
Cincinnati	415,436	318,160	337,330
Louisville	243,941	180,449	180,449
Milwaukee	163,000	130,000	172,626
Total	1,736,112	1,304,468	1,617,690

LIVE STOCK.

The development of our Western system of railroads has greatly expanded our stock market, and the proportions it must assume in the future, with the completion of the bridge, the opening of other railroad lines, and of the agricultural wealth of the rich and boundless country to the west of us, must be enormous. The receipts and exports for the year and other figures of interest and importance will be found in the following tables:

RECEIPTS AND SHIPMENTS OF CATTLE, SHEEP AND HOGS FOR SIX YEARS

YEAR.	RECEIPTS.			SHIPMENTS.		
	Cattle.	Sheep.	Hogs.	Cattle.	Sheep.	Hogs.
1870	201,422	94,477	310,850	129,748	11,649	17,156
1869	124,565	96,626	344,848	59,867	12,416	39,076
1868	115,352	79,315	301,569	37,277	6,415	16,277
1867	74,146	62,974	293,241	26,799	19,022	28,627
1866	103,259	64,047	217,622	24,462	15,194	13,358
1865	94,307	52,133	99,663	46,712	8,680	17,869

EXPORTS FOR THE YEAR.

ROUTES.	Cattle.	Sheep.	Hogs.
By River	5,065	7,322	4,466
St. Louis, Alton and Chicago Railroad	44,916	735	3,152
Indianapolis and St. Louis Railroad	40,653	2,630	4,055
St. Louis, Vandalia and Terre Haute Railroad	11,564	535	1,692
Ohio and Mississippi Railroad	22,226	39	2,987
Toledo, Wabash and Western Railroad	1,936	......	509
Other Routes	3,386	388	295
Total Exports	129,748	11,649	17,156

GROCERIES.

The following table gives a general glance at this important department of trade:

Receipts and Exports of Molasses, Coffee and Rice.

YEARS.	MOLASSES.								COFFEE.		RICE.		
	RECEIPTS.				EXPORTS.				RECP'S	EXP'TS	RECEIPTS.		EXP'TS.
	Bbls.	½ Bbls.	Kegs.	Hds.	Bbls.	½ Bbls	Kegs	Hds.	Bags.	Bags.	Sks.	Bbls.	Sks.
Total 1870......	13,819	693	5,221	6	21,754	12,275	21,361	7	113,950	112,621	2,298	5,150	10,971
Ttoal 1869......	26,468	1,994	5,053	512	21,040	9,634	20,365	13	135,491	107,855	1,308	5,287	10,804
Total 1868......	15,377	2,382	4,189	450	15,338	9,047	17,596	......	92,699	91,615	4,284	3,736	9,781
Total 1867......	8,565	473	996	......	10,925	7,728	14,763	......	98,617	80,344	5,883	1,181	7,560
Total 1866......	6,100	1,033	761	......	9,582	4,981	11,132	......	90,367	65,985	4,977	Pkgs.	5,344
Total 1865......	10,098	998	1,461	531	9,379	2,130	11,095	......	60,106	56,963	3,035	"	....

It is impossible to speak of the grocery trade of St. Louis without adverting particularly to the Belcher Sugar Refinery and establishment, which, in magnitude of operations and mercantile influence, is among the first of the kind in the country. The business which resulted in the establishment of the refinery was commenced in 1840, and by the persistent energy of Messrs. W. H. and Charles Belcher was steadily increased, and has now attained a colossal character reflecting credit upon our city. The buildings of the refinery cover nearly four squares. We have not space to enter into any detailed description of this establishment, but the extent of the business of the company is fairly indicated by the following figures:

Sales of refined sugar by Belcher's Sugar Refining Company in the home market:

Years.	Pounds.	Years.	Pounds.
1856	13,700,000	1864	7,900,000
1857	11,800,000	1865	13,100,000
1858	12,900,000	1866	17,300.000
1859	18,800,000	1867	17,300,000
1860	15,000,000	1868	18,300,000
1861	9,500,000	1869	22,400,000
1862	7,400,000	1870	25,500,000
1863	7,900,000		

The amount of duty paid to the government by the refinery is shown as follows:

Years.	Amounts.	Years.	Amounts.
1865	$378,015	1868	$637,371
1866	463,727	1869	754,649
1867	651,924	1870	801,140

The refined sugars and syrups made by this refinery find a sale here and in the leading towns and districts west of St. Louis. Formerly it sold many goods to Chicago and Milwaukee and the upper Mississippi towns, but that trade has all gone to New York and other Atlantic cities. The growth of St. Louis and the country west of it, however, compensates for this loss.

The following are the present directors and officers of the company:

Directors—R. J. Lackland, D. A. January, James Smith, Carlos S. Greeley, Joseph C. Cabot, Geo. S. Drake, Chas. Belcher.

Officers—Chas. Belcher, president; Ed. Y. Ware, secretary.

The grocery trade of St. Louis is fully representative of the best business enterprise and the soundest commercial principles. Our merchants import largely from all quarters, availing themselves of the fullest range of the trade. To illustrate the extent of the business, we may say that there are in this city seven firms doing a business of about $1,000,000 each annually, and two or three whose operations reach $1,750,000 each per annum. The wholesale trade of this year will be fully twenty-five per cent. over that of last year. The total annual wholesale trade for the past year reached $27,600,000, and the retail sales about $9,000,000, making the grand total annual sales $36,000,000. The wholesale merchants are now importing more heavily than during any previous year, and the expansion of the business corresponds with that observable in the other departments of our commerce.

DRY GOODS TRADE.

The past year was satisfactory in its results in reference to this most important department of trade — more so, indeed, than any since the close of the year. It was characterized by a steady shrinkage in values; but the business done, although accompanied by a reduction of profits, was conducted on sound principles, with no tendency to over-trading. While the operations of the year afford unmistakable evidence of a general expansion in the trade, corresponding to the increase observable in every department of our city's commerce, it is indeed an undeniable fact that already our dry goods merchants sell to a larger territory than any other city in the United States. Previous to the war the dry goods business ranged from $10,000,000 to $12,000,000, while now it aggregates $38,000,000. The aggregate wholesales of dry goods and fancy goods reaches $29,000,000, retail sales about $9,000,000. The retail sales of two of our houses reach over $1,000,000 each, annually, and four (including the two) about $500,000 each. The wholesale trade, heretofore confined to Main street, now indicates a decided movement toward Washington avenue and Fifth street, and the four magnificent stores now all but completed on the latter thoroughfare, near St. Charles street, will be occupied this Fall by Main street houses, while other buildings in the same locality, for wholesale purposes, are in contemplation. The yearly increase in the dry goods trade of St. Louis can not be less than 30 per cent.

HARDWARE.

The hardware trade was largely increased in volume during 1869, and suffered no falling-off in 1870, while there are satisfactory evidences of a constant expansion. The value of production during the past year was nearly $2,500,000, and the amount invested in manufacture is about $1,000,000. The business of each of our more important houses shows a material increase over that of the preceding year. The annual sales of seven wholesale firms are represented respectively by the following figures: $600,000, $150,000, $234,000, $100,000, $135,000, $400,000, $550,000. In a city destined to become famous in the working of metals the hardware trade must necessarily assume a proportionate magnitude and importance.

LUMBER.

The receipts of all kinds of lumber during the year 1870 were as follows:

	Feet.		Feet.
White Pine	199,569,000	Cypress	70,000
Yellow Pine	30,350,000	Shingles	140,434,000
Poplar	3,775,000	Lath	27,514,000
Walnut	3,679,000	Pickets	1,210,000
Oak	2,866,000	Logs	29,400,000
Ash	457,000		

The total number of feet of all kinds of lumber and logs on hand in St. Louis, January 1, 1871, was 119,882,265. The sales in 1870 exceeded those of 1869, 53,110,000 feet of lumber, and the aggregate during the season is 229,110,000, demonstrating an increase in the trade of 30 per cent. Alluding to the lumber resources of Missouri, Mr. Joseph Bogy, in a statement respecting the trade, published in the annual report of the Union Merchants' Exchange, speaks as follows: "This business in our State has not received the attention it deserves. The fine timber regions of the Gasconade, Washington, Madison, Iron, and other sections, have not been developed to any extent beyond their home demand and that of our own market. While a large business should be done, and capital attracted to these regions, we hope to see, by the extension of new railroads, which will soon penetrate those sections of our State where timber is abundant, these causes obviated. It is a well-known fact that the pine regions of the North are fast giving out, and that we have reached that period where the demand for lumber is increasing and supply diminishing, and, sooner or later, the yellow pine must take its place as a substitute for most of the white pine now used.

The following figures show the receipts and shipments of lumber, logs, shingles, etc., during the months named of the present year:

RECEIPTS.

JANUARY—White Pine	544,000
Shingles	3,158,000
Yellow Pine Flooring, 335,000; Dimension, 77,000	412,000
Poplar, 150,000; Oak, 200,000; Walnut, 145,000	495,000
Red Cedar, 108,000; Ash, 12,000; Hickory, 9,000	129,000
FEBRUARY—White Pine	2,016,000
Shingles	4,665,000
Yellow Pine Flooring and Dimension	641,000
Poplar, 358,000; Oak, 293,000; Walnut, 337,000	988,000
Cedar, 185,000; Ash, 20,000; Hickory, 16,000	221,000
Sycamore, 10,000; Maple, 5,000	15,000
Walnut Logs, 100,000; Oak Logs, 100,000	200,000
MARCH—White Pine	6,231,000
Shingles	8,919,000
Lath	3,930,000
Poplar, 764,000; Oak, 515,000; Walnut, 380,000	1,659,000
Yellow Pine Flooring and Dimension	1,147,000
Red Cedar, 784,000; Ash, 47,000	831,000
Oak Logs, 216,000; Walnut Logs, 350,000; Ash Logs, 50,000	616,000
All other kinds of Lumber	7,000
Fence Posts	12,000

APRIL—White Pine........ 8,978,000
Yellow Pine........ 1,573,000
Shingles........ 9,558,000
Lath........ 1,601,000
Pickets........ 20,000
Oak, 272,750; Walnut, 269,600; Poplar, 656,000,........ 1,198,350
Red Cedar, 165,000; Ash, 66,352........ 831,352
Other Lumber........ 20,000
Oak Logs, 389,000; Walnut Logs, 245,000; Cottonwood Logs, 247,000.... 881,000
MAY—Total Logs and Lumber........42,667,300
Shingles........ 7,690,000
Lath........ 3,600,000
JUNE—Total Logs and Lumber........30,575,000
Shingles........ 9,075,000
Lath........ 3,211,000

Total Lumber and Logs received, in feet........101,640,402
" Shingles " 43,065,000
" Lath " 12,342,000
" Fence Posts " 12,000

The shipments were as follows:

JANUARY—White Pine and other Lumber........ 3,163,000
Shingles........ 3,270,000
Lath........ 1,100,000
FEBRUARY—White Pine and other Lumber........ 3,566,000
Shingles........ 3,575,000
Lath........ 1,620,000
MARCH—Pine and other Lumber........ 7,904,000
Shingles........ 9,608,000
Lath........ 5,250,000
APRIL—All kinds Lumber........ 5,892,000
Shingles........10,616,000
Lath........ 3,798,000
MAY—Lumber of all kinds........ 9,134,000
Shingles........12,265,000
Lath........ 8,163,000
JUNE—Lumber of all kinds........10,661,000
Shingles........11,868,006
Lath........ 6,664,000

TOBACCO.

A general glance at the condition of the trade in this important article is appended in the following tables:

Monthly Receipts of Hogsheads of Tobacco for Past Four Years.

YEARS.	Jan.	Feb.	March.	April.	May.	June.	July.	Aug.	Sept.	Oct.	Nov.	Dec.	Total.
1867........	35	82	427	1,360	1,719	3,342	3,712	3,599	2,734	887	437	250	18,584
1868........	65	148	857	1,449	1,966	3,170	1,310	1,489	1,156	351	229	76	12,266
1869........	123	349	641	911	1,420	2,642	1,307	1,181	717	423	220	194	10,128
1870........	146	394	625	1,226	1,714	2,815	1,548	1,449	640	323	165	148	11,193

1870......Boxes and packages Leaf Tobacco........ 1,257

Monthly Exports of Hogsheads of Tobacco for Past Four Years.

YEARS.	Jan.	Feb.	March.	April.	May.	June.	July	Aug.	Sept.	Oct.	Nov.	Dec.	Total.
1867........	90	182	626	636	983	2,548	3,183	2,469	2,512	1,655	1,080	309	16,273
1868........	72	122	418	601	1,381	1,399	889	1,123	1,413	703	626	147	8,896
1869........	153	99	238	683	1,005	1,765	1,130	858	1,197	637	233	216	8,214
1870........	69	129	233	692	913	1,513	1,250	800	643	766	413	221	7,642

Total sales at public auction, including reviews......................	7,261 hhds.	
Total rejections sold privately or shipped elsewhere................	3,147 "	
		10,408 hhds.
Stock on hand January 1st, 1870..	403 hhds.	
Receipts during 1870..	11,193 "	
		11,596 hhds.
Exports during 1870, direct...	1,593 hhds.	
" " " from warehouses....................................	4,230 "	
" " " to adjacent manufacturing establishments	1,819 "	
City consumption..	3,153 "	
		10,795 hhds.
Stock on hand January 1st, 1871..		801 hhds.

WOOL, HIDES, PELTRIES AND FURS.

The table appended gives a compact view of trade operations in the articles above named, during the year 1870 and the five years preceding :

YEAR.	WOOL.		HIDES.				PELTRIES.		FURS.	
	REC'PTS.	EXP'TS.	RECEIPTS.		EXPORTS.		REC'TS.	EX'PTS.	REC'TS.	EXP'TS.
	Pkgs.	Bales.	Pcs.	Bundles.	Pcs.	Bundles	Bd s.	Bdls.	Pkgs.	Pkgs.
1870...........	13,486	17,882	120,739	37,425	55,896	132,321	12,903	4,238	2,[illegible]23	3,612
1869...........	14,905	20,738	103,906	17,170	66,173	81,048	11,584	4,279	4,051	1,897
1868...........	17,756	18,530	150,245	16,362	81,546	47,083	11,278	4,042	6,536	4,992
1867...........	12,040	11,928	146,421	11,910	85,291	45,113	10,278	3,807	6,093	2,820
1866	9,205	8,557	160,470	6,981	165,580	22,481	.....	......	......	......
1865...........	10,599	9,394	187,591	7,310	267,119	....	.....	......	......	......

Receipts of Highwines for Fifteen Years.

Year.	Barrels.	Year.	Barrels.	Year.	Barrels.
1870....................	61,754	1865	38,014	1860	102,356
1869....................	52,103	1864	50,407	1859	100,092
1868....................	23,419	1863	54,862	1858	122,295
1867	38,455	1862	70,374	1857	125,547
1866....................	58,157	1861	72,790	1856	95,821

LEATHER MANUFACTURES.

In this, as in various other manufacturing branches of this city, to fully delineate its character and magnitude it would be necessary to treat it far more in detail than is possible in this condensed commercial *resume*, and we can only present a few significant facts. From reliable statistics it appears that there is over $5,000,000 invested in the business, and that the annual sales range between $15,000,000 and $20,000,000, including, of course, all branches of the business. Indeed, if we include saddlery and the other departments which may correctly be comprised in the leather trade, the capital invested will reach nearly $8,000,000. There is no market in the United States where a greater variety and better articles are placed at the disposal of buyers.

COTTON.

St. Louis is not at present as active or extensive a cotton market as it should properly be, but the obstructions to the development of the trade are transitory in character and the prospects for the future are decidedly encouraging. The establishment of the proper means of compressing, increase of storage facilities, and the perfecting of the railroad system south into the cotton-producing territory removed from river transportation, will unquestionably expand operations at this point. The cotton consumed by our manufacturers during the past year was :

By St. Louis Cotton Factory	3,300 bales.
By Brown, Marriott & Co	900 "
By Wm. B. Edgar	200 "
By Brooks Bolton	95 "
Total	4,495 bales.

The amount of bagging manufactured during the year 1870 was 3,377,845 yards.

Receipts and Exports of Flax Tow for Two Years.

RECEIPTS.			EXPORTS.		
Articles.	1870.	1869.	Articles.	1870.	1869.
Flax tow, bales		9,035	Flax tow, bales	1,635	73

Receipts and Exports of Rope and Cordage.

RECEIPTS.				EXPORTS.		
Articles.	1870.	1869.	1868.	Articles.	1870.	1869.
Rope, coils	93	50	636	Rope and Cordage, coils..	40,001	41,471
Cordage	19,093	24,107	14,466			

Receipts of Hemp and Tow for Twenty Years.

Year.	Bales.	Year.	Bales.	Year.	Bales.	Year.	Bales.
1870	12,716	1865	40,846	1860	68,673	1855	91,326
1869	24,468	1864	64,078	1859	63,796	1854	69,629
1868	25,699	1863	56,337	1858	81,423	1853	62,692
1867	30,750	1862	78,317	1857	80,094	1852	48,819
1866	18,759	1861	25,568	1856	53,737	1851	65,471

MANUFACTURE OF COTTON AND WOOLEN GOODS.

A few facts in relation to the relative advantages of St. Louis for the manufacture of staple cotton and woolen goods will be of interest. It is situated in the center of the great and inexhaustible coal region of the West, and our proximity to the cotton and woolen belt, and the cheap transit of the Mississippi river and railways, insures an average price of two cents per pound less for middling cotton than at New York or Boston, thus enabling the manufacturer to produce his goods in St. Louis at less than the Eastern mills can produce them, and at an additional saving of a half cent per yard for the transportation of the manufactured product. Through the rare productiveness of our soil, we can prosperously support a larger population to the square mile than any other country in the world. Our destiny, therefore, is a matter of fact, and not a question of argument. We are to be the center of a manufacturing district in textile fabrics, which is to supply the wants of the Mississippi Valley, the Southwest, the Northwest and the Pacific Slope.

In the manufacture of staple goods, where the raw material and fuel are the leading items in the cost, a very small difference in the cost of production turns the scale for or against any locality—thus, if the raw material can be converted into manufactured goods in one week at a profit of one per cent., it amounts to the enormous profit of fifty-two per cent. per annum.

There are already established a large number of cotton mills in the Mississippi Valley, and three-fourths of all the sheetings sold in this market during the last year have been the production of these mills. The increase of woolen mills during the last five years, in the section of which St. Louis is the commercial center, is beyond parallel in the history of this country. There have been mistakes made in the excessive production of some kinds of goods, but the fact has been proven that we have the ability to produce such goods at less cost than Eastern mills. For the future the wool will be grown here and west of us, and can only reach the Atlantic seaboard under the heavy tax of double first-class freight for wool in the grease and dirt, equal to four or five cents per pound upon scoured wools. With these facts in view, it must be apparent that it is only a question of time when the great manufacturing interest of the United States will be in the Mississippi Valley, and St. Louis its center.

MISSOURI WINES.

Elsewhere we have spoken of Missouri as a wine-producing State, and none, indeed, can question her extraordinary natural advantages in this respect. The wine and liquor trade in this city is one of increasing importance, but the most interesting feature is the development in quantity and quality of the manufacture of our native wines. The following foreign testimony from a critical pen illustrates the growing opinion abroad as to Missouri wine. It is taken from the London *Globe* of a comparatively recent date, and of course alludes to the product of the American Wine Company, Isaac Cook, President:

"While the vineyards of France are trodden down by the Prussian invader, and those of the Rhineland are not so carefully tended as they would be in days of peace, the United States are largely extending their vinticulture, and with remarkable success. To the fair sisterhood of vine-crowned rivers, which includes the Maine and Loire, the Moselle and Rhine, must now be added the mightier streams of America, and especially the Missouri. We have recently tasted a champagne from St. Louis, which seems to us unsurpassable in purity and flavor; and the flavor is entirely distinct from that of any European wine within our knowledge. Any *gourmet* who wants a new palatal sensation should try this wine, which possesses that exquisite freedom from heat and acidity which belongs only to the choicest continental vintages. It has the bouquet of vernal flowers, so that as you raise the glass to your lips you are reminded of the April woodlands, faintly fragrant with hidden violets. Longfellow boasts concerning the Catawba wine that it is free from the intoxicating qualities of some European vintages, and this wine of Missouri is said to be of a still finer type. Probably this result is due to its being grown upon a virgin soil. The best vintages wear out in time. Ask an epicure coeval with the century if he ever tasted the Chateau Lafitte which he remembers in his youth. The constituents of the soil which gave the grape its high qualities, conferring purity and fragrance on the wine, are gradually exhausted; and attempts to renew them artificially, or to give strength by the use of manure, end only in the production of a coarse liquor, unworthy of dedication to Dionysius."

IRON MANUFACTURE IN ST. LOUIS.

The existing magnitude of the iron interests in this city and the great importance attaching to their further development in the future give a particular attraction to any intelligent views and thoughts on the subject, and the following communication from Mr. John Magwire, an excellent authority, will be read with interest:

L. U. Reavis, Esq.:

Sir—You have requested me to give in writing my views concerning the manufacturing of articles at St. Louis, especially iron. In September, 1866, by request of several gentlemen connected with the St. Louis Agricultural and Mechanical Fair, I wrote an essay upon the advantages and adaptability of St. Louis as a manufacturing city of all articles manufactured in other cities of the United States. When the Lindell Hotel was burned, the essay, which they had published in pamphlet form, was destroyed, except the few copies that had been distributed. The State Agricultural Society had the essay published in their report for that year, and you will find it commencing on page 122 of the Agricultural Report of the State of Missouri. That essay contains, as I believe, the facts sufficient to show the advantages at St. Louis for establishing manufactories of all fabrics needed by the people, and the advantages as a point for distributing without the intervention of commission merchants or middle-men. I do not think that I can add anything of importance to what you will find in that essay, except to advert to the results in making iron, so abundantly proved by the working of the furnaces that have gone intooperation since 1866. These results, however, are so well known now by all persons familiar with making iron that it is hardly necessary to write them in a book. Everybody now knows that, owing to the richness and fusibility of Missouri ores, furnaces using those ores and raw Illinois coal mixed with coke, yield from twenty-five to thirty per cent. more iron per day than furnaces of the same dimensions in any other locality of this country or in Europe, and that the quality of the iron is excellent; that enough good iron can be produced from Missouri ores and Illinois coal to supply the wants of the country; and the fact is now also well known that good pig-iron can be produced in Missouri and Illinois at a cost of labor varying not far from that required in Wales (England), which is the most favorable country of Europe for making iron. There are greater facilities for obtaining ore and coal in Wales than any other country of Europe, but neither in Wales nor upon any other part of the earth's surface, so far as my information goes, are ore and coal so accessible as in Missouri and Illinois. It must be borne in mind that all manufacturing, especially iron, is produced by labor; and in the production of iron, until the discovery by Bessemer, the refining of iron from the pig into the bloom, or bringing it to "nature," as the refiners term it, was the hardest and most toilsome labor that man had ever been required to perform. This labor must be performed upon our pig-iron as now made in order to produce merchantable iron or rails, and the cost of producing pig-iron is better determined by the quantity one man can make in a day than by the amount of dollars and cents or shillings and pence he is paid. It requires, in Wales, the labor of one man for thirteen days to produce a ton of pig-iron, or thirteen men one day. In Missouri and Illinois the labor of one man eight days, or eight men one day, can make a ton of pig-iron, which will make a rail that will last three times as long as the ordinary Welsh rail. In Wales the subsistence of the thirteen men, their food and shelter, is equal to the labor of five men; in the Mississippi Valley, subsisting eight men requires the labor of three men. Now here is the difference in cost of producing iron: eighteen men in Wales and eleven in Illinois and Missouri, and the Missouri rail will last three times as long as the common Welsh rail. Good rails are made in Wales, but at additional expense over the ordinary mode, which makes an inferior rail. Bad rails cannot be made of Missouri iron, if proper attention is given, in the ordinary mode.

In the face of these facts our railroad companies are compelled to import rails from Wales. This raises a question which, when inquired into, puts a terrible responsibility upon our American statesmen. That the responsibility of depriving the American manufacturer of the facilities to make all the rails needed in this country, must rest upon the conscience of our American statesmen, I am prepared to demonstrate unmistakably; the proof is at hand, but it would be out of place in your book. The working of the furnaces in Missouri and Illinois have proved that a sufficiency of iron can be produced, and although the iron is of a superior quality, now since steel can be made from the pig-iron by using the elements which nature has provided, and machinery that the genius of man has invented, doing away with the labor of puddling, and our Missouri ore is, with one other exception in the United States, the only ore adapted to making steel by the Bessemer or pneumatic process, our iron business will not be complete until that mode is fully put into operation here, and in place of the uncertain iron rail, steel rails can be furnished that will last seventeen times as long as iron rails. The Pennsylvania Central road is now, I am informed, re-laid with steel rails, and the pig-metal, or a portion of it, used at the mills in this country to make rails for the Pennsylvania road, was imported from England, where the ore is inferior to Missouri ore, and the coal no better, and not as accessible as Illinois coal. The explanation is this: steel cannot be successfully made by the Bessemer or pneumatic process unless the pig-iron is free from sulphur or phosphorus; two per cent. of sulphur will not hurt, but one-tenth of one per cent. of phosphorus is fatal. Such metal could not be obtained in this country in sufficient quantity. None of the stone-coal iron would answer, and the quantity of charcoal pig is small and every day decreasing, and there is not much of it that will answer. But next to Bessemer's discovery, and one that will revolutionize the iron business, is the process of freeing mineral coal from sulphur and all other foreign substances, leaving pure carbon to go into the coke oven. The coke made from coal that has been freed from sulphur and other substances, leaving only the carbon, is as good in one locality as another; the carbon of coal is alike everywhere, and pig-iron made from Missouri ore, with coke from coal that has undergone the purifying process, will answer for making Bessemer steel. The Illinois Patent Coke Company in East St. Louis, Theodore Meier, President, have erected works for making coke by the Osterspeys patented process, and will in a short time be prepared to deliver to furnace-men 2,500 bushels per day, and there is no limit to the quantity that can be made. The process of purifying the coal, the crushing and washing, is done by machinery, only requiring the labor of three men and the machinery one day to receive from the cars and deliver the purified coal into the coke ovens. The coke made from the pure carbon is compact and heavy; it will carry a seventy per cent. ore on a twenty-foot bosh, and a furnace of that size using this coke will yield daily fifty tons of metal. There will be no uncertainty as to the quality; it will be uniform day in and day out; every ton may be relied upon with perfect certainty as suitable for Bessemer steel. The working of a furnace with raw coal is a lottery; some days the metal will be good and the next day bad. Uniformity is not to be expected, and never could be had with all the skill that could be applied.

By the discovery of Osterspeys, the making of pig-metal with Missouri ore will become an exact science. And since the coal of one locality can be made as good as any other, and it having been demonstrated that Missouri ore is peculiarly well adapted for making steel, ought to settle the question you propose.

JNO. MAGWIRE.

St. Louis, *July 10, 1871.*

In a previous part of this book we have given some general statistics respecting the iron furnaces at present in operation. The following additional facts are of interest, showing the iron produced in 1870:

Pig-Iron produced by Pioneer Carondelet Furnace	6,000 tons.
" " " " Kingsland "	12,000 "
" " " " South St. Louis "	6,500 "
" " " " Lewis Iron Co.'s "	6,000 "
" " " " Iron Mountain "	8,553 "
" " " " Pilot Knob "	2,425 "
" " " " Irondale "	3,993 "
" " " " Scotia Iron Co.'s "	2,440 "
" " " " Moselle "	3,000 "
" " " " Meramec "	4,000 "
Aggregate production of Pig-iron in 1870	54,911 tons.

	1868.	1869.	1870
Tons ore mined	105,000	195,000	316,000
Tons ore shipped	47,000	120,000	246,555

The magnificent Vulcan Iron Works have commenced operations.

COAL.

The total receipts of coal for 1870 were 957,259 tons, or 23,931,475 bushels. The coal resources contiguous to St. Louis are inexhaustible, and nature appears to have prophetically provided them to assist the full development of our iron manufactures.

ZINC.

The product of this metal in this State during the years mentioned was:

	1869.	1870.
Zinc ore produced, lbs	4,270,400	8,240,000
Zinc metal—spelter	723,000	1,545,930
Value of "	$70,470	$131,404
Zinc slabs exported	12,449	49,549

LEAD.

The total amount of lead received at St. Louis during the year 1870 was 17,010,410 pounds. The Missouri product was 13,640,370.

Buildings Erected in St. Louis from January 1 to December 1.

WARDS.	Brick and stone.	Frame.	Dwellings.	For business purposes.	Value.
First Ward...	154	63	133	84	$1,255,540
Second Ward	59	9	45	23	183,365
Third Ward	61	1	43	19	283,525
Fourth Ward	90	6	73	23	504,750
Fifth Ward	39	2	29	12	699,400
Sixth Ward	31	....	4	27	1,371,600
Seventh Ward	110	7	68	49	1,304,720
Eighth Ward	36	....	7	29	173,025
Ninth Ward	124	2	113	13	421,250
Tenth Ward	50	....	12	38	153,900
Eleventh Ward	187	13	162	38	521,000
Twelfth Ward	79	11	66	24	435,450
Total	1,020	114	755	379	$7,307,525

Most of these structures are of a very substantial character, built of iron, brick, stone, or marble, and one of them costing upwards of $300,000, and numbers of others more than $50,000 each.

List of Steamers and Barges plying between St. Louis and other Ports during 1870, with their Value and Carrying Capacity.

Steamers, 209; barges, 229; total, 438. Value, $6,844,200; carrying capacity, 236,960 tons. This showing of St. Louis tonnage is largely in advance of previous years.

OPERATIONS AT THE CUSTOM HOUSE.

The following table shows the comparative receipts from all sources of the port of St. Louis during the decade ending December 31, 1870:

Year.	Import Duty.	Tonnage Tax.	Hospital Tax.	Inspections.	Storage.	Official Fees.	Collections in Coin.	Collec'ns in Currency	Total Collections
1861	$ 14,425 15	....	$2,304 60	$ 771 00	$ 523 00	$ 585 50	$ 14,425 15	$ 4,184 58	$ 98,609 73
1862	20,404 70	....	4,660 60	3,341 25	950 33	1,661 80	20,404 70	10,614 98	31,019 68
1863	36,922 09	$3,228 00	3,644 60	4,194 00	436 50	1,785 15	36,622 09	13,288 25	49,910 34
1864	76,448 43	4,191 20	6,185 55	5,636 00	408 45	1,890 30	76,448 43	18,311 50	94,759 93
1865	586,407 07	24,916 85	10,271 10	18,848 05	729 74	5,410 40	586,407 07	60,176 14	654,583 21
1866	785,651 30	24,104 00	8,465 50	11,745 70	424 98	4,541 30	785,651 30	49,284 48	834,935 78
1867	1,236,798 06	30,259 25	8,656 18	15,571 00	2,413 24	3,558 15	1,236,793 06	60,457 82	1,297,255 88
1868	1,403,997 64	28,435 22	6,244 64	14,044 83	1,383 18	3,880 15	1,403,997 64	53,988 02	1,457,985 66
1869	1,711,256 19	27,491 70	6,619 93	14,366 92	2,487 42	1,890 00	1,711,256 19	52,856 12	1,764,112 31
1870	1,996,083 49	16,483 57	7,003 64	14,040 49	1,390 31	2,482 65	1,996,083 49	41,400 66	2,037,448 15

A STATISTICAL AND FINANCIAL VIEW OF THE GROWTH OF ST. LOUIS.

TABLE *showing the Census in different years, assessed value of Property, taxes collected, and the revenue from various sources.*

Years.	Census.	Assessed value of property.	Taxes assessed.	Taxes collected.	Merchants, dram shops and other licenses.	Water-works.	Wharfage	Miscellaneous sources.	Total revenue.
1811	....	$134,516 00	$ 672 58	....	....	....	....	....	....
1812	....	134,313 00	447 71	....	....	....	....	....	....
1818	....	1,218,390 62	4,873 56	$ 700 00	$ 200 00	....	....	$407 11	$1,307 11
1819	....	1,132,163 83	3,396 49	4,454 77	415 00	....	....	355 00	5,224 77
1820	4,928	1,024,440 00	3,585 54	3,486 77	[illegible]	....	....	227 81	4,164 58
1821	....	955,950 00	3,828 80	2,211 62	567 50	....	....	421 87	3,200 99
1822	....	956,170 00	3,824 68	2,228 44	631 66	....	....	574 62	3,435 22
1823	....	810,064 00	4,050 32	....	....		....	....	....
1824	....	1,028,217 00	5,137 54	7,788 62	4,273 82	....	$ 686 37	4,418 25	17,161 02
1825	....	788,168 00	1,970 42	486 09	1,966 96	....	197 07	567 32	3,217 44
1826	....	1,003,876 00	2,509 69	1.281 07	2,114 13	....	611 60	734 70	4 631 50
1827	....	1,175,380 00	2,938 45	2,108 40	5,686 63	....	1 607 71	1,984 48	11,387 22
1828	5,000	1,510,332 00	3,775 83	1,750 91	4.034 12	....	1,268 17	10,365 60	17,436 80
1829	....	1,906,392 00	4,765 95	3,410 62	6,887 98	....	1,350 97	9,310 60	20,960 17
1830	5,852	1,830,616 00	4,576 54	1,674 87	6,085 97	....	1,285 38	5,245 67	14,291 89
1831	....	2,080,062 00	3,466 77	2,880 20	8,596 57	....	1,594 99	5,585 52	18,654 28
1832	....	2,338,584 00	3,897 64	2,274 55	....	....	....	....	....
1833	6,397	2,196,672 00	3,745 84	....	....		....	....	....
1834	....	2,063,688 00	2,759 61	818 06	7,955 00	....	3,236 90	7,281 49	24,564 64
1835	8,316	2,221,888 00	8,332 08	3,827 16	9,819 87	$4,588 73	5,151 32	8,050 69	31,432 77
1836	....	8,138,104 00	20,615 41	11,614 63	13,270 28	5,338 21	9,485 26	5,554 61	44,263 94
1837	14,252	7,425,618 00	24,752 06	22,924 88	21,317 30	8,372 13	10,649 43	14,802 77	78,066 51
1838	....	8,169,657 00	33,408 75	28,257 79	18,415 75	12,694 11	10,441 97	13,710 41	83,520 03
1839	....	7,736,260 00	39,000 55	48,738 54	21,087 50	20,517 25	11,516 70	23,048 43	125,988 48
1840	16,469	8,573,662 00	43,291 56	40,195 96	....	20,672 16	....	....	....
1841	....	8,957,198 00	45,088 61	39,408 57	24,469 00	14,954 31	15,187 16	29,622 08	123,044 42
1842	....	....	....	42,113 55	25,336 00	12,507 81	14,115 19	36,622 68	130,225 23
1843	....	8,308,480 41	74,795 23	92,683 51	25,357 28	13,402 10	17,407 86	14,662 76	163,514 51
1844	34,140	13,983,923 30	122,411 82	116,774 19	24,238 00	14,518 60	20,739 25	18,578 11	194,848 24
1845	36,721	14,519,591 53	145,185 91	145,672 26	23,843 87	15,442 47	22,449 23	19,925 07	227,332 90
1846	....	15,202,120 37	152,021 20	143,513 31	31,356 99	17,858 50	25,210 44	18,142 04	236,081 28
1847	....	16,665,145 75	174,983 99	170,629 68	34,796 09	25,538 48	31,231 05	19,840 40	261,035 70
1848	....	....	....	....	....	21,967 92	35,886 16	....	....
1849	63,471	....	....	....	....	....	33,701 72	....	....
1850	74,439	29,676,649 27	214.045 30	257,899 80	62,048 06	30,943 78	46,912 26	120,328 16	518,132 06
1851	....	35,615,855 19	386,824 45	354,241 96	73,570 91	30,824 85	47,064 35	53,750 08	559,452 15
1852	94,000	38,281,668 96	403,619 36	379,097 44	81,459 82	36,995 38	55,506 69	62,510 88	615,576 21
1853	....	39,397,186 33	425,586 22	403,241 60	85,212 60	49,865 04	58,402 37	129,245 23	725,956 84
1854	....	41,104,921 13	425,497 01	417,587 51	89,276 47	51,735 29	60,069 99	212,874 76	831,544 02
1855	97,672	42,456,757 00	459,068 14	449,639 06	98,025 50	70,380 47	62,613 46	273,089 49	954,647 57
1856	125,000	59,600,000 00	....	553,711 74	119,025 50	68,597 20	74,061 68	205,473 69	1,020,869 91
1857	....	73,062,043 94	667,421 62	580,208 33	128,522 49	84,021 96	72,345 72	181,717 85	1,016,816 25
1858	135,330	82,160,449 00	752,457 99	720,175 41	127,719 10	87,352 20	64,808 18	161,541 76	1,167,596 65
1859	143,800	92,340,870 00	947,235 03	904,281 69	147,414 99	99,501 88	69,615 72	124.058 74	1,345,773 02
1860	160,773	102,408,232 00	1,033,019 01	924,427 13	132,898 66	114,760 35	67,544 66	134,784 59	1,374,415 39
1861	....	90,975,497 00	836,049 74	558,237 47	112,886 59	123,690 25	28,635 85	78,834 51	902,284 67
1862	....	63,770,000 00	598,448 15	528,354 03	146,484 16	147,120 95	43,997 36	107,447 87	933,404 37
1863	....	66,619,292 00	631,934 20	678,125 92	132,064 77	170,313 30	54,152 90	106,477 79	1,131,134 63
1864	164,456	74,422,533 00	858,752 71	868,617 56	125,682 84	208,340 00	72,290 97	176,870 92	1,463,895 92
1865	....	99,031,563 00	1,105,031 12	1,111,039 20	194,512 81	248,268 33	84,384 60	135,447 39	1,773,652 24
1866	204,327	108,565,391 00	1,460,385 99	1,122,433 23	206,178 67	248,575 30	78,226 88	165.217 56	1,820,631 64
1867	....	106,845,340 00	1,432,481 93	1,243,755 95	256 791 46	288,910 07	66,293 45	169,609 00	2,025,360 02
1868	....	110,190,930 00	1,423,789 65	1,427,316 31	261,464 31	321,412 50	85,965 43	147,613 01	2,213,771 56
1869	....	130.553,120 00	1,875,899 55	1,879,700 35	317,409 53	323,102 00	92,365 72	163,445 75	2,776,018 35
1870	310,864	143.847.950 00	2,135,400 80	2,012,936 20	315,564 46	335,626 91	93,827 37	215,341 12	2,973,296 06

Blank spaces indicate that the records are incomplete or lost.

TABULAR STATEMENT,

Showing the Financial and Taxable Condition of some of the Principal Cities of the United States.

CITIES.	Area Sq. Miles in City Limits.	Population for 1870.	Assessed Value for 1870.	State Tax.	County Tax.	City Tax.	School Tax.	Total Taxation.	Total amount of Taxes, 1870.	Tax per Capita, 1870.	Bond Debt for 1870.	Floating Debt, 1870.	Debt per Capita, 1870.
New York	22.65	954,613	871,911,327	0.4375	None.	2.1375	0.125	2.70	$23,541,605.69	$24.66	$46,811,208.50	$7,746,918.94	$79.61
Boston	16.25	231,479	569,827,300	0.165	0,455	0.455	0.455	1.53	8,718,357.69	37.66	16,959,500.91	4,858,911.02	94.25
Philadelphia	120	657,179	507,987,900	0.1130	None.	None.	None.	1.80	9,143,812.20	13.91	42,401,933.94	3,368,367.64	69.64
Brooklyn	....	396,300	201,326,746	0.70	0.76	3.87	....	....	7,897,538.00	....	26,434,247.38	4,000,000.00	....
St. Louis	19.9	312,619	187,345,420	0.50	0.40	1.50	0.40	2.80	4,366,948.73	....	12,379,500.00	1,313,707.81	44.31
Chicago	34.5	297,718	275,954,660	0.65	1.50	1.50	0.00158	3.65	10,072,344.23	32.85	12,931,000.00	None.	45.43
Baltimore	16	267,599	214,807,062	0.1925	None.	1.50	0.30	1.6925	3,635,610.17	10.32	25,762,826.05	None.	73.16
Cincinnati	48	218,900	136,107,236	0.40	0,365	2.395	0.39	3.16	4,130,610.12	19.21	4,956,000.00	250,000.00	24.21
New Orleans	91	195,000	127,942,781	0.75	None.	2.375	0.1	4.215	5,437,578.19	27.88	18,000,000.00	None.	92.31
San Francisco	....	140,000	104,280,483	0.865	0.99	0.99	None.	2.845	2,966,779.74	21.05	4,606,500.00	None.	32.90
Louisville	....	100,206	90,806,712	0.45	None.	2.12	0.33	2.90	2,633,394.65	26.28	4,720,000.00	70,000.00	47.80
Memphis	....	40,230	24,783,190	0.20	0.8625	1.70	0.30	3.0625	758,985.19	18.87	3,567,000.00	704,892.15	106.19
Detroit (36 per ct. c. v.)	....	79,879	23,603,327	0.209444	0.74563	2.357412	0.749739	4.19717	990,671.76	12.40	661,127.31	None.	8.28
Buffalo...(33 per cent.)	....	118,050	37,640,050	1.	455	2.426	None.	3.891	1,464,577.35	12.41	2,584,698.00	None.	21.89

CENSUS OF THE STATE OF MISSOURI.

A Complete Exhibit—Returns of each County as Certified by the Census Superintendent

Counties.	Pop'n
Adair	11,449
Andrew	15,137
Atchison	8,440
Audrain	12,307
Barry	10,373
Barton	5,087
Bates	15,960
Benton	11,322
Bollinger	8,162
Boone	20,765
Buchanan	35,109
Butler	4,298
Caldwell	11,390
Callaway	19,202
Camden	6,108
Cape Girardeau	17,558
Carroll	17,445
Cass	19,296
Carter	1,455
Cedar	9,474
Chariton	19,135
Clark	13,667
Clay	15,564
Clinton	14,663
Cole	10,292
Cooper	20,692
Christian	6,707
Crawford	7,982
Dade	8,683
Dallas	8,383
Daviess	14,410
DeKalb	9,858
Dent	6,357
Douglas	3,915
Dunklin	5,982
Franklin	30,098
Gasconade	10,093
Gentry	11,607
Greene	21,549
Grundy	10,567
Harrison	14,635
Henry	17,401
Hickory	6,452
Holt	11,652
Howard	17,233
Howell	4,218
Iron	6,278
Jackson	55,041
Jasper	14,929
Jefferson	15,380
Johnson	24,649
Knox	10,974
Laclede	9,380
Lafayette	23,623
Lawrence	13,067
Lewis	15,114
Lincoln	14,073
Linn	15,900
Livingston	16,730
Macon	23,230
Madison	5,849
Maries	5,915
Marion	22,504
McDonald	5,226
Mercer	11,557
Miller	6,616
Mississippi	4,982
Moniteau	11,335
Monroe	17,149
Montgomery	10,405
Morgan	8,434
New Madrid	6,357
Newton	12,821
Nodaway	14,751
Oregon	3,287
Ozark	3,363
Osage	10,793
Pemiscot	2,059
Perry	9,877
Pettis	18,706
Phelps	10,506
Pike	23,076
Platte	17,352
Polk	12,445
Pulaski	4,714
Putnam	11,217
Ralls	10,510
Randolph	15,908
Ray	18,700
Reynolds	3,756
Ripley	3,175
St. Charles	21,304
St. Clair	6,742
St. Francois	9,741
Ste. Genevieve	8,384
St. Louis	351,189
Saline	21,672
Schuyler	7,987
Scotland	10,670
Scott	7,317
Shannon	2,339
Shelby	10,119
Stoddard	8,535
Stone	3,253
Sullivan	11,908
Taney	4,407
Texas	9,618
Vernon	11,246
Warren	9,673
Washington	11,719
Wayne	6,068
Webster	10,434
Worth	5,004
Wright	5,684
Total	1,717,258

FRANCIS A. WALKER, *Superintendent of Census.*

A Closing Word.

Thus have I written a new record — a new prophecy of a city central to a continent of resources, whose productive energies are greater than those possessed by all the world besides, and upon which is destined to reside a population greater than now exists on the globe — of a city which I know will stand upon the American continent "in the latter day" the grandest material achievement of the civilization of the world — a city destined to become the all-directing head and the central moving heart of the great family of man — a city from out whose throbbing life and comprehensive brain will go forth new laws and new principles of civilization for the better government of states and nations — a city destined to control the commerce of more than one hundred thousand miles of railway, reaching with equal facility to every extremity of the continent, to gather the surplus products of more than one hundred populous States, and to whose central life more than one hundred continental cities, populous and powerful, as all the present existing cities of the globe, will contribute prosperity and greatness — a city which, in its perfect development, its territorial expanse, its architectural elaboration, its industrial growth, its commercial supremacy, its financial power, its achievements in art, its fame in literature, its mental strength, its moral purity, and its perfect government, will flash upon the mind of the human race, and the world will behold in America the city of prophecy — the Apocalyptic City —

> *"The New Jerusalem, the ancient seer*
> *Of Patmos saw."*

All hail! mistress of nations, and beautiful queen of civilization! I view thee in the light of thy destiny. Thou art transfigured before me from thy present state to one infinitely more grand, and which overshadows and dwarfs all civic forms in history.

The influence of thy empire will pervade the world with invisible and electric force. Yet, vivifying and benignant capital — emporium of trade and industry, seat of learning and best-applied labor, pivotal point in history, supreme and superb city of all lands — I behold thy majesty from afar, and salute thee reverently as the consummation of all that the best human energies can accomplish for the elevation and happiness of our race.

All hail! Future Great City of the World, and "GLORY TO GOD IN THE HIGHEST, AND ON EARTH PEACE, GOOD-WILL TOWARD MEN!"

www.ingramcontent.com/pod-product-compliance
Lightning Source LLC
LaVergne TN
LVHW011208110826
845150LV00006B/1359